The Complete Osmond Family Illustrated Discography

Compiled By Daniel Selby

The Complete Osmond Family Illustrated Discography
©2020 Daniel Selby / BearManor Media. All Rights Reserved.
All photographs / illustrations are copyright of their respective owners, and are reproduced here in the spirit of publicity. While we have made every effort to acknowledge photograph credits we apologize for any and all omissions, and will make every effort to make any appropriate changes in future editions of this book if necessary.

No part of this book may be reproduced in any form or by any electronic or mechanical means, including information storage and retrieval systems, without written permission from the publisher or author, except in the case of a reviewer, who may quote brief passages embodied in critical articles or in a review.

Note: Many foreign 45 releases were issued with the same catalog # and picture sleeves for different countries, especially neighboring. Also some were re-issued with a different design / number at a later time. Not all are presented here. Additionally, this book does not show the hundreds of compilation (Greatest Hits) LP's that were issued worldwide on MGM, Polydor, Mercury and various other labels.

Published in the USA by:

Printed in the United States of America
Cover Layout & Interior Design: Daniel Selby.

ISBN: 978-1-62933-614-5

Special Thanks To:

Allan Beatty for the help with all my computer problems and putting up with my meltdowns over them during the writing and formatting of this book! And for the love these last 33 years.

To the *many* people who pitched in and helped with my collecting of information on the recorded history of the Osmonds over the last 15-20 years. Due to several computer losses I no longer have the names, emails or original files— only the old print-outs! Some that were scanned for use here!

To the many fans of the Osmonds all over the world who encouraged and offered help with the writing, compiling and suggesting of photos in this book without asking for anything in return!

eBay, Amazon and Discogs where I have been able to find and buy so many Osmond import records that I never knew existed!

And last, but certainly not least, The Osmonds for recording all this material making my book possible! You rock! Literally!

All personal proceeds of this book are being donated to Children's Miracle Network.

Introduction / Dedication

With as vast a career, spanning many, many decades it would be impossible to present every single 45 and LP release in the careers of a family with at least 5 different performing groups who recorded in eight languages: Swedish, Japanese, Samoan, German, Spanish, French, Latin and of course English. They've also had five recording acts on the charts at the same time with the Osmond Brothers, Donny & Marie, and Donny, Marie, and Jimmy as individual artists. But I have attempted to locate and present a vast majority of the work by this famous musical family who has sold more than **100+ million albums** world wide. Collectively and individually they have had approximately 200 albums released. ***Two hundred albums!*** Jimmy was the first to receive a gold record at five years old. Collectively, Jimmy as a solo artist and with his family, share an astounding 56 gold and platinum records and many other prestigious entertainment awards!

Like a lot of popular musical groups, scratch that— like *all* popular musical groups the Osmond's have been both loved and loathed by the public. But they have certainly had the last laugh. Countless gold and platinum records, a highly rated TV series, sell out shows around the world as recently as 2019, the number one show in Las Vegas for years (not an easy feat!), a star on the Hollywood Walk of Fame as well as one on the Las Vegas Walk of Stars. Though the Osmonds have changed over the years their popularity never really has. Though there were lean times, this family has remained loved by fans around the globe. And while most of the fans may have stepped away for a few years to start families of their own or go to school, the Osmonds were always there in the back of the fan's minds. And how nice it was for the family to have waited for fans to come back… in droves!

I remember how thrilling it was back in the 1970's to receive a hand written letter from Mother Osmond after I wrote to her in 1974 to say how much Marie meant to me. I took that letter *everywhere* I went in the original envelope until it literally fell apart and turned to dust! Mother Osmond's words of support meant everything to me. They still echo in my mind.

'Mother Osmond' was how many fans addressed the Osmond's mother and she liked that title. Many years went by and I wrote to her again. I had come to find out that in the Osmonds lineage was the name Evans. That was my mother's maiden name. My mother was from Utah and was Mormon. I felt we had to be related somehow. Unfortunately just as things were coming together to start searching out the answers Mother Osmond fell ill. I didn't feel it was my place to continue to write and ask questions. Shortly thereafter Mother Osmond passed away. It was like a sword in my heart. I can only imagine the pain of the family. This dear lady had always treated me kindly and with respect when I would see her at concerts or visit the Osmond Studios in Orem, Utah, which at the time was in the middle of empty Utah land. It has since been built up all around the former production studio I came to find when I again took a visit there in 2009 to drive past it.

The same was true with Father Osmond. He was a very welcoming man with a quick smile, a firm handshake and a "How are you?" Same with Mother Osmond. And they waited for your reply. I spoke with Mother Osmond more since I felt very comfortable with her. Not that I didn't with Father Osmond, it's just hard to explain. In my own life I was closer to my mother as well. Mother Osmond was also around more it seemed. And Mother Osmond always encouraged others to go after their dreams and use their minds. That is what I have done with this book. I dreamed big and did thousands of hours of research. Even if this book goes nowhere but my own bookshelf I put a dream on paper thanks to her encouragement. I dedicate this book to Mother Osmond who was always encouraging, thoughtful, steady and calming. A rock. Without her this book would not have been possible.

Without her the music would have never been played. I can't thank her enough. ♥

Father and Mother
OSMOND

Above: Backstage with Marie in her dressing room at The Flamingo after a wonderful show!

About the Author

    Though I enjoy writing and have written three other books centering around my life, dealing with anorexia and based on my journals, this book has been the most difficult to write. Not because the subject matter was difficult or boring, but because I wanted everything to look neat and uniform and I wanted the Osmond's catalog to be as complete as possible. I did hours upon hours upon hours of research and compiling of Osmond records, catalog numbers, recording dates, etc. Several people knowing this sent me much information for the Osmond Archive! Though I can't recall names now I do thank them! In all honesty I stated this book way back in 2007/2008 with initial compiling. I had not intended to write this book for anyone other than myself, but *so* many people (and I mean from *all* over the world) wrote me saying they wanted a copy after seeing the cover I designed. I spent eight to twelve hours a day most days working on this book during April, May and *far* into summer 2020. Everyone in the country was home due to the recent crisis. I started seriously putting this book together on the night of Wednesday, April 22, 2020.

    I was born in California where I did a lot of acting and enjoying the sunny weather. I went to high school in Salt Lake at Granite High where many family members went before me. I spent time at Osmond Studios in Orem going to the Donny & Marie and later Osmond Family Show tapings there as often as I could. I had also went to tapings at KTLA in Los Angeles since I lived in Anaheim in the 1970's at the time the show was produced there.

    My friendship with Marie Osmond now extends into many years. It was because of Marie that I really started to notice music. I had heard of the Osmonds before 1973 - 1974 when I first became aware of Marie. My sister Kelly was a **huge** Donny fan and had all his records. In 1974 she received his new album "Donny" for her birthday on December 11th. I had found the LP the day before her birthday in our mother's dresser when I was snooping for Christmas gifts and I brought Kelly in to see it… such a bad brother. Kelly was **very** excited and spent that day before her birthday making sure the stylus on her stereo was clean…. I think she even calibrated it if that is possible! She wanted to make sure she heard every breath that Donny took between lyrics on his new album. I recall her using a magnifying glass and toothbrush on it!

    Many times Kelly had received Donny's records as birthday or Christmas gifts through the years. You can see the photo strip below of her getting and showing off her copy of *Donny Osmond Superstar* in December 1973. Our mother knew how it was to be a teen and have an idol. Our mother loved Elvis Presley. But for me it was all about Marie. From the first time I heard her voice in late 1973 I was hooked. I bought her first album, Paper Roses, on 8-Track tape with my allowance money one week. Just the first few notes of *Paper Roses* can bring me pure happiness. Those early memories flood back. I had that tape until the player in our car chewed it up in June 1974 on our way to visit family in Utah. My mother replaced it with an LP copy soon afterwards. After that first 8-Track I started collecting anything and everything that concerned Marie. I clipped the tiniest photos of her out of TigerBeat, TV Guide or any publication. To me Marie was the epitome of class, grace, beauty, talent and style. Totally incomparable. That has not changed.

    So becoming friends with Marie has been one of the most exciting things that has ever happened to me. Forget me seeing my own acting on TV or in the movie theater being exciting! My father was a highly successful business man who had a machinery and steel company in the bay area and we lived well. I was often given a choice of what I wanted for my birthday or for good grades, etc, and by the time 1976 rolled around there was plenty of Osmond merchandise on the market. I wanted one of everything… and that is basically what I received over time and sometimes two or more from relatives. In a span of two years I had hundreds of Osmond items in my room on custom shelves. I kept everything in the boxes un-played with. Decades later when I heard Marie had a fire at her house and lost a lot of personal career items I gave her a bulk of my Osmond archives that I used to have on-line at landofos.com that so many of you say you remember. I felt it was a part of Marie's history and many actors and singers do (and should!) collect on their careers!

This musical family has touched *so* many people throughout the world. Their music is woven tightly into the very fabric of America. I now know many, many people who used to put the Osmonds down, but now reveal that they secretly watched *The Donny & Marie Show* on Friday nights. Closet Osmond Fans! And why not? Anyone who was anyone was on it! I wrote just a bit about the show at the back of the book and included Marie's 1980/1981 limited run NBC-TV show and The Osmond Brothers 1972 ABC-TV Saturday morning cartoons as well. I didn't care what people thought of me for watching Donny & Marie and I told people that. Not many people at all said anything disparaging. And I proudly wore my Marie Osmond T-shirts to school.

Both Marie and Donny received copies of this book and I heard back from Marie that she loved it! That alone is payment enough for me! My proceeds donated anonymously to charity. It is my hope that you will enjoy reading and looking at this commemorative book as much as I had writing it and looking at it for months on end, day in and day out as I edited and assembled it. It has been a labor of pure love.

~Daniel

Kelly gasps at the huge poster of DONNY OSMOND!

My sister Kelly and her excitement over *Donny Osmond Superstar*.
(Forgive my mother's cigarette… she no longer smokes.)
Christmas 1973

A few favorite photos of Marie and I from just a few years ago!

Marie Osmond — One of the most genuine people I know!

Family Matters

No Osmond book would really be complete without mentioning the family members who worked so hard behind the scenes, and also performed with the family on occasion!

Virl Osmond and Tom Osmond

Virl was born on October 19, 1945 in Ogden, Utah as George Virl Osmond Jr. Two years later on October 26, 1947, Thomas Rulon Osmond was born. Very early in their childhood it was discovered both children were born severely hearing impaired. Their parents were initially told to place the boys in a home for the deaf but they would not consider doing that. Upon testing it was discovered Virl was 45% deaf. Tom was discovered to have almost no hearing. Though through medical treatments Tom has gained some hearing ability.

Neither brother was treated differently within the family. Once the two brothers were old enough for school, Mother Osmond set up a room in their house to home school them where they thrived under her guidance and unwavering love.

It was also advised that Father and Mother Osmond not have anymore children. This did not sit well with either of them since they had hoped to have many children. Going against medical advice the two loving parents would continue to have children. It would not matter to them if they all had hearing loss or some other affliction, they wanted a house full of love and that to them meant having more children.

At the time Virl and Tom had been tested in 1949 Mother Osmond was carrying another child who would be born on June 22nd and be named Alan Ralph Osmond. Later Wayne, Merrill and Jay, along with Alan, would make up the original four performing Osmond brothers.

Virl and Tom would go on to learn sign language which later in their lives they would teach their brothers and sister. It would also be a way that the family could communicate from across a room or in noisy environments so they would not have to yell.

Later still Virl would teach his brothers to dance after Mother Osmond enrolled him in dance class so he would feel left out when the other brothers started singing. Tom also picked up easily on dance. A lot of the early dances that you see the brothers doing, Virl and Tom had taught the brothers.

The family seemed to be musical naturally. Both parents had natural music ability that they in turn passed on to their children. The performing brothers had originally started singing to raise money for costly hearing aids for Virl and Tom.

Both Virl and Tom learned to play multiple musical instruments too and during the 1970's and 1980's appeared with the family in concerts and on television, most notably on the family's Christmas Specials on ABC-TV. Tom and Virl were also the first deaf missionaries from the LDS Church. Tom worked 28 years for the US Postal service. A job he was very proud of. Virl received an art degree from BYU and later designed and prepared the graphics on the Donny and Marie album known as *Featuring Songs From Their Television Show* (titled *Deep Purple* in the European market) and work on other Osmond designs. Virl also wrote *The Untold Story of Olive Osmond* which was published in early 2010. Virl used his mother's early journals as the basis for the book. Many rare family photos were included in the book.

So it could be said that without Virl and Tom there would not have been a performing Osmond family that we all know and love. The 1982 TV film "**Side by Side: The True Story of the Osmond Family** " is one that should be required watching for any Osmond fan.

The Albums

The Osmond Brothers

Songs We Sang On The Andy Williams Show
E/SE-4146

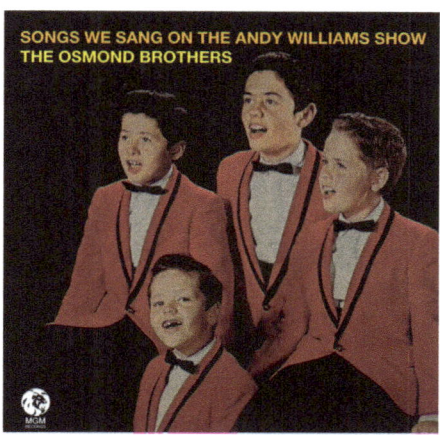

Track Listings:
Be My Little Baby Bumble Bee / Mighty Lak' A Rose / Keep Your Eye On the Girlie You Love / Just A Song At Twilight / I Wouldn't Trade The Silver In My Mother's Hair / Kentucky Babe / Bye The Light Of The Silvery Moon / Aura Lee / In The Good Old Summertime / Take Me Back To Babyland / Down Our Way

Production Information:
Produced by: Jesse Kaye
Recorded at: United Recording Corporation, Hollywood, CA
Recording Engineers: Bill Putnam and Ben Jordan
Director of Engineering: Val Valentin
Recorded April 18, 25 and 29, 1963

Orchestra Conducted by: George Wyle

Original Liner Notes: Andy Williams

    Not too many months ago, my father, who is in the Real Estate business in Los Angeles, called me and said he had heard a vocal quartet that he thought would be good for my television show. An audition was set up and I met, for the first time, the Osmond Brothers.
    The minute I saw them I realized why my father was so taken with this group. They were four boys ranging in age from seven to twelve. The four Osmond Brothers were about the same ages as the four Williams Brothers were when we started singing on the radio back in Des Moines, Iowa. The resemblance was uncanny.
    When they finished their first song, I was still somewhere back in Iowa singing with my brothers. In Jay I could see myself. He was the youngest and the smallest and had two teeth missing and winked a lot. He captured me right away.
    I put them on the show that week and they were an immediate hit with the cast and the crew and the studio audience. But I didn't know until the following week, when the mail started to come in, how much these boys had captured the hearts of the American public in only one appearance. Everybody wanted to see more of the Osmond Brothers.
    I thought at first that their appeal was mostly to mothers and fathers – but their clean-cut, scrubbed look and natural charm reached everyone. After a few appearances on my show, people from all walks of life would stop me and ask if the boys were going to be on the show

that week. It could be a golf caddy, a middle-aged woman, a group of teenagers...it didn't seem to matter. Everybody liked the Osmond Brothers and wanted to see more of them.

With the success of the Osmond Brothers on my show, it was inevitable that they would be asked to record. This album, their first, promises to be the start of what looks like a long and tuneful career.

Besides their new MGM Records contract, they have been signed by MGM-TV to appear regularly on the new TV adventure series, "The Travels of Jaimie McPheeters," which is scheduled to be aired every Sunday night on ABC-TV starting in the fall of 1963.

George Wyle, prominent West Coast arranger and conductor, and Don Williams, their agent, played prominent roles in the production of this album. Mr. Wyle wrote the arrangements for the album, and worked with the boys at his home. He is tremendously proud of them and says, with almost fatherly pride, that along with their talent, they are without doubt the most gentlemanly and respectful boys he has ever met.

Four of the songs in this album are performed just as the boys sing on my show, without orchestral accompaniment. The remaining eight tunes have subtle instrumental backing. About the only difficulty encountered at the recording sessions what that of height. Each brother is about three inches taller than the younger brother next to him – reading high to low, it's Alan, Wayne, Merrill, and Jay. To get their heads on one level for microphone balance an intricate system of platforms had to be arranged. But musically, the boys had no problems at all ...as you will soon hear. When you listen to this album, I know you'll love it, and the Osmond Brothers, as I do.

—Andy Williams

Cover Photo: Studio Five Incorporated

Singles Released from this album:

Be My Little Baby Bumblebee / I Wouldn't Trade The Silver In My Mothers Hair - K13162 (US)

Notes:

- Released: June 1963

Trivia:

The Osmond Brothers first appeared on The Andy Williams Show on December 20, 1962. They performed a version of "I'm A Ding Dong Daddy From Dumas."

PREVIEW
PM-7 / MGM Records

Preview TV'S Newest Young Singing Stars The Osmond Brothers / Preview TV'S Newest Adventure Series The Travels Of Jaimie McPheeters. Show premiered September 1963.

**This is the back jacket featuring The Osmond Brothers.
Finding a copy of this LP without ring wear is nearly impossible given the dark colors.**

Track Listing:
Be My Little Baby Bumble Bee / By Light of the Silvery Moon / Aura Lee / In The Good Old Summertime / Down Our Way / Bye Bye Blues

Side two consists of promotional narrative about the TV program. The Osmond Brothers do not appear.

Production Information:
Produced by: Jesse Kaye
Music recorded at: United Recording Corporation, Hollywood, CA
Recording Engineers: Bill Putnam and Ben Jordan
Director of Engineering: Val Valentin
Orchestra Conducted by: George Wyle
Recorded April 18 and 25, 1963

From Front Cover:
Preview TV's Newest Adventure Series The Travels of Jaimie McPheeters

Produced by Metro-Goldwyn-Mayer and presented by the ABC-TV Network starting Sunday, September 15. A record TV cast of 14 continuing players, staring …Dan O'Herlihy as "Sardius McPheeters," Kurt Russell as "Jaimie McPheeters," Donna Anderson as "Jennie." This exciting new full-hour show launches AC Spark Plug Division's 10th consecutive year on TV!...Another dramatic example of the strong and continuing selling support you receive from AC.

From Back Cover:
Preview TV's Newest Young Singing Stars: The Osmond Brothers!
Selected songs from their first record album recently released… Be My Little Baby Bumble Bee – By The Light of the Silvery Moon – Aura Lee – In The Good Old Summertime – Down Our Way – Bye Bye Blues. The youthful Osmond Brothers: Alan, Wayne, Merrill, and Jay are cast as the Kissel Brothers, "Micah, Leviticus, Deuteronomy, and Lamentations" in "The Travels of

Jaimie McPheeters." Their unique singing will add another highlight to this great new television show brought to you by AC Spark Plug.

Notes:

- The theme song "The Travels of Jaimie McPheeters" does not appear on the album but was released as a single in 1964 with Aura Lee on the "B" Side.

- Released: July 1963

The 1964 US picture sleeve for *The Travels of Jaimie McPheeters*.

We Sing You A Merry Christmas
E/SE 4187

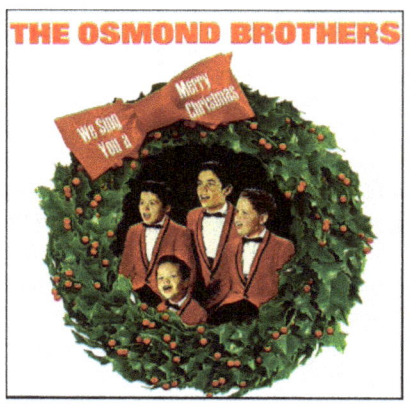

Track Listings:
Silent Night / Winter Wonderland / The Little Drummer Boy / Jingle Bells / O Little Town of Bethlehem / Santa No Chimney / Joy To The World / White Christmas / Deck The Halls With Boughs of Holly / Christmas Means More Ev'ry Year / The First Noel / O Come All Ye Faithful

Production Information:
Produced by: Jesse Kaye
Recorded at: United Recording Studios, Hollywood, CA
Recording Engineer: Ben Jordan
Director of Engineering: Val Valentin
Music arranged and conducted by: George Wyle
Recorded August 19 and September 12, 1963

Original liner notes:
When silent snow sifts slowly over the land and the days are warm with good feeling, the spirit of Christmas is with us. Like a beacon in the night of winter, Christmas sustains us, nourishes us, warms us with the hope of spring. The ways of celebration vary from land to land, but one of the constant elements of Christmas is the lovely music of the season. Another is the joy and wonder it brings to children.

So when children raise their voices in the songs of Christmas, we are doubly blessed because they sing of their happiness with the enthusiasm and the innocence of the young.

The Osmond Brothers – Alan, Wayne, Merrill, and Jay, reading from the tallest and eldest down – have enjoyed the warmth of a family Christmas ever since they can remember. They are four of the nine Osmond children, all of whom play and sing together, and their Christmas has always been filled with the music of the holiday. They sing the sacred songs and the popular songs, and they make them ring with what can only be described as the true spirit of Christmas.

When the Osmond Brothers first appeared on the Andy Williams TV show, their singing touched off an avalanche of mail demanding more. Their popularity led, inevitably, to a regular berth on the bright, new MGM TV series, "The Travels of Jaimie McPheeters," on ABC, and to a recording contract with MGM Records. Wherever they sing, they always perform the old favorites and the newest tunes with that wonderful quality called heart.

It seems fitting, somehow, that the Osmond Brothers recorded this album of Christmas music during the hottest hot spell Hollywood had encountered in years. But the lucky spectators, including Don Williams, brother of Andy and contributor of valuable support and advice, experienced a mid-summer Christmasy feeling as the boys sang these wonderful songs.

So when you play this album by the Osmond Brothers, it may turn out to be the happiest of your Christmas gifts on that wonderful day. Because the Osmond Brothers will be sharing with you their greatest gift – the charm and sincerity of boys singing the songs they know and love best. And, after all, isn't Christmas the day for the giving of gifts with love?

Notes:

- There are actually three different versions of this album with three different record numbers. All of the front covers have the same design overall.

- The first one, listed above (E / SE 4187) contains 12 tracks.

- The second one (M / MS 543) was released on the Metro Label - a division of MGM. This album has left off White Christmas. It also lists The First Noel and O Come All Ye Faithful as one track instead of two like the other two albums do.

- The third one, (PM-9) was released on the MGM label. Although it shows 11 tracks, Santa No Chimney was left off of this recording and The First Noel and O Come All Ye Faithful were split into separate tracks instead of being listed together as they are on the first two albums. This album also contains the following statement in the liner notes: "This record is brought to you with the cooperation of AC Spark Plug Division. AC Spark Plug sponsors "The Travels of Jaimie McPheeters" on ABC-TV Sunday night." The youthful Osmond Brothers appear regularly on the program - which indicates that this record was also used as a promotional tool to promote The Travels of Jaimie McPheeters. Copies of this album also had an easel cut out on the back of the album, which allows the listener to prop the album up on a table.

- The narrative (as seen above) on the back of each album is pretty much the same, although the narrative on the second album was edited quite a bit.

- Released: November 1963

Sing The All Time Hymn Favorites
E/SE-4235

Track Listings:
In The Garden / Softly Now the Light of Day* / My Task* / Come, Come Ye Saints* / Lead Me Gently Home Father / Now The Day is Over* / Whispering Hope* / Abide With Me* / Softly and Tenderly* / Oh My Father / I Need Thee Every Hour* /At The End of the Road

Production Information:
Produced By: Jesse Kaye, Don Williams
Recorded at: United Recording Studios, Hollywood, CA
Recording Engineer: Ben Jordan
Director of Engineering: Val Valentin
*Adapted by: George Wyle
Conducted by: George Wyle
Album recorded May 8, 1964

Original liner notes:

The recording of this album of hymn favorites was a work of dedication and love for the Osmond Brothers. The four boys, from the eldest, Alan, Wayne, Merrill, and Jay, have a deep and abiding faith and that faith is eloquently demonstrated in their singing of these inspirational melodies.

The hymns included in this album were chosen because they are familiar to everyone; they are among the best-loved sacred songs of all time. These particular selections were also chosen because their melodic content was most suited to the boys' voices and type of harmony. Then too, they were chosen because of their joyful quality, the kind of hymns young people are most likely to enjoy singing.

The producers of The Osmond Brothers Sing The All-Time Hymn Favorites, Jesse Kaye and Don Williams, did everything humanly possible to preserve the naturalness – the spontaneous warmth and sincerity – of the boys singing in this album.

The boys were encouraged to sing these great songs of faith as they felt them – much as they would sing them at a service in their very own church. The musical adaptations (by George Wyle) and arrangements (by Wyle, Val Hicks and Dick Williams) were scrupulously prepared with the single thought of preserving the natural warmth and sincerity of the performances.

The Osmond Brothers have become family favorites since their first appearance on the Andy Williams TV show, and since then, have appeared regularly in the MGM TV series The

Travels of Jaimie McPheeters. They appeal to families across the nation because they have the healthy, happy look of wholesome family life themselves. As a matter of fact, the music is a very important part of their family life. The Osmond family has nine children and all but one are boys. Every Thursday evening is "Family Night" when the entire family gets together for a musicale. Each of the children plays some kind of musical instrument and each sings, dances, and recites. The selections in The Osmond Brothers Sing The All-Time Hymn Favorites are an integral part of these Thursday night musicales for the Osmond's are a devout family in which each member is always ready to raise his or her voice in praise of the Almighty.

As has been pointed out above, great care was taken in the making of this album. Everything that was done at the recording session was pointed at capturing the love and the honesty with which the Osmond Brothers sing the great songs of faith and transferring that quality to this album.

As co-producer Jesse Kaye said in the production notes of this recording: "These boys are constant churchgoers where they sing hymns regularly; consequently, it was not difficult to transfer their love and sincerity to this phonograph record…nothing was done to change their understanding of the great hymns and so, there emerged an album of hymns sung right from the hearts of these wonderful little fellows which should please old and young alike."

Notes:

- This album was originally released on LP and open reel tape formats.

The Osmond Brothers on *The Andy Williams Show* 1964

The New Sound Of The Osmond Brothers
E/SE-4291

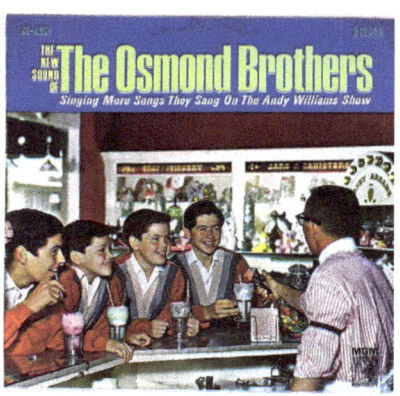

Track Listings:
Chim Chim Cher-ee / My Mom*+ / Hello, Dolly / Sing A Rainbow / Ragtime Cowboy Joe
Life is Just A Bowl of Cherries / Downtown / May Each Day / Mister Sandman*+ / Sweet and Low / That's What I Want / When the Red, Red Robin Comes Bob, Bob, Bobbin' Along

Production Information:
Album produced by: Jesse Kaye and Don Williams
Recorded at: United Recording Corporation Hollywood, CA
Engineers: Ben Jordan, Hal Linstrot and Bones Howe
Conducted and arranged by: George Wyle
*Conducted and arranged by: Terry Melcher
Recorded: +July 20, 1964, March 17 and 30 1965
Released: May 1965

Cover photograph: John Engstead

Original liner notes:

This is the new sound of the Osmond Brothers!

Yes…new! The boys have added some brand new vocal sounds to the barbershop harmonies that categorized their earlier offerings and are expanding into all sorts of new areas.

You know the Osmonds of course. They're the four young brothers – Alan, Wayne, Merrill, and Jay, reading from the oldest and tallest, down – who have starred on the Andy Williams TV Show and on the dramatic series the Travels of Jaimie McPheeters. And it all began just two years ago with a one-shot appearance on the Andy Williams television program. The simple harmonic blend of their fresh young voices drew huge amounts of mail. They appeared again…and again...and again. With each appearance Andy recognized the innate showmanship of these four young fellows, and he was instrumental in helping them develop into the stars they are today.

Soon after their first appearance on the Williams show, MGM records signed the boys for records and TV. Since that time they have learned to act, to do comedy, to play several musical instruments and to dance. They have added special material designed for personal appearances and have become, in a very real sense, a polished singing act. In this album you can hear the way in which they have continued to develop musically, for in this album they have expanded their singing to include today's sound – rock and roll and rhythm and blues tunes.

Just listen to the Osmond's rock and roll interpretations of the recent popular smash hit, Downtown; their wild arrangement of Mister Sandman and That's What I Want. The boys also wail My Mom in rhythm and blues style. These last two songs were written specifically for them.

To round out the package of fine singing, The Osmond Brothers also sing a few typically American standards like Hello, Dolly, Life is Just A Bowl of Cherries, Ragtime Cowboy Joe, and Red, Red, Robin.

Then these same boys sing such sensitive and appealing compositions as May Each Day, the sign-off theme from the Andy Williams Show; Chim Chim Cheree, from Walt Disney's Mary Poppins motion picture success; Sing A Rainbow, a nearly forgotten beauty from the film, Pete Kelly's Blues; and the almost hymnal standard Sweet and Low. Such versatility is extremely rare among young singers.

All of the selections in this album were arranged and conducted by George Wyle with the exception of My Mom and Mister Sandman which were arranged by Terry Melcher. Melcher, incidentally, is Doris Day's son and a fine young record producer, song writer and performer in his own right.

The boys – and their singing style – are growing up. The lads are developing a rich warm sound that is flexible enough to sing any kind of song material. They've come a long way in just two years and they will be going a lot farther.

This album was designed for the great American public – all ages and all walks of life from six to sixty – so sit back and listen to the fine New Sound of The Osmond Brothers.

Singles Released From This Album:
Mr Sandman / My Mom - K13281 - US (PS)
Mr Sandman / My Mom - 13281X (Canada)
Chim Chim Cher-ee - DM - 1059 (Japan) (PS)

The Japanese picture sleeve for *Chim Chim Cher-ee*.

The Wonderful World Of The Osmond Brothers
SONX-60144 - (JAPAN)

Track Listings:
I've Got Lovin' On My Mind / Mollie "A" / Make The Music Flow / Clouds (Both Sides Now) / Mary Elizabeth / Speak Like A Child / Takin' a Chance on Love / Groove with What You Got / Good News / Beauty and the Sweet Talk / Takin' on a Big Thing

Production Information:
Recorded in Japan

Notes:

- Released March 1969

The Japanese picture sleeve for *Both Sides Now* (Clouds).

Merry Christmas
MM-1184 - (Japan)

Track Listings:
Silent Night / The Little Drummer Boy / In The Garden / Jingle Bells / O Little Town of Bethlehem / Come Come Ye Saints / Joy To The World / Whispering Hope / Deck The Halls With Boughs of Holly / Christmas Means More Ev'ry Year / The First Noel / O Come All Ye Faithful / Softly and Tenderly / Winter Wonderland / Santa, No Chimney

Production Information:
Produced By: Jesse Kaye, Don Williams
Recorded at: United Recording Studios, Hollywood, CA
Recording Engineer: Ben Jordan
Director of Engineering: Val Valentin
Music arranged and conducted by: George Wyle

Notes:

- Released: November 1969

- This album is a compilation of We Sing You A Merry Christmas and The Osmond Brothers Sing The All-Time Hymn Favorites.

Hello! The Osmond Brothers
CD-7004 - (JAPAN)

Track Listings:
Golden Rainbow / Keep The Customer Satisfied / Open Up Your Heart / Raindrops Keep Falling On My Head (Donny & Marie) / Bridge Over Troubled Water / My Little Darling / Young Love Swing / Movin' Along / Chance / Sha La La / Scarborough Fair / Aquarius / Let the Sunshine In

Production Information:
Recorded in Japan

Singles Released From This Album:
Young Love Swing / Sha La La - CD-77 (Both songs sung in Japanese) (PS)
Chance / Greensleeves - CD-92 (PS)
Movin' Along / Open Up Your Heart - Moving Along / Open Up Your Heart - K-14159 (US)

Notes:

- Released: September 1970
- On this album, Donny & Marie make their recording debut together singing *Raindrops Keep Fallin' On My Head.*

The Japanese picture sleeve for *Sha La La.*

Christmas Holiday With The Osmonds
(CD-7006) - (JAPAN)

Track Listings:
Santa Claus Is Coming To Town / Rudolph The Red Nose Reindeer / White Christmas / Santa, No Chimney / Silent Night, Holy Night / This Christmas Eve / I Hope You Have a Very Merry Christmas / Jingle Bells / O Come All Ye Faithful / I Saw Mommy Kissing Santa Claus / Blue Christmas / Winter Wonderland / God Rest Ye Merry Gentleman / The Night Before Christmas

Production Information:
Producer: Y. Aoyama
Director of Recording: K. Maeda
Recorded at: United Recording Hollywood, CA

Arrangers: K. Hattori, Jimmy Dale, George Wyle

Musicians:
Piano: Don Randi
Guitar: Louie Shelton
Bass: Don Baldwin
Drums: Peter Lvlis

Notes:

- Released: November 1970

- Reissued with different cover art as: The Osmonds & Jimmy Osmond "Merry" Christmas **MM-2041 / January 1973 (Japan)**

Osmonds
SE-4724

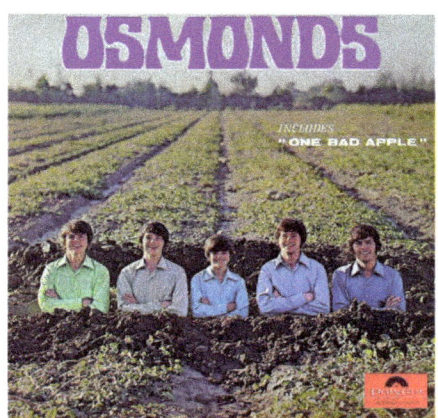

(Canadian version on the Polydor label)

Track Listings:
Think / One Bad Apple / Catch Me Baby / Lonesome They Call Me, Lonesome I Am / Motown Special / Sweet and Innocent / He Ain't Heavy, He's My Brother / Find' em, Fool' em, Forget' em / Most Of All / Flirtin'

Production Information:
Produced by: Rick Hall
Recorded at: Fame Studio Home of the Muscle Shoals Sound, 603 E. Avalon Muscle Shoals, Alabama and Independent Recorders Studio City, CA
Engineers: Jerry Masters, Mickey Buckins and Rick Hall
Recorded: October 26, 1970 – November 13, 1970

Musicians:
Drums: Fred L. Pouty
Guitars: Albert S. Lowe, Jr. and Travis Wammack
Steel Guitar: Leo Leblanc
Keyboard: Clayton Ivey
Baritone Sax: Ronnie Eadies
Trombone: Dale Quillen
Trumpet: Harrison Calloway and Jack Peck
Tenor Sax: Harvey Thompson

Vocal Arrangements by: Earl Brown, The Osmonds, and Rick Hall

Photography / Design: Ron Raffaelli

LP Data:
Billboard Chart Debut: Jan 30, 1971
Highest Chart Position: #14
# of Weeks on Chart: 42

Singles released from this album:
One Bad Apple / Flirtin' - 20 06 026 (Spain)
One Bad Apple / He Ain't Heavy ...He's My Brother - 2006-021 (UK)
One Bad Apple / He Ain't Heavy ...He's My Brother - 3014 (Costa Rica)
One Bad Apple / He Ain't Heavy ...He's My Brother - 2065 044 - Polydor (Canada)
One Bad Apple / He Ain't Heavy ...He's My Brother - 2006021 (New Zealand)

The following releases were issued with a picture sleeve:
One Bad Apple / He Ain't Heavy ...He's My Brother - K14193 (US)
One Bad Apple / He Ain't Heavy ...He's My Brother - 2006 021 (France)
One Bad Apple / Movin' Along - 2006 025 (Greece)
One Bad Apple / He Ain't Heavy ...He's My Brother - 2006 021 (Norway)
One Bad Apple / He Ain't Heavy ...He's My Brother - MG 70.040 (Italy)
One Bad Apple / Flirtin' - 2006 026 (Germany)
One Bad Apple / He Ain't Heavy ...He's My Brother - CD-104 - Feb.1, 1971 (Japan)

Notes:

- This album was originally released on LP, cassette, 8-Track and open reel tape formats in January 1971.
- This album was awarded a gold record for sales in excess of 500,000 copies on September 13, 1971.
- Sheet music was marketed for this album and Whole Album Songbook

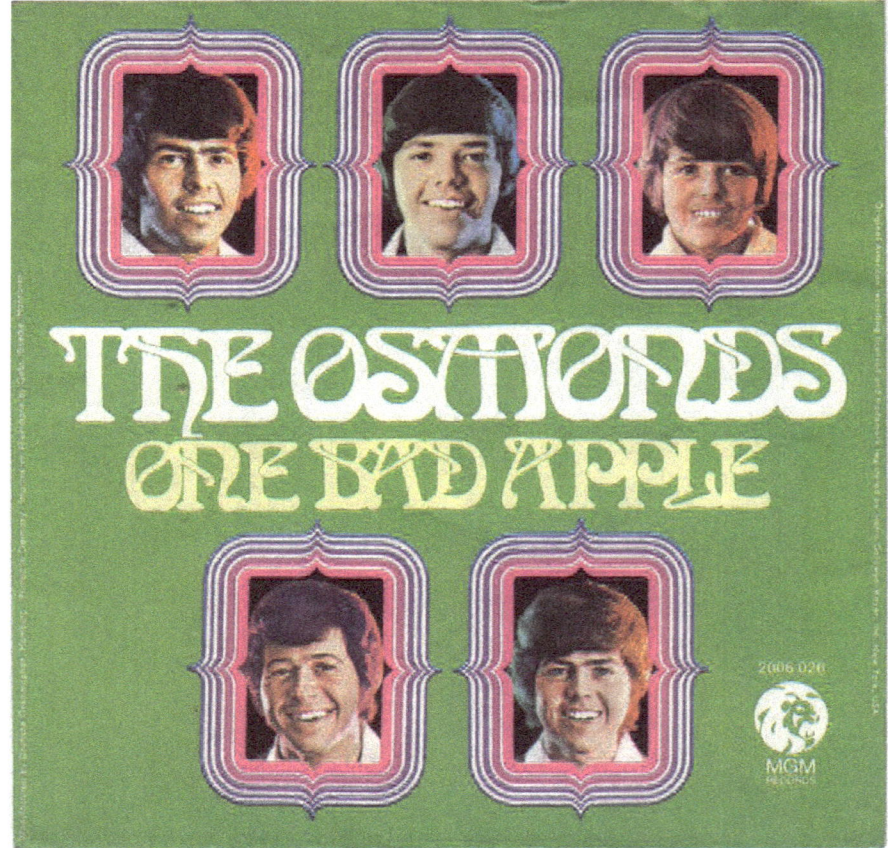

The German picture sleeve for *One Bad Apple*.

Homemade
SE-4770

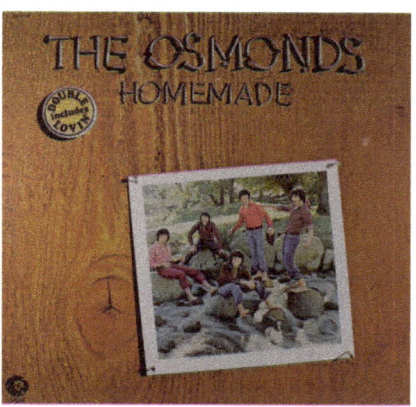

Track Listings:
The Honey Bee Song / Carrie / Double Lovin' / Chilly Winds / Shuckin' and Jivin' / The Promised Land / If You're Gonna Leave Me / We Never Said Forever / She Makes Me Warm / Sho Would Be Nice

Production Information:
Produced by: Rick Hall
Recorded at: Fame Recording Studios Home of the Muscle Shoals Sound, 603 E. Avalon Muscle Shoals, Alabama.
Engineer: Rick Hall
Recorded: February 16, 17, 18, 20 and 21, 1971

String Arrangements by: Peter Carpenter
Horn Arrangements by: Harrison Calloway, Jr.

Singles Released From This Album:
Double Lovin' / Chilly Winds - 2065 066 Polydor (Canada)
Double Lovin' / Chilly Winds - 2006 058 (Australia)

The following releases were issued with a picture sleeve:
Double Lovin' / Chilly Winds - K-14259 (US)
Double Lovin' / Chilly Winds - 2006 058 (Germany)
Double Lovin' / Chilly Winds - 2006 058 (Norway)
Double Lovin' / Chilly Winds - CD-1003 (Japan)

Notes:

- This album came with a poster inside.
- Sheet music was marketed for this album and whole album songbook.
- The German album had the same album cover, but different back cover art.
- Some printings of the album cover titled the first song as "A Taste of Honey" and others titled the first song as "The Honey Bee Song."
- This album was originally released on LP, cassette, 8-Track and open reel tape formats on June 19, 1971.

- This album was awarded a gold record for sales in excess of 500,000 copies on January 20, 1972

LP Data:
Billboard Chart Debut: 06/26/71
Highest Chart Position: #22
# of Weeks on Chart: 34
Billboard Chart: Top Selling LP's

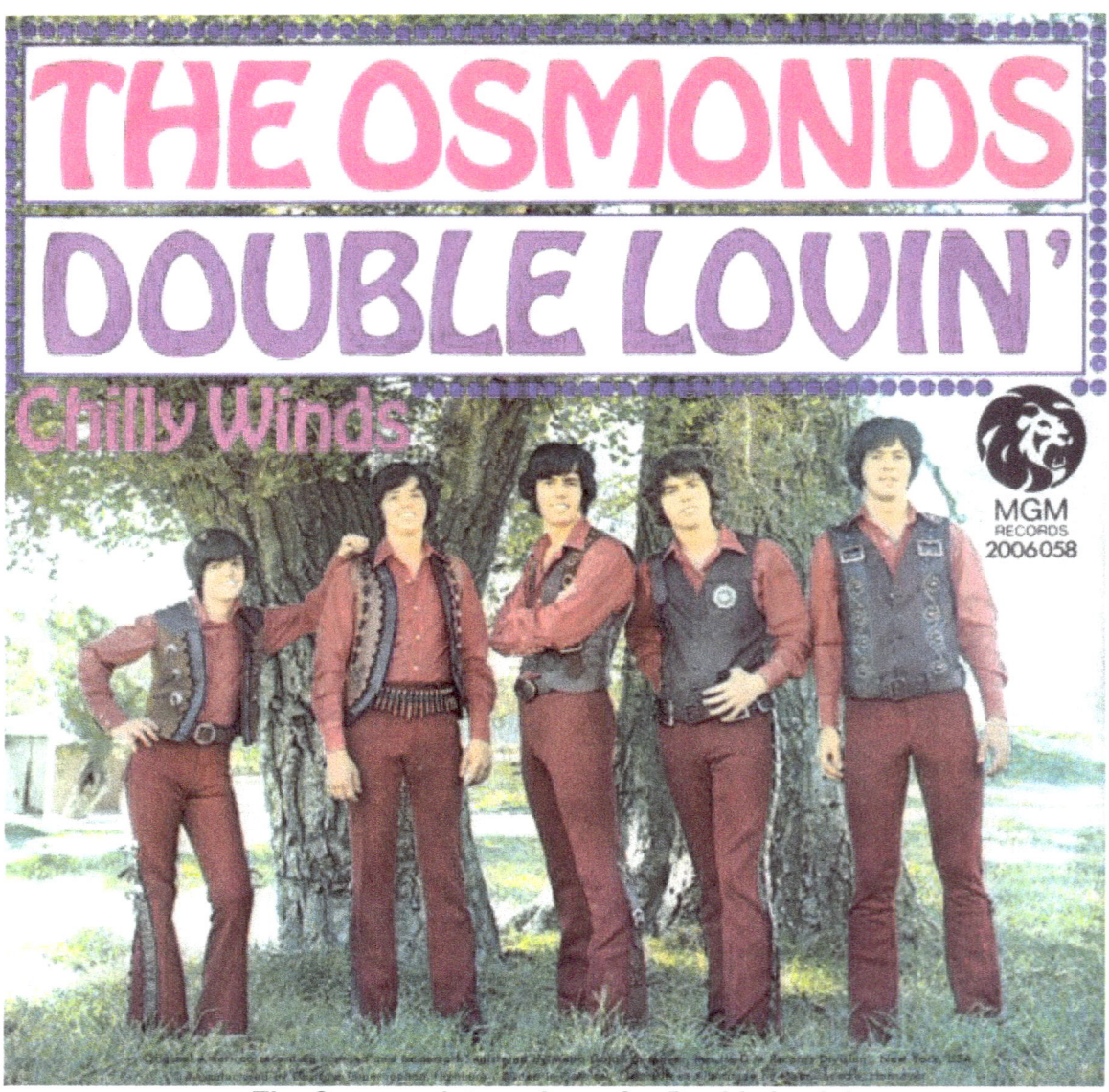

The German picture sleeve for *Double Lovin'*.

The Osmonds Live In Tokyo
(CD-7015) May 1971 - (JAPAN)

Track Listings:
Movin' Along / Motown Special / Close To You / Sweet and Innocent / He Ain't Heavy, He's My Brother / Evil / I Got A Woman / Put Your Hand In the Hand / My Little Darling / Jimmy's The Happy Robbers / Your Song / We Got To Live Together / Gospel Medley / One Bad Apple

Production Information:
Music Accompaniment – Toshiyuki Mayama & His New Band

Notes:

- Recorded in Tokyo, Japan.

The Osmond Brothers in 1971

Phase III
SE-4796

Track Listings:
Down By The Lazy River / Business / Love Is / A Taste of Rhythm and Blues / Yo-Yo / He's the Light of the World / My Drum / It's You Babe / In The Rest of My Life / Don't Panic

Production Information:
Down By The Lazy River / Business / Love Is / My Drum / It's You Babe / Don't Panic
Produced by: Michael Lloyd
In the Rest of My Live
Produced by Osmonds / Curb / Costa
A Taste of Rhythm and Blues / Yo-Yo
Produced by Rick Hall
He's The Light of The World
Produced by Ruff / Curb / Osmonds

Recorded at: Fame Recording Studios Home of the Muscle Shoals Sound, 603 E. Avalon Muscle Shoals, Alabama and Independent Recorders, Hollywood, Ca
Engineers: Rick Hall and Ed Greene
Recorded: June 21, 1971 – September 25, 1971

Photography: Emerson – Loew
Montages: Ron Raffaelli
Art Direction: Saul Saget
Special thanks to: The American Underground and The Fame Gang

Singles Released From This Album:
Yo Yo / Keep On My Side - K-14295 (US)
Yo Yo / Keep On My Side - PS 170 (South Africa)
Yo Yo / Keep On My Side - 2006 075 (Australia)
Yo Yo / Keep On My Side - 20 06 075 (Spain)
Yo Yo / Keep On My Side - 2006 075 (UK)
Yo Yo / Keep On My Side - 2006 075 (France)
Yo Yo / Keep On My Side - 2006 075 (New Zealand)
Yo Yo / Keep On My Side - 2006 075 (Germany)
Yo Yo / Keep On My Side - 2065 082 Polydor (Canada)
Down By The Lazy River/ He's The Light Of The World - K 14324 (US)

Down By The Lazy River/ He's The Light Of The World - 2065-096 Polydor (Canada)
Down By The Lazy River/ He's The Light Of The World - 2006-096 (UK)
Down By The Lazy River/ He's The Light Of The World - 2006 096 (Australia)

The following releases were issued with a picture sleeve:
Yo Yo / Keep On My Side - 2006 075 (Belgium)
Yo Yo / Keep On My Side - CD-1011-IN (Japan)
Yo Yo / Keep On My Side - MG 70044 (Italy)
Yo Yo / Keep On My Side - S 53639 (Yugoslavia)
Down By The Lazy River/ He's The Light Of The World - 2006 096 (Norway)
Down By The Lazy River/ He's The Light Of The World - CD-1016-IN (Japan)
Down By The Lazy River/ He's The Light Of The World - 2006 096 (Portugal)
Down By The Lazy River/ He's The Light Of The World - 2006 096 (France)
Down By The Lazy River/ He's The Light Of The World - 2006 096 (Belgium)
Down By The Lazy River/ He's The Light Of The World - 2006 096 (Netherlands)
Down By The Lazy River/ He's The Light Of The World - 2006 096 (Germany)
Down By The Lazy River/ He's The Light Of The World - 2006 200 (Dutch)
Down By The Lazy River/ He's The Light Of The World - CD-1016-IN (Japan)

LP Data:
Billboard Chart Debut: Jan 29, 1972
Highest Chart Position: 10
# of Weeks on Chart: 35
Billboard Chart: Top Selling LP's

Notes:

- Sheet music was marketed for this album.
- This album was originally released on LP, cassette, 8-Track and open reel tape formats on January 29, 1972.
- This album was awarded a gold record for sales in excess of 500,000 copies on May 29, 1972.

The Italian picture sleeve for *Yo-Yo*.

The Best Of The Osmonds
CD 4038-9 (Japan)

Track Listings:
Chilly Winds / He Ain't Heavy, He's My Brother / Put Your Hands In the Hand / Double Lovin' / One Bad Apple / Father Told Me / Sweet and Innocent / Flirtin' / Movin' Along / Most Of All / Find' em, Fool' em, Forget' em / Motown Special / Golden Rainbow / Catch Me Baby / Bridge Over Troubled Water / Think / Open Up Your Heart / Scarborough Fair / My Little Darling / Chance / Jimmy's The Happy Robbers / Young Love Swing / Sha La La / Aquarius / Let the Sunshine In

Notes:

- Released: March 1972

The Osmond Brothers 1972

The Osmonds Live
2SE-4826 - (2 LP Set)

Track Listings:
Osmond Special – Motown Special / Double Lovin' / Your Song / Sweet and Innocent / You've Lost That Lovin' Feelin' / Proud Mary / Free / Go Away Little Girl / Sometimes I Feel Like A Motherless Child / Where Could I Go But to the Lord / Every time I Feel The Spirit / We Gotta Live Together / Trouble / I Gotta Woman / Hey Girl / Down By the Lazy River / Yo-Yo / One Bad Apple

Production Information:
Produced by Alan Osmond and Michael Lloyd
Recorded in concert at the Forum Los Angeles, CA, December 4, 1971
Tapes assembled at MGM Recording Studios, Hollywood, CA
Engineer: Ed Greene

Photography: Emerson – Loew

Notes:

- This two album set was originally released on LP, cassette, 8-Track and open reel tape formats on June 5, 1972.
- This album was awarded a gold record for sales in excess of 500,000 copies on December 30, 1972

LP Data:
Billboard Chart Debut: June 17, 1972
Highest Chart Position: 13
# of Weeks on Chart: 29
Billboard Chart: Top Selling LPs

Crazy Horses
SE-4851

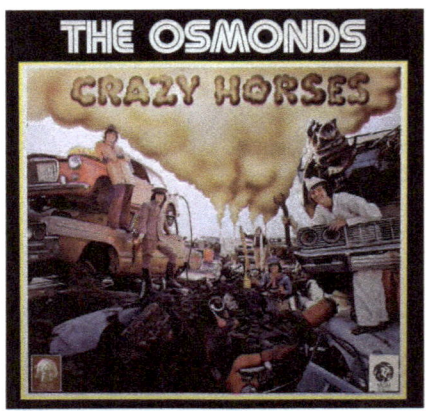

Track Listings:
Hold Her Tight / Utah / Girl / What Could It Be / We All Fall Down / And You Love Me / Crazy Horses / Life Is Hard Enough Without Goodbyes / Hey Mr. Taxi / That's My Girl / Julie / Big Finish

Production Information:
Produced by: Alan Osmond and Michael Lloyd
Recorded at: MGM Recording Studios, Hollywood CA
Engineered by: Ed Greene
Horns Arranged by: Jim Horn
All Songs Written, Sung, and Played by: The Osmonds
All Songs Published by Kolob Music (BMI)
Album Photography & Design by: Ron Raffaelli
Recorded: March 17, 1972 – June 23, 1972

Singles Released From This Album:
Hold Her Tight / Love Is - K 14405 (US)
Hold Her Tight / Love Is - 2006 115 (Australia)
Hold Her Tight / Love Is - 2065 137 Polydor (Canada)
Hold Her Tight / Love Is - 2006-115 (UK)
Hold Her Tight / Love Is - 2006-115 (Scandinavia)
Crazy Horses / That's My Girl - K 14450 (US)
Crazy Horses / That's My Girl - MGM-14-016 (Philippines)
Crazy Horses / That's My Girl - 2006 142 (New Zealand)
Crazy Horses / That's My Girl - 2006 142 (Norway)
Crazy Horses / That's My Girl - 2065 156 - Polydor (Canada)
Crazy Horses / That's My Girl - 2006-142 (UK)
Crazy Horses / That's My Girl - 2006 142 (Ireland)
Crazy Horses / That's My Girl - 2006 142 (Australia)
Crazy Horses / That's My Girl - 2006 142 (Netherlands)
Crazy Horses / That's My Girl - PGP RTB – S 53 677 (Yugoslavia)
Crazy Horses / That's My Girl - 2006 142 (Turkey)

The following releases were issued with a picture sleeve:
Hold Her Tight / Love Is - DM-1231 (Japan)
Hold Her Tight / Love Is - 2006 115 (France)
Crazy Horses / That's My Girl - 2006 142 (Germany)
Crazy Horses / That's My Girl - DM 1236 (Japan)
Crazy Horses / That's My Girl - 2006 142 (Belgium)

Notes:

- Released in France in 1975.
- Sheet music was marketed for this album and whole album songbook.
- It was cited by author Chuck Eddy as one of *The Five Hundred Best Heavy Metal Albums in the Universe.*
- This album was originally released on LP, cassette and 8-Track tape formats on October 14, 1972.
- This album was awarded a gold record for sales in excess of 500,000 copies on January 24, 1973.

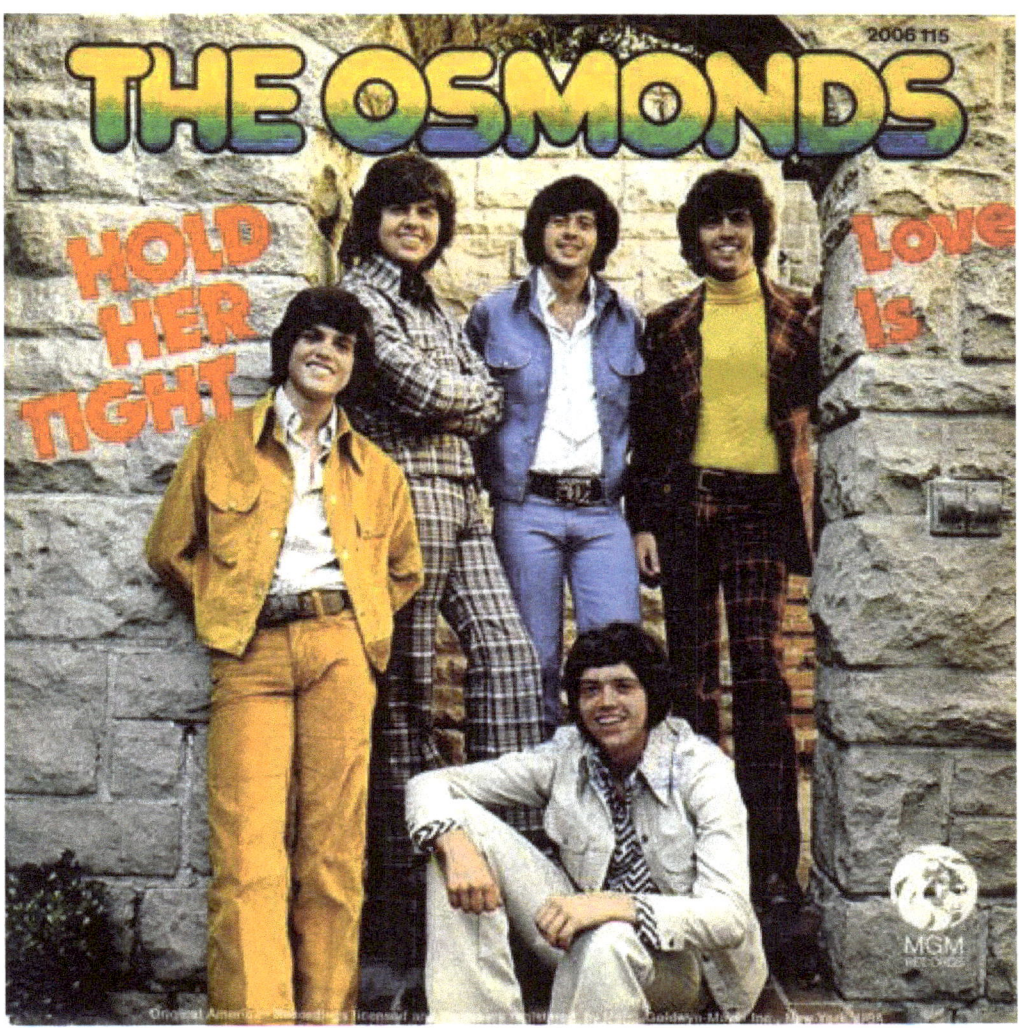

The French picture sleeve for *Hold Her Tight*.

The Plan
SE-4902

Track Listings:
War In Heaven / Traffic In My Mind / Before The Beginning / Movie Man / Let Me In / One Way Ticket To Anywhere / Are You Up There / It's Alright / Mirror, Mirror / Darlin' / The Last Days / Goin' Home

Production Information:
Produced by: Alan Osmond
Recorded at: Kolob Studios, Los Angeles, CA in March-April 1973
Engineer: Ed Greene
Strings Arranged by: Tommy Oliver, Pete Carpenter, Reg Powell
Special thanks to Mike Curb, Ed Greene, and the baby.
Art Direction: Saul Sager
All songs composed and played by The Osmonds

Singles Released From This Album:
Goin' Home / Are You Up There - K 14562 (Canada)
Goin' Home / Are You Up There - 2006 288 (New Zealand)
Goin' Home / Are You Up There - 2006 288 (Australia)
Goin' Home / Are You Up There - 2006 288 (Belgium)
Goin' Home / Are You Up There - 2006 288 (UK)
Hold Her Tight / Movie Man - 2006 438 (France / Belgium)
Hold Her Tight / Movie Man - 2006 438 (UK)

The following releases were issued with a picture sleeve:
Goin' Home / Are You Up There - 2006 288 (Germany)
Goin' Home / Are You Up There - 2006 288 (Italy)
Goin' Home / Are You Up There - S 53 702 (Yugoslavia)
Goin' Home / Are You Up There - 2006 288 (France)
Goin' Home / Are You Up There - 2006 288 (Netherlands)
Goin' Home / Are You Up There - DM-1245 (Japan)
Let Me In / One Way Ticket To Anywhere - K 14617 (US)
Movie Man / Traffic in My Mind - 2006 357 (France / Belgium)

Notes:

- Sheet music was marketed for this album and whole album songbook.
- This album was originally released on LP, cassette and 8-Track tape formats on June 30, 1973.

The US picture sleeve for *Let Me In*.

Love Me For A Reason
SE-4939

Track Listings:
Having a Party / The Girl I Love / Love Me For A Reason / Ballin' the Jack / Send A Little Love / Peace / Gabrielle / I Can't Get Next To You / Sun, Sun, Sun / I Can See Love In You and Me / Fever

Production Information:
Produced by: Mike Curb
Executive Producers: The Osmonds
Recorded at: Kolob Studios, Provo Utah,
MGM Recording Studio, Los Angeles, CA,
Polydor Records London Studio, London, England
Engineered by: Ed Greene
Arranged and Conducted by: H.B. Barnum

Alan Osmond: vocals, Yamaha piano, guitar
Wayne Osmond: vocals, Gibson lead guitar, woodwinds
Merrill Osmond: vocals, bass
Jay Osmond: vocals, Ludwig drums, percussion
Donny Osmond: vocals, Arp Synthesizer

Wardrobe designed by: Bill Belew
Cover Design by: David Wiseltier, Kameny Associates, Inc.
Photography by: Leandro Carrea / Rod Dyer Inc.

Singles Released From This Album:
Having A Party / Wanted - 2006 492 (UK)
Having A Party / Wanted - 2006 495 (Italy)
Having A Party / Wanted - 2006 492 (New Zealand)
Having A Party / Wanted - 2006 492 (Australia)
Love Me For A Reason / Fever - M 14746 (US / Canada)
Love Me For A Reason / Fever - 2006 458 (UK)
Love Me For A Reason / Fever - 2006 458 (Austria)
Love Me For A Reason / Fever - 2006 458 (Ireland)

Love Me For A Reason / Fever - 2006 458 (Australia)
Love Me For A Reason / Fever - 2006 458 (New Zealand)
Love Me For A Reason / Fever - MGM-14-076 (Philippines)
Love Me For A Reason / Fever - 2006 458 (Mexico)
Love Me For A Reason / Crazy Horses - 2006 469 (Brazil)

The following releases were issued with a picture sleeve:
Love Me For A Reason / Fever - S 53 794 (Yugoslavia)
Love Me For A Reason / Fever - 2006 458 (Netherlands)
Love Me For A Reason / Fever - 2006 458 (France)
Love Me For A Reason / Fever - 2006 458 (Belgium)
Love Me For A Reason / Fever - 2006 458 (Germany)
Having A Party / Wanted - 2006 495 (Netherlands)
Having A Party / Wanted - 2006 495 (Spain)
Having A Party / Wanted - 2006 495 (Germany)
Having A Party / Wanted - S - 53 862 (Yugoslavia)
Having A Party / Sun Sun Sun - 2006 495 (France)
Having A Party / Sun, Sun, Sun - 2006 495 (Belgium)

Billboard Chart Debut: Nov 2, 1974
Highest Chart Position: 47
# of Weeks on Chart: 14
Billboard Chart: Top Selling LPs

Notes:

- This album was originally released on LP, cassette and 8-Track tape formats on November 2, 1974.
- Sheet music was marketed for this album.

The German picture sleeve for *Love Me For A Reason*.

The Proud One
SE-4993

Track Listings:
I'm Still Gonna Need You / Where Would I Be Without You / Kind of a Woman That A Man Wants / Thank You / Someone To Go Home To / Take Love If Ever You Find Love / The Proud One (Recorded November 12, 1974) / Frightened Eyes / The Last Day Is Coming / Where Are You Going To My Love (Recorded November 12, 1974)

Production Information:
Produced by: Mike Curb
Executive Producers: The Osmonds
The Last Day Is Coming Produced by: Alan Osmond and Michael Lloyd
Recorded at: Kolob Recording Studios, Provo, Utah and
MGM Recording Studios, Hollywood, California
Engineered by: Ed Greene and Umberto Gatica
Arranged by Tommy Oliver and Gene Page
Strings and Horns Arranged by: Michael Lloyd and Jerry Styner

Photography: Albert Mckenzie Watson
Design: Vigon, Nahas, Vigon
Art Direction: Sheri Leverich

Singles Released From This Album:
The Proud One / The Last Day Is Coming Is Coming - M 14791 (Canada)
El Orgulloso (The Proud One) / El Final Se Acerca (The Last Day Is Coming Is Coming) - MGM-562 (Mexico)
The Proud One / The Last Day Is Coming Is Coming - 2006 520 (Australia)
The Proud One / The Last Day Is Coming Is Coming - 2006 520 (New Zealand)
The Proud One / The Last Day Is Coming Is Coming - 2006 520 (Ireland)
The Proud One / The Last Day Is Coming Is Coming - 2006 520 (UK)
I'm Still Gonna Need You / Thank You - M 14831(Canada)

The following releases were issued with a picture sleeve:
The Proud One / The Last Day Is Coming Is Coming - DM-1267 (Japan)
The Proud One / The Last Day Is Coming Is Coming - 20 06 520 (Spain)
The Proud One / The Last Day Is Coming Is Coming - 2006 520 (France)
The Proud One / The Last Day Is Coming Is Coming - 2006 520 (Austria)

The Proud One / The Last Day Is Coming Is Coming - 2006 520 (Germany)
The Proud One / The Last Day Is Coming Is Coming - 2006 520 (Belgium)
The Proud One / The Last Day Is Coming Is Coming - 2006 520 (Netherlands)
I'm Still Gonna Need You / Thank You - M 14831 (US)
I'm Still Gonna Need You / Thank You - 2006 551(Germany)

Notes:

- This album was originally released on LP, cassette and 8-Track tape formats on August 30, 1975.
- This album was titled "I'm Still Gonna Need You" in the UK.

Songs recorded for this album but not released:
Believin' in Love (Recorded November 12, 1974)

The US picture sleeve for *I'm Still Gonna Need You*

Brainstorm
PD-6077

Track Listings:
I Can't Live A Dream (Recorded May 17, 1976) / Back On The Road Again# / Boogie Down### (Recorded July 22, 1976) / Gotta Get Love# / Walkin' In The Jungle# / At The Rainbow's End / Learnin' How To Love Again / It'll Be Me (Recorded May 17, 1976) / Check It Out### (Recorded July 22, 1976) / Medicine Man##

Production Information:
Produced by: Mike Curb and Michael Lloyd
Executive Producers: The Osmond Brothers
#Produced by: The Osmond Brothers
##Produced by: Alan Osmond and Michael Lloyd
###Produced by: Wayne Osmond, Mike Curb, and Michael Lloyd

Recorded at: Kolob Recording Studios, Los Angeles, California,
and Provo, Utah
Engineered by: Ed Greene, Humberto Gatica, Wayne Osmond and Michael Lloyd
Remix Engineer: Humberto Gatica

Musicians:
Jay Graydon, Michael Lloyd, John D'Andrea, Steve Olitzky, Ben Benay, James Hughart, Ron Krasinski, Dan Sawyer, Reginald Powell, Shaun Duffey Harris

Art Direction: Beverly Parker
Design: Brian Hagiwara
Photography: Kenneth McGowan

Singles Released From This Album:
I Can't Live A Dream / Check It Out - PD 14348 (US / Canada)
I Can't Live A Dream / Check It Out - 2066 726 (UK)
I Can't Live A Dream / Check It Out - 20 66 726 (New Zealand)

The following releases were issued with a picture sleeve:
I Can't Live A Dream / Check It Out - 2066 726 (Netherlands)

Notes:

- This album was originally released on LP, cassette and 8-Track tape formats.

Songs recorded for this album but not released:
Put The Light On (Recorded May 17, 1976)

The Netherlands picture sleeve for *I Can't Live A Dream*.

Steppin' Out
SRM-3766 - 1979

Track Listings:
Steppin' Out / Emily / You're Mine / Baby's Back / Love On The Line / Rainin' / I, I, I / Love Ain't An Easy Thing / Hold On / Rest Your Love

Production Information:
Produced by: Maurice Gibb and Steve Klein For Osbro Productions
All rhythm tracks and vocals recorded at: Kolob Recording Studios and
Osmond Entertainment Center, Provo, Utah (except Emily)
Strings, horns, and additional overdubbing Criteria Recording Studios, Miami, FL
Engineered by: Steve Klein
Remixed at Criteria Studio "D" Miami, FL
Assistant Engineer (In Miami): Mike Guerra
Mastering: Mike Fuller, Criteria Recording Studios Miami, FL

All selections except: Love Ain't an Easy Thing and Rest Your Love on Me written by Alan, Wayne, Merrill, and Jay Osmond.
All selections except: Love Ain't an Easy Thing and Rest Your Love published by Osmusic Publishing Co, (BMI)
Rest Your Love written by: Barry Gibb, Stigwood Music, Inc. (Uni-Chappel Music Admin) BMI
Love Ain't An Easy Thing written by Neil Sadaka – Phil Cody
(Kiddio Music Co, BMI and Top Pop Music Co, ASCAP

Musicians:
Keyboards and Synthesizers: Denny Crockett, Blue Weaver, George Bitzer, Bruce Nazarian
Bass: Ike Egan, Bruce Nazarian, George "Chocolate" Perry
Guitars: George Terry, Bruce Nazarian, Rich Dixon, Joey Murcia
Drums: Sam Foster
Percussion: Joe Lala, Fred Wickstrom, Richie Puente, Ken Hodges
Horns: Boneroo Horns
Sax: Whit Sidener, Chris Colclesser
Trombones: Peter Graves, Russ Freeland
Trumpets: Ken Faulk, Vinne Tanno
French Horn: Jerry Peel
Strings: Miami String Section

Sax Solo on Steppin' Out: Mike Lewis
Strings and horns arranged by: Mike Lewis
Female Vocal on Love on the Line: Kitty Woodson

Special thanks to: The Entire Criteria Staff.
The Aphex Aural Exciter appears on this record.
Art Direction, Photography and Design: Ed Caraeff Studio.

Singles Released From This Album:
You're Mine / Put Your Love On The Line - Mercury-74056 (US)
Steppin' Out / Put Your Love On The Line - Mercury - 6167 761 (UK)
Rainin' / Hold On - Mercury - 6167 782 (France)
You're Mine / Hold On - Mercury - 6837 569 (France)
Emily - Mercury 74079 (Promo) (US)

12" Singles Released From This Album:
I, I, I / You're Mine - Mercury MK-91 (US)

Notes:

- This album was originally released on LP, cassette and 8-Track tape formats.

1979 promotional ad as seen in Billboard magazine

The Osmond Brothers
60180 - 1982

Track Listings:
Never Ending Song of Love / You'll Be Seeing Me / I Think About Your Lovin' / Take This Heart / Bring On The Sunshine / It's Like Falling In Love (Over and Over) / Ease The Fever / Two Kinds of Crazy / Your Leaving Was The Last Thing On My Mind / Blue All Over You

Production Information:
Produced by: Rick Hall
Recorded at: Fame Recording Studios, Muscle Shoals, AL
Background Vocals recorded at Osmond Teleproduction Center, Orem UT
Recording Engineers: Rick Hall, Jerry Masters, Johnny Sandlin, Walt Aldridge
2nd Engineer: Ralph Ezell

Art Direction: Ron Coro
Design: Denise Minobe
Photography: Jim Shea

Musicians:
Keyboards: David Briggs, Pigg Robbins, Steve Nathan, Chalmers Davis
Drums: Owen Hale
Bass: Bob Wray, Ralph Ezell
Guitars: Fred Newell, Ken Bell, Walt Aldridge
Steel Guitar and Dobro: Sonny Garrish
Banjo: Fred Newell
Harmonica: Bill Darnell
Sax: Ronnie Eades
Fiddle and Tamborine: Rick Hall
Additional background vocals: Hershal Wiggington

Singles Released From This Album:
I Think About Your Lovin' / Workin' Man Blues - E-47438
Pienso En Tu Amor (I Think About Your Lovin') / Blues Del Trabajador (Working Man's Blues)
Elektra F-ELK 0047438.9 (Peru)
Never Ending Song of Love For You / You'll Be Seeing Me - 7-69883
It's Like Fallin' Love / Your Leavin' Was The Last Thing On My Mind 7-69969

Notes:

- This album was originally released on LP, cassette and 8-Track tape formats.

Songs recorded for this album but not released:
"I Got You (Now and Forever)" and "Over the Yukon."

1982 promotional ad as seen in Billboard magazine

One Way Rider
1-25070 - 1984

Track Listings:
She's Ready For Someone To Love Her / Come Back To Me / What Do The Lonely Do / One Way Rider / If Every Man Had A Woman Like You / We Work Hard (To Make Love Easy) / She Danced Her Way Into My Heart / Where Does An Angel Go When She Cries / She's Back In Town Again / You Be The Judge

Production Information:
Produced by Jim Ed Norman for JEN Productions, Inc.
Recorded at: Audio Media Recorders, Nashville, TN
Magnolia Sound Studio, Nashville, TN
The Record Lab, Provo, Utah
Soundstage Studio, Nashville, TN
Redwing Studio
Music Mill Studios, Nashville, TN
Engineers: Marshall Morgan / Eric Prestidege / Cliff Maag
Assistant Engineers: Giles Reeves / Tom Crosswait / Tim Kish / Joe Scaite
Additional overdubbing at: Woodland Sound Studio Nashville, TN
Engineer: Tracy Jorgensen
Mixed by: Eric Prestidge at the Music Mill Studios, Nashville, TN
Originally mastered by: Glenn Meadows at Mastertonics, Nashville.
This album was digitally mixed and mastered.

Musicians:
Bass: Joe Osborn, Bob Glaub
Keyboards: Dennis Burnside, Brian Whitcomb
Electric Guitar: Steve Gibson, Paul Worley, John Hug, Randy Mitchell, Josh Leo
Acoustic Guitar: Paul Worley, John Hug, Randy Mitchell
Drums: Eddie Bayers, Michael Huey
Strings: Nashville String Machine with Carl Gorodetzky; concertmaster.
Strings Arranged and conducted by: Bergen White

Art Direction / Design: Laura Li Puma
Photography: James Goble
Personal Management: United Management Associates, Karl Engemann

Singles Released from This Album:
Where Does An Angel Go When She Cries / One More For Lovers - 7-29387
She's Ready For Someone To Love Her / You Make The Long Road Shorter - 7-29594
If Every Man Had A Woman Like You / Come Back To Me - 7-29312

Notes:

- This album was originally released on LP and cassette tape.

1984 Osmond Brothers Country T-Shirt.
Promotion is very important in the music business and shirts, tour books and more helped move records!

Today
5118 - 1985 Range Records (UK)

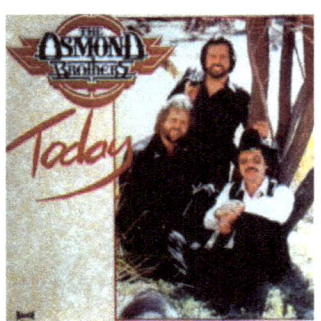

Track Listings:
I Think About Your Lovin' / It's Like Fallin' In Love (Over and Over) / Never Ending Song of Love / Take This Heart / Ease The Fever / Your Leaving Was The Last Thing on My Mind / Blue All Over You / She's Ready For Someone To Love Her / If Every Man Had A Woman Like You / What Do The Lonely Do / We Work Hard (To Make Love Easy) / Where Does an Angel Go When She Cries / She's Back in Town Again / One Way Rider

Production Information:
Produced by: Rick Hall and Jim Ed Norman
Recorded at: Fame Recording Studios, Muscle Shoals, AL
Audio Media Recorders, Nashville, TN
Woodland Sound Studios, Nashville, TN
Background vocals recorded at Osmond Teleproduction Center, Orem Utah
Recording engineers: Rick Hall / Jerry Masters / Johnny Sandlin / Walt Aldridge / Marshall Morgan / Tracy Jorgensen / Eric Prestidge
Assistant Engineer: Ralph Ezell / Giles Reeves / Ken Briblez

Musicians:
Keyboards: David Briggs / Hargus "Pig" Robbins / Steve Nathan / Chalmers Davis / Dennis Burnside / Brian Whitcomb
Drums: Owen Hale / Eddie Bayers / Michael Huey
Bass: Bob Wray / Ralph Ezell / Joe Osborn / Bob Glaub
Guitars: Fred Newell / Ken Bell / Walt Aldridge
Acoustic Guitars: Paul Worley / John Hug / Randy Mitchell
Electric Guitars: Steve Gibson / Paul Worley / John Hug / Randy Mitchell / Josh Leo
Steel Guitar and Dobro: Sonny Garrish
Banjo: Fred Newell
Harmonica: Bill Darnell
Saxophone: Ronnie Eades
Fiddle and Tamborine: Rick Hall
Additional background vocals: Hershal Wiggington

String arrangements and conducting: Bergen White
Strings: The Nashville String Machine
Concertmaster: Carl Gorodetzky

Album compilation: Tony Byworth / Wootton International

Album coordinator: Marguerite Luciani

Personal Management: Karl Engemann, United Management Associates
Public Relations: Ronald J. Clark

Singles Released From This Album:
One Way Rider / I Think About Your Lovin' RANS-74 (UK)

A rare photo of the brothers mid career.

Baby Wants
(Unreleased Album)
1986 EMI Records

Known Track Listings:
Baby Wants / Lovin' Proof / You Look Like The One I Love / It's Only Heartache / Looking For Suzanne / Back In Your Arms Again / Slow Ride / The Price You Pay / You're Here to Remember, I'm Here to Forget / Anytime / Desperately / Baby When Your Heart Breaks Down / Love Burnin' Down

Production Information:
Produced By Terry Choate and Dennis Wilson
Associate Producer: Merrill Osmond
Recorded in Nashville, TN and St. Louis, MO

Notes:
- Most, if not all, of the material from this unreleased album has been released on singles.

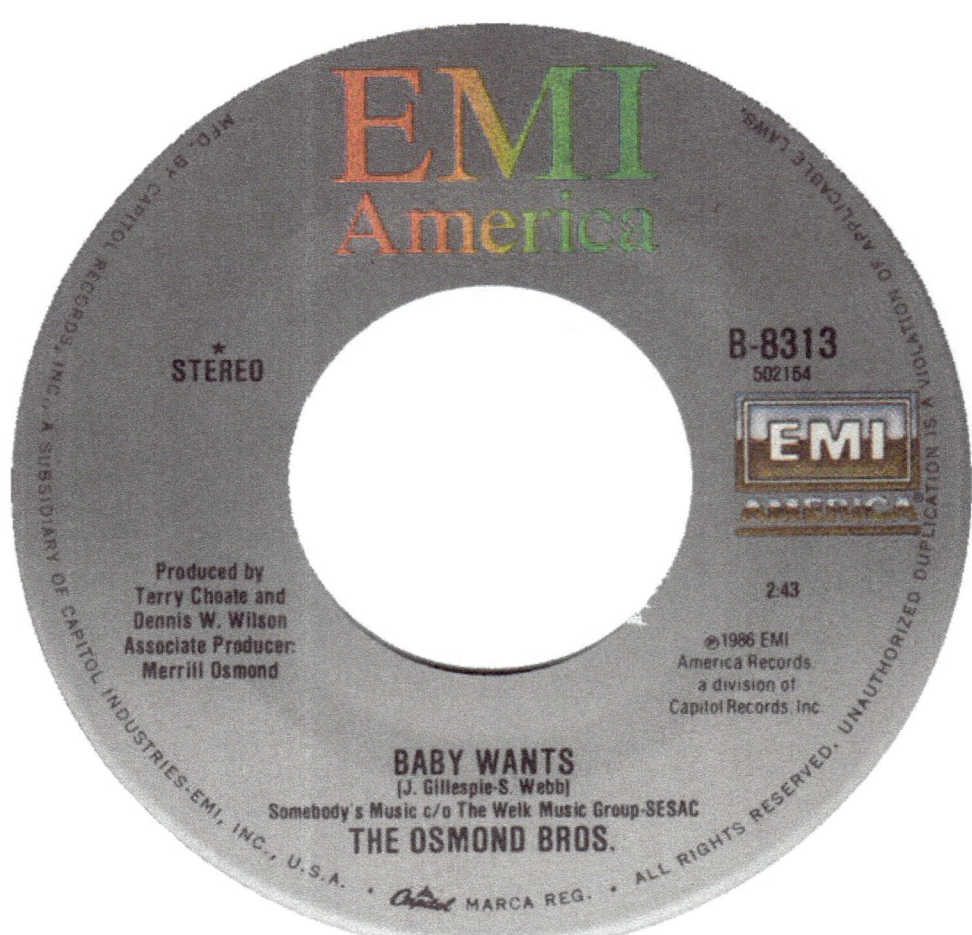

The US single of *Baby Wants*.

Back Home
1993

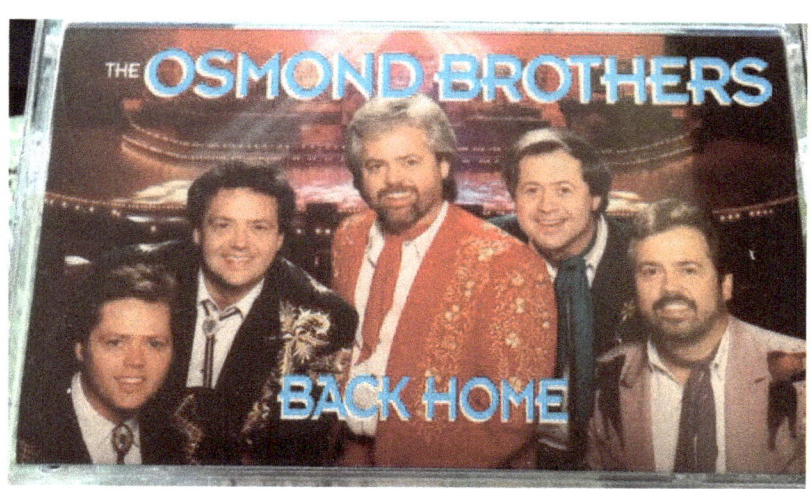

Track Listings:
Takin' Country To The City / Dream A Little Dream of Me / Mama Don't Allow / Lester Leaps In / The Jayson Beat / The World Is Waiting / For The Sunrise / If You Knew Susie / When The Saints Go Marching In / Boil That Cabbage Down / Dancin' In Branson / Mountain Music / Is It Only Love? / I Think About Your Lovin' / One Way Rider / Hits Medley: One Bad Apple - Yo Yo - Down By The Lazy River - Crazy Horses - Love Me For A Reason / And You Love Me / Back Step Lovin' / He Ain't Heavy, He's My Brother

Production Information:
Produced by: The Osmond Brothers
Recorded at: The Record Lab, Orem, Utah
Engineer: Cliff Maag

Thanks to: G&O Records, George and Olive Osmond

Notes:

- Cassette Only Release
- Sold exclusively through the Osmond Theater in Branson, MO

Live In Concert
Osmond Entertainment - 1997

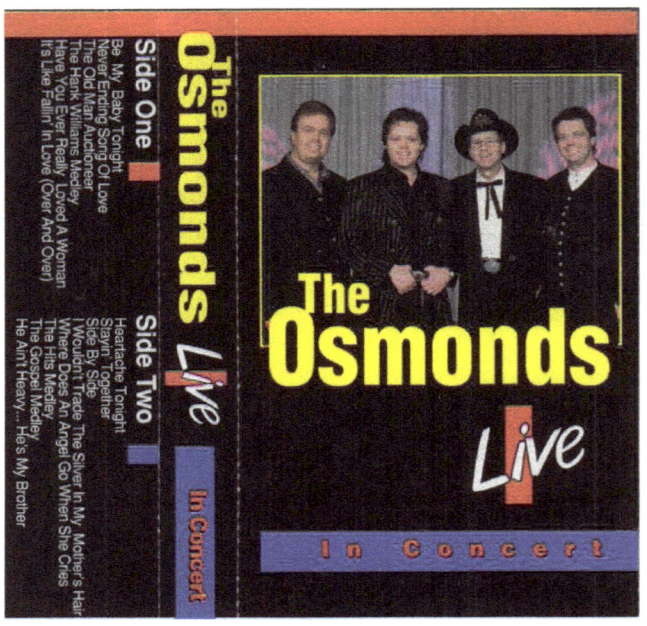

Track Listings:
Be My Baby Tonight / Never Ending Song Of Love / The Old Man Auctioneer / Hank Williams Medley: Your Cheatin' Heart - Hey, Good Lookin' - I'm So Lonesome I Could Cry - Jambalaya / Have You Ever Really Loved A Woman / Heartache Tonight / Stayin' Together / Side By Side / I Wouldn't Trade The Silver In My Mothers Hair / Where Does An Angel Go When She Cries / Hits Medley: One Bad Apple - Love Me For A Reason - Yo Yo - Down By The Lazy River / Gospel Medley: I Am A Child Of God - Because I Have Been Given Much - I Need Thee Ev'ry Hour - How Great Thou Art - God Be With You 'Til We Meet Again / He Ain't Heavy, He's My Brother

Production Information:
Produced by: Jimmy Osmond
Co-Producer: Whit Privette
Recorded at: Osmond Family Theater, Branson, MO
Engineer: Bob Jernigan

Musicians:
Bass, Backing Vocals: Whit Privette
Electric and Acoustic Guitar: Mike McAdoo
Fiddle, Trumpet, Acoustic Guitar, Backing Vocals: George Mason
Saxophone, Harmonica, Synthesizer, Acoustic Guitar: Jay Brandon
Piano and Synthesizer: Ken Michaels and Jay Snyder
Drums and Percussion: Casey Smith

Notes:

- Released on cassette tape and CD.

Gospel Favorites
Top of the World Entertainment - 1999

Track Listings:
Friends / I Am A Child of God / I'll Fly Away / The Refiner's Fire / Let Me In / Amazing Grace / Oh Happy Day / The Anchor Holds / Swing Low, Sweet Chariot / More Than Anything / How Great Thou Art / Love One Another / God Be With You Til We Meet Again

Production Information:
Produced By: The Osmond Brothers (Wayne, Merrill, Jay & Jimmy)
Executive Assistance: Marian Hile
Co Produced: Ric Williams and Whit Privette
Recorded and mixed entirely with Pro Tools 24 Mixplus system on location at the Osmond Family Theater Recording Studios, Branson, MO
Engineered and Mixed By: Ric Williams
Drums: David Osmond
Bass: Whit Privette
Guitar: Mitch Keirsey
Keyboard: Gregg Gray
Horns: Rich Duston, Louis Thierbach, Bryon Westerman, Jay Parks, Brent Vaugham
Flute: Claude Coffman
Strings: Tina Sibley, James Robertson, Jane Shurty, Joan Salts
Musical Arrangements: Greg Gray
Research: Janice Smith
Technical Assistance: Danny Watson at Ozark Pro Audio
Special thanks to: RoDak / Mike Dowdle

Cover photo: Deborah J Kew
Graphic Design By: Newkirk Design Group

This Album Is Dedicated To Our Loving Parents

Notes:

- Sold at Osmond Family Theater and Fan Club outlets

Christmas Memories
Top of the World Entertainment - 1999

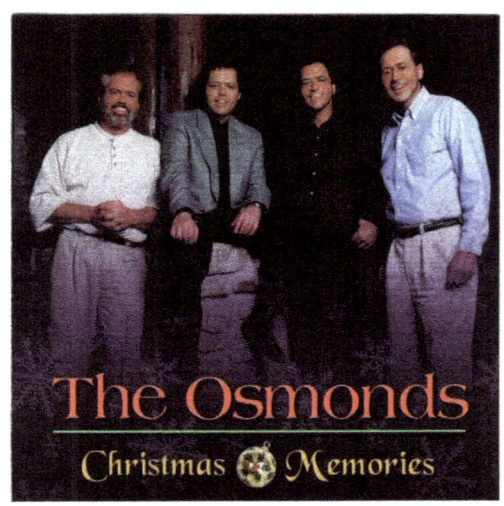

Track Listings:
It Came Upon a Midnight Clear / It's the Most Wonderful Time of the Year / Jingle Bell Rock / Happy Holiday / Winter Wonderland / Santa Claus is Coming to Town / The Gift / Christmas Medley: White Christmas - Rockin' Around the Christmas Tree - Have Yourself a Merry Little Christmas - Feliz Navidad - We Need a Little Christmas - Little Drummer Boy - Silver Bells - Angels We Have Heard On High / Caroling Medley: Caroling, Caroling - Here We Come a Caroling - Christmas is Coming - We Wish You A Merry Christmas / Kay Thompson's Jingle Bells / Mary Did You Know / O Holy Night / Silent Night / Sing Out the Glories of Christmas

Production Information:
Produced by: The Osmond Brothers (Wayne, Merrill, Jay & Jimmy)
Co-Produced by: Ric Williams and Whit Privette
Recorded and Mixed entirely with Pro Tools 24 Mixplus System on location at Osmond Family Theater Recording Studio, Branson, MO
Engineered and Mixed by: Ric Williams
Assistant Engineer / Editor: Whit Privette
Vocal Arrangements: The Osmond Brothers

Executive Assistance to the Osmond Brothers: Marian Hile
Research: Janice Smith
Technical Assistance: Danny Watson at Ozark Pro Audio
Graphic Design by: Mark W. Roy

Musicians:
Piano/Keyboard: Gregg W. Gray
Acoustic/Electric Guitar: Mitch Keirsey
Bass Guitar: Whit Privette
Drums: David Osmond
Vocals: The Osmond Brothers
Horns: Verle Ormsby, Ned Wilkinson, Jim Murphy, Wesley Marshall, Carl Hose, David Johnson, Jim Miller, Jay Davera, Neil Brocker
Percussion: Ned Wilkinson

Handbells: Eric Gaden, Brandon Williams
Background Vocals: The John Morton Choir
Strings: Tina Sibley, Jane Shurtz Ronna Adema, Juliana Georgiades, Melissa Horine, Carol Harrison, Suzanne Gasaway, Starla Blair, Dorothy Straw, Esther Henry, Joan Gasaway

This album is dedicated to our leader, brother Alan. We love you.

Notes:

- Sold at Osmond Family Theater and Fan Club outlets.

An outtake from the cover photo session of *Christmas Memories*.

Back On The Road Again Live
RBF Incorporated - 2001

Track Listing:
I Can't Get Next To You / Yo-Yo / Down By The Lazy River / Two Kinds Of Crazy / Back On The Road Again / Old Man Auctioneer / I'll Be Good To You / Hold Her Tight - Yes Ma'am / An American Trilogy / The Proud One / Crazy Horses / Love Me For A Reason / Friends / Brothers Medley: Lazy River - Bye, Bye Love - All The Gold In California - Do You Remember These - You've Lost That Lovin' Fellin' - Too Much Heaven - A B C - One Bad Apple - He Ain't Heavy, He's My Brother / Gospel Medley: How Great Thou Art - God Be With You Til We Meet Again

Bonus Track: Bring Back The American Dream

Notes:

- All tracks except, Bring Back The American Dream, recorded live at Mystic Lake Celebrity Palace, Prior Lake, Minnesota on March 7, 2001
- A Fan Club Only Release

Distributed by RBF Incorporated.
© 2001 Crazy Horses, LLC

Live By Request
AJR200701 - 2007

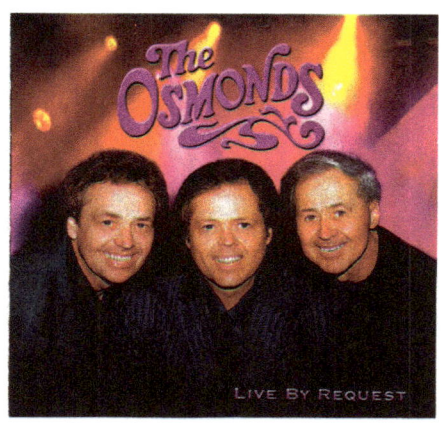

Track Listing:
Crazy Horses / The Proud One / Havin' A Party / At The Rainbow's End / Down By The Lazy River / 100 Days, 100 Nights / Rock And Roll Music / Let Me In / I Can't Live A Dream / Rainin' / You Take Me To Heaven / 70's Medley: Yesterday, September - Take A Chance On Me - Crocodile Rock - That's They Way (I Like It) - Superstition - Too Much Heaven - Tragedy - ABC - I Want You Back - One Bad Apple - Bohemian Rhapsody / Love Me For A Reason / He Ain't Heavy, He's My Brother

Production Information:
Recorded at: The Mansion Studio, Branson, Mo
Engineers: Daniel Stone and Stephan John

CakeWalk Studios Branson, Mo
Engineers: Mark Owen

Brunson Brothers Studios, Provo, Utah
Engineer: Gaynor Brunson

Mixed at Brunson Studio, Provo, Utah
Re-Mix Engineer: Gaynor Brunson
Assistant Engineer: Shauna Flynn

Musicians:
Guitars: Gene Puckett / Jimie Glaser
Bass: Bryan Lawson / Marty Wilhite / Jamie Glaser
Drums: Steve Mason / Pete Generous
Keyboards: Aaron Smith / Gregg W. Gray
Strings: Tina Sibley / Jane Shurtz / Carol Harrison / Alezsis Zarins / Kirsten Weiss
Horns: Don Smith / Doyle Miller / Gaynor Brunson Carl Hose / Bill Reder
Backvocals: Wayne Osmond, Merrill Osmond, Jay Osmond and Jimmy Osmond.
Cover Photo: Sophia Osmond.
Back and liner photos: Tom McFarland
Cover Graphics: Shauna Flynn

I Can't Get There Without You
OSMONDSCD 1

Track Listings:
Break Your Fall / Can't Get There Without You / Save Me / I Need You / Fall To Fly / Take Me Home / Breakable / Will You Go With Me / Gotcha Goin' My Way / Remember Me

Notes:

- Released: September 18, 2012

Back CD Tray Insert

Up Close and Personal
The Final Tour
2013

For over five decades The Osmond Brothers have entertained sold out crowds throughout the world and 2012 marked the year of their biggest ever UK Tour. Now you can see Merrill, Jay and Jimmy Osmond perform all their hits and new songs from their latest CD I Can't Get There Without You, together with backstage film footage, and introductions by Jimmy Osmond. The programme is on two DVD's. Also included in this set is an audio CD with selected live tracks from the concert tour. The packaging is a deluxe hardback book with photos covering over 50 years of The Osmonds entertainment career and never before seen candid photos taken behind the scenes on this final UK tour. Additionally there is a printed certificate signed by Merrill, Jay and Jimmy Osmond making this an exclusive edition.

Notes:

- 2 DVDs of the Final Tour Concert (in the UK), with behind the scenes footage and narrated by Jimmy Osmond
- 1 CD (audio) with selected live tracks from the concert
- Booklet with a pictorial history of The Osmonds and never before seen backstage photos
- A printed signed certificate
- Packaged in a hardback book style with the discs mounted inside front and back covers and the booklet in the middle.

Merry Christmas
OSMONDSCD3

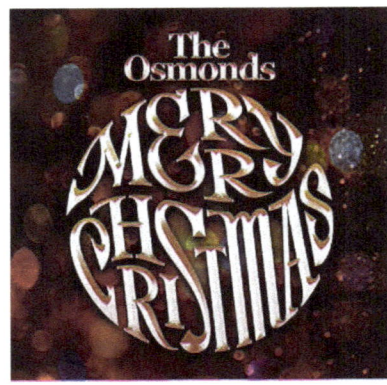

Track Listing:

Medley: It Came Upon a Midnight Clear - It's the Most Wonderful Time of the Year - Jingle Bell Rock / Happy Holidays / You Meet the Nicest People / Last Christmas / Medley: White Christmas - Rockin' Around the Christmas Tree - Have Yourself a Merry Little Christmas - Feliz Navidad - We Need a Little Christmas / Lonely This Christmas / Hallelujah / Little Drummer Boy / Kay Thompson's Jingle Bells / Merry Xmas Everybody / Medley: O Holy Night - Silent Night - Sing Out the Glories of Christmas / Caroling Medley: Caroling, Caroling - Here We Come a Caroling - Christmas Is Coming - We Wish You a Merry Christmas / Winter Wonderland / The Gift / Santa Claus Is Coming to Town / Silver Bells / Mary, Did You Know?

Notes:

- Released: November 13, 2015
- Features Osmond Brothers - Merrill, Jay and Jimmy in all new recordings.

Very Merry Rockin' Good Christmas
Jay & Merrill
Curb Records

Track Listing:
Very Merry Rockin' Good Christmas / Winter Wonderland / Jingle Bells / Santa Claus Is Coming To Town / Christmas Must Be Tonight / Merry Christmas Everyone / Run Rudolph Run / Last Christmas / Christmas Star / Sleigh Ride / Merry Christmas Everybody / Little Drummer Boy / Silent Night

Notes:

- Released: November 16, 2018

Jay & Merrill

Merrill
Osmond

What I Like
1989

Track Listings:
Heartbreak Radio / Sly Little Fox / Save That Dress / Hope of America / This Is America / Yes Ma'am / Takin' Country To The City / Step By Step / Waltzin' in 4/4 Time / Singin' Again / There's a Man Who Loves You / Stayin' Together

Production Information:
Producer: Merrill Osmond
Recorded at: The Record Lab, Orem Utah
Sound Engineer: Cliff Maag

Cover Photo: Chris Galloway

Special Thanks to: Carole Oldroyd, LuAnn Brobst, Jerry Williams

Manufactured by: Merrill Osmond Enterprises

Notes:

- Cassette Only Release

I Love America
1994

Track Listings:
Hope of America / This Is America / Standing Up For Freedom / Armed Forces Medley / Unselfish Heart / A Thousand Points of Light / Family / Shake It / One World, One Voice / Hope of America

Notes:

- Cassette only release

Merrill Osmond Family Christmas
1995

Track Listings:
Memories of Christmas / Jingle Bells / Winter Wonderland / Rudolph / I'm Gettin' Nothin' For Christmas / The Greatest Gift / Christmas Is / Silent Night

Notes:

- Cassette only release

How Great Thou Art
1997

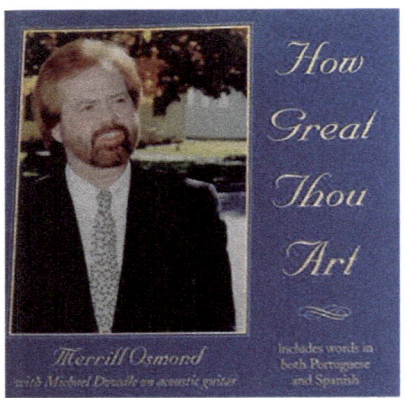

Track Listings:
*How Great Thou Art / Did You Think to Pray / I Need Thee Every Hour / *I Am A Child of God / *Teach Me To Walk In The Light/ I'll Go Where You Want Me To Go / I Know That My Redeemer Lives / More Holiness Give Me / *Because I Have Been Given Much *Our Savior's Love / I Stand All Amazed / Abide With Me 'Tis Eventide / *Love One Another/ God Be With You Till We Meet Again

Production Information:
Produced and engineered by: Cliff Maag,
Recorded at: The Record Lab, Provo Utah

"How Great Thou Art," Stuart K Hine, Manna Music Inc.

*Copyright permission granted.

Notes:

- All other hymns public domain and recorded as printed in the Hymn Book of the Church of Jesus Christ of Latter-day Saints.

From My Heart To Yours
MJM Entertainment

Track Listings:
The Anchor Holds / Friends / Amazing Grace / His Name is Wonderful / I Pledge Allegiance To The Lamb / Household of Faith / More Than Anything / Stayin' Together / The Refiners Fire

Production Information:
Produced by: Mike & Jane Malcom
Co-Produced by: Merrill Osmond

Recorded and Mixed at: Crystal Recording & Sound, Branson, MO
Recording Engineer: Chris Jones
Mixing & Mastering by: Stephen John

Background tracks courtesy of: The Right Trax by Word Music
Additional Tracks courtesy of Christian World

Cover Design by: Mike Malcom
Cover Photo by: Teresa Heard
CD Photo by: Sue Scholl

Special Thanks to: Peggy Jones

Notes:

- Released: March 23, 1999

Never Say Never
CURCD147- (UK)

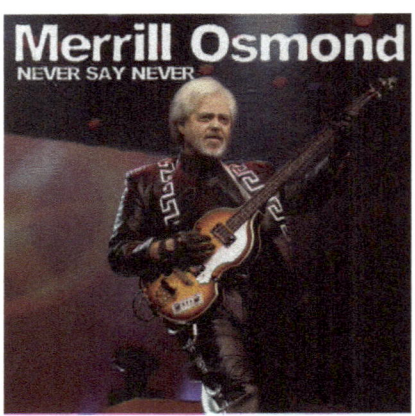

Track Listing:
If You Believe / All Tied Up / Medicine Man / Never Say Never / Save That Dress / I'll Be Good To You / O In Love / My Girl / Girl Medley / You're Here to Remember, I'm Here to Forget / Plan Medley / Hold Her Tight / Mighty Mighty Love / Up Over The Yukon

Notes:

- Released: March 15, 2004

May All Your Wishes Come True
Limited Edition

Track Listing:
Jingle Bells (with Heather Hallows) / Blue Christmas / Walking In A Winter Wonderland / Mary Did You Know / Memories Of Christmas / Rudolph The Red Nose Reindeer / The Greatest Gift / Christmas Is / Silent Night

Notes:

- Released: 2006

The Voice
MPH Records - MPHCD281 (UK)

Track Listing:
You Take My Breath Away / Coming Home / One Bad Apple / Love Me For A Reason / The Proud One / Yo-Yo / Let Me In / Darlin' / He Ain't Heavy He's My Brother / Down By The Lazy River / Crazy Horses / Move A Mountain

Bonus Track:
Shiloh

Notes:
- Released: May 23, 2008

Unplugged

Tracking List:
Yo-Yo / At The rainbows End / Proud One / Let Me In / Darlin / If Every Man Had A Woman Like You / Here To Remember / That's My Girl / Born to be Wild / I Think About Your Lovin' / Crazy Horses / Love Me For A Reason / One Bad Apple / Heartbreak Radio / Where Does An Angel Go When She Cries

Notes:

- Released August 2009

Swing Time
2009

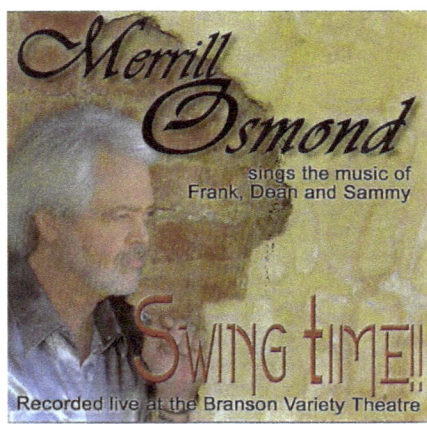

Track Listing:

The Lady Is A Tramp / Come Fly With Me / That's Life / Candy Man / Fly Me To The Moon / You Make Me Feel So Young / Ain't That A Kick In The Head / You Don't Know Me / Mack The Knife / Luck Be A Lady / New York, New York

Notes:
- Recorded live at Branson Variety Theater

Merrill Osmond Sings Broadway

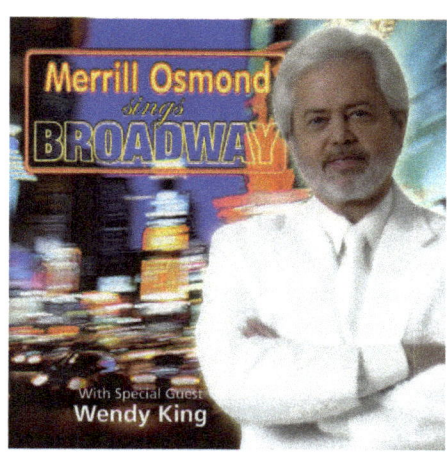

Tracking List:
Close Every Door / Copacabana / Impossible Dream / Lullaby of Broadway / Mame / Oh What a Beautiful Morning / Magic Of The Night / Razzle Dazzle / Some Enchanted Evening / This Is The Moment

Notes:

- Released: 2009

A Tribute To Classic Rock

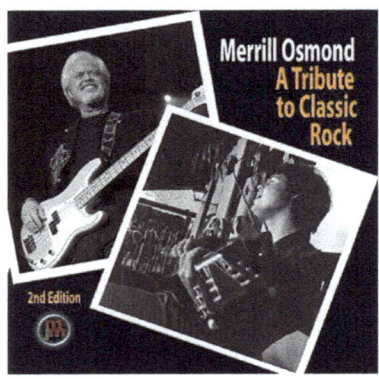

Tracking List:
Rock And Roll / Sharp Dressed Man / Ain't No Sunshine / Old Time Rock & Roll / Travelin' Band / Hold Her Tight / Free Ride / Superstition / I Don't Want To Miss A Thing / Can't You See / Takin' Care of Business / Born To Be Wild

Notes:

- Released: October 1, 2010

Merrill working on the album.

Heart and Soul
March 18, 2011

Track Listings:
A Million Love Songs / I Who Have Nothing / When A Man Loves A Woman / The Power of Love / I'll Be There / Hero / If You Don't Know Me By Now / You Take My Breath / Away / I'll Never Fall In Love / If You Leave Me Now / Hearts Bound 4Ever / You Are So Beautiful / Hard To Say Goodbye

Production Information:
Producer: Merrill Osmond
Co-Producer: Mary Osmond
Recorded at: Nick Sibley Recording Studio, Springfield MO
Engineer: Nick Sibley

Musicians:
Lead Vocals: Merrill Osmond
Bass: Bryan Lawson
Drums & Percussion: Steve Mason
Guitars: Gene Puckett
Horns: Ned Wilkinsen
Keyboard: Scott Taylor
Sax: Todd Estes
Violin: Tina Sibley

Additional Vocals: Mal Pope
Backing Vocals: Greg Frazier, Allie Hutsell, Gene Puckett, Tina Sibley, Ned Wilkinson
Project Coordinator: Gene Puckett
Production Assistants: Donna Cahill, Sherri Lippoldt
Tracks: Scot Lancaster, Lyman Clark
Photos: Ina Mourik

From Merrill:
This CD has been a labor of love for me. So many wonderful friends over the years have encouraged me to record such a collection of songs. In fact, as I look back at my journal entries, this subject goes back 10 years. There were so many emotions that filled my heart and mind as I sang these songs.

I remembered places and conversations where I either heard the original song played, or a memory that popped into my thoughts that reminded me of a personal conversation or an experience I had that mirrored the words I was singing. Choosing the songs was not an easy task. Thousands of suggestions from websites to Facebook entries put a spotlight on so many incredible songs. But when I made the final decision each song made sense to me. They represented where I am today and the feelings of my heart and soul. So to those who have supported me over the years, and given me a reason to keep singing, this CD is for you.

Enjoy, The Bear – Merrill

Merrill and Mary

I'm On Fire

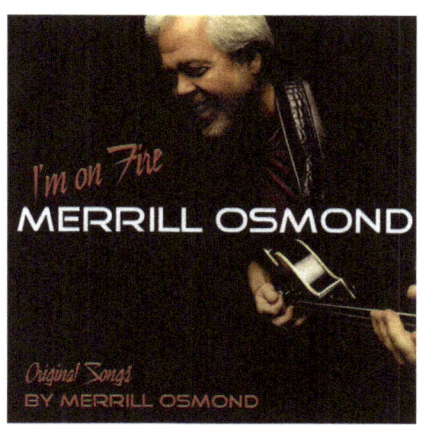

Track Listing:
Looking for Zion / You Gotta Have Hope / I'm on Fire / Still My Heart Believes / Pure Glory / Shake It Up

Production Information:
Produced by: Merrill Osmond and Gregg Gray
Recorded at: The Record Lab, Provo, Utah and Elitel Music Group, Branson, MO
Engineered by: Cliff Maag and Gregg Gray

All material written by: Merrill Osmond and Cara Thompson-Weir

Musicians:
Drums: Mike Lacy and Jay Laurence
Guitars: Mark Boyd, Mitch Keirsey and Rich Dixon
Bass: Matt Larson
Percussion: Pete Generous
Sax: Bill Caldwell
Keyboards: Gregg Gray
B3: Steve Lindiman

Cover Design: Teresa Heard
Photography: Rubberball.com
Distributed by: Black Bear Publishing

Notes:

- Released: 2012
- All original songs by Merrill Osmond

Remembering Elvis
Black Diamond Records - 40931

Track Listing:
One Night / Blue Suede Shoes / Always On My Mind / Can't Help Falling In Love / Are You Lonesome Tonight / I Just Can't Help Believing' / In The Ghetto / It's Now Or Never / Jailhouse Rock / Love Me Tender / Return To Sender / She's Not You

Bonus Track:
Suspicious Minds

Notes:

- Released: 2012

Merrill and Tesca

Track Listing:

Meet Me in Montana / You're Here to Remember / Play the Music Loud / Emily

Notes:

- Released 2012

Jay
Osmond

It's About Time
JO-B-9694 - 1994

Track Listings:
Even Cowboys Like A Little Bit of Rock N Roll / That's My Girl / Girl / Fallin' In Love Again / Wipeout / Country Boy / Topsy / And You Love Me / My Drum

Production Information:
Produced by: Jay Osmond, Mike McAdoo, Casey Smith and Whit Privette for Big Idea productions, Inc.
Recorded at: Crystal Recording Studio, Bryant, AR
Engineer: Bert Jones

Musicians:
Drums, Lead & Backing Vocals: Jay Osmond
Bass & Backing Vocals: Whit Privette
Acoustic & Electric Guitars, & Backing Vocals : Mike McAdoo
Accordion, Synthesizer: Ken Michaelis
Piano, Trombone, & Synthesizer: Myles Mylenbush
Tenor Sax, Harmonica and Flute: Jay Brandon
Percussion and Drum set: Casey Smith
Violin: George Mason
Backing Vocals: Tami Art and Babette Young

For many years it has been my desire to release an album with some of my favorite songs. This album is about rhythms, seasons, yesterdays, and tomorrows … It's about time. – Jay Osmond

A special thanks to my family, Crystal Recording Studio, Big Idea Productions, photographer Jim Lersch, and of course the band and their families.

In memory of Bert Jones, Engineer

Notes:

- Released on cassette tape only.

It's About Time Again
2009

Track Listing:
Crazy Horses / Smile, When You're Smiling / Sugar, Sugar / That's My Girl / Girl / A Taste of Rhythm and Blues / My Drum / You're Not Alone / Wipe Out / And You Love Me / Fallin' In Love / Topsy / Dream / Friends / Rock and Roll Music / Bonus Track: Wembley Drum Solo

Production Information:
Producer, Vocals, Drums: Jay Osmond
Co-Producer: Gaynor Brunson
Recorded at: Brunson Brothers Studios, Provo, Utah

Background Vocals on Friends & Rock And Roll Music: Osmond Brothers
Instrumentals: Brunson Brothers and Jamie Glaser
Arranger on Friends: Gregg Gray
Keyboard on You're Not Alone: Sam Cardon
Female Vocalist, Sugar, Sugar: Jenny Frogley

Concept & Project Director: Terri Shoemaker
Art Director: Eric Osmond
Art Designer: Jennifer Bjornstad

Photographer: Brandon Osmond

Project Consultant: Jackie Skinner

From the Original It's About Time:
Female Voice on Phone, Girl: Kandilyn Osmond
Female Vocalist Fallin' Love Again: Babette Young
Female Vocalist And You Love Me: Tami Art

Tenor Sax, Harmonica, Flute: Jay Brandon
Violin: George Mason
Acoustic and Electric Guitar: Mike McAdoo
Accordion, Synthesizer: Ken Michaels
Keyboards and Trombone: Myles Mylenbush
Bass: Whit Privette
Percussion / Drums And You Love Me: Casey Smith

From Jay:

About Crazy Horses:
Crazy Horses was our family's biggest worldwide hit. I love performing it on stage, and just had to include it as one of my all-time favorites. There are so many memories attached to the music and words of this song. I thought it would be appropriate to do my own personal version…and add a little twist to it!

About Smile / When You're Smiling:
I have a picture of my wife, Kandilyn, where she has this beautiful smile on her face. It has always made me smile when I look at it. She has helped me realize how important smiling is, even in a difficult situation. She believes a smile can ease the pain of others and lift them when they are down. I would like to dedicate these two songs as a medley in honor of her, for having the courage and strength to smile through some very challenging times. Ironically, the day after I finished recording this medley, I learned that Smile was Michael Jackson's favorite song. I find it interesting how this song has touched so many people.

About Sugar, Sugar:
One of my favorite dance tunes of the 70s was Sugar, Sugar. I loved this song! So, when Terri (my assistant) brought up this tune to be included on the CD, I thought it would be groovy and fun to remember the good old days at high school dances. As I went to the studio, I sat down at the drums and asked Gaynor (my recording engineer) to set up the drum microphones and record me as I started playing (and singing this song in my mind). I then put my voice on it and turned it over to Jamie (my band arranger), who took my voice and drum track and put the band to it. Then, Jenny (the female vocalist) came into the studio and put her cool voice on. Finally, we put the vocal backgrounds on. This song made my list, not just because of the song itself, but because of how all the elements came together in an amazing way! (Also, because my wife Kandilyn likes the way I sing, You are my Kandi girl – ha!)

About: That's My Girl
My brother Alan wrote this song with this future wife Suzanne in mind. I thought it was a wonderful description of his feelings. This song was included on my 1994 cassette, and I thought I would include it on this CD as well. This time though, I though it would be fun to record my voice now (in a duet style), echoing my voice from 15 years ago. I wanted to show a then and now difference in style and tonality. See if you can hear the differences between the original voice (then) and the echo voice (now). To this day, it rates as one of my favorite songs.

About: Girl
I always thought this tune, which we wrote as brothers had a cool Beatles sound. It reminds me of all the many times back in the 70s when my brothers and I flirted with girls and used dumb pickup lines on them. My very talented son Eric loved this song when he heard it on my 1994 cassette. When he was putting the artwork together for this CD, he insisted that I included this song. It not only brings back some fun memories of the 70s for me, but brings a happy feeling to

Eric every time he hears it.

About: A Taste of Rhythm and Blues
Years ago, I was invited to dance on the show, Soul Train with Chaka Khan's sister. I love it! The dance moves I learned there inspired me to start choreographing songs for my brothers to put into our concerts. This also helped me as I choreographed the opening numbers and concert spots for The Donny and Marie Show. I want to apologize to my brother Donny for some of the funky moves I made him do on the show – ha! (He was a great sport.) I kept developing different moves as I would go to different dances. Sometimes at these dances, I'd notice people who just stood on the sidelines and watched. I always tried to encourage them to get out on the dance floor. I'd tell them that it didn't matter how well they danced, it was just fun to feel the groove. So, this song reminds me of the fun times I had, as I helped others to have fun too.

About: My Drum
As a kid (and now as an adult), I would find great emotional relief as I started to play my drums. My brothers knew this (especially when I was feeling anxious, frustrated or worried), and they wrote this song about me. I find it interesting that my son Marcus (who is a great bass player) tends to pick up his bass, especially when he is feeling emotional. Marcus has helped me to remember that no matter how young or old we are, we all need to let go and do something that is fun and stress reducing.

About: You're Not Alone
When I first heard John Canann sing this song, it impressed me so much. It reminds me that whether you are male, female, single, or married, we all have bouts of loneliness. No one is immune to this feeling. I have learned that the Savior Jesus Christ is always there to help and strengthen us in our moments of struggle. If only we remember to fall back into His arms. I dedicate this song to my sweet little sister, Marie. She has felt alone many times in her life, but has found the truth that lies in the lyrics of this song through trial and prayer.

About: Wipe Out
Back in the late 60s and early 70s, Wipe Out was a pretty hip song. Being a drummer, people would often ask, Can you play Wipe Out? The perception was that the drum beat seemed difficult, when it is actually a very simple rhythm with a catchy beat. It is more than a drum lick though, it is a groove that excites everyone. My son Jason (who is an amazing drummer) used to teach people how to play the drums. He was great at helping them find their inner rhythms. Every time I hear this song, it reminds me so much of him. I dedicate this song to Jason, which includes a drum solo at the end that he and I created together.

About: And You Love Me
I think my brother Wayne has written some of the best songs that have ever been recorded. He is a mega talent. I've always felt my brothers Alan and Merrill were like Lennon and McCartney, and Wayne was like George Harrison. I have that kind of respect for them as writers. This is one of Wayne's major cool songs. I want to thank my friend Tami Art (who is an amazing singer) for recording this song with me.

About: Fallin' In Love Again
This was my first song I wrote (back in the 70's). However, there is one spot in the song where I got stuck on a couple of lyrics. My brother Alan fixed a word or two in order make the song flow, so I wanted to give him credit and thank him for his help. This song was selected for the 1978 movie Goin' Coconuts. During one scene in the movie, my brother Donny played the piano and sang this tune with my sister Marie. I was honored they wanted to include my song in the film. I

made a few more lyric changes and later recorded it as a duet with the very talented Babette Young. This song makes my list of favorites.

About: Topsy
Years ago, I was a representative for Ludwig Drums, along with Karen Carpenter and her drummer, Hal Blaine. Hal (known as one of the world's greatest studio drummers) released an album which included Topsy when I was about 18 years old. I remember being fascinated with his steady drumming and creative soloing. I made a promise to myself that someday I would play like that. I knew that one day I wanted to record Topsy in my own way. I dedicate this song to Hal and the other great drummers who made a strong impression on me as a kid, and motivated me to develop my own drumming style.

About: Dream
This was one of my mother's favorite songs. In honor of her, I wanted to include it as one of my favorite songs too. She was always so positive and peaceful to be around. I remember when I was a kid and things didn't go as I planned, she would say, Oh well, just look at it this way…, or This too shall pass. She always encouraged our family to dream big and use our imaginations. The varied drumming throughout this song is for my mother, who spent a lot of time listening to me pound away on those drums. Both of my wonderful parents were, and still are, an inspiration to our family and friends throughout the world.

About: Friends
My brothers and I have performed this song for years. It really emphasizes the importance of being a friends, whether you're in a family situation or not. We have made many great friendships with numerous fans throughout the years. It is also wonderful to see how many of our fans have developed friendships with each other. This song brings a reality to the fact that life is really short, and that being a friend is so very important. I never get tired of hearing or singing it. I hope you will always keep its message close to you.

About: Rock and Roll Music
The groove is what I love most about this song. It sits here, as musicians say, in the pocket. I often perform this song in our shows, and it has become a favorite of mine. As I look at the audience, I feel like they are having as much fun with it as I am!

About: Wembley Drum Solo
I will always remember the feeling I had while performing my drum solo at our Wembley concert. This concert tour was our 50th Anniversary celebration as a family in show business. So many memories were running through my mind while I was playing this solo. It was truly an amazing feeling to look out into the crowd, hear the screams, see the cameras filming, taking a glimpse of the video screens, hearing the sound of the drums booming in the speakers and in my ears, and focusing on playing – all at the same time. Talk about pressure. Ha! Seriously, it was a moment in time for me that I will never forget. I was taken back to memories of the early days when our amazing older brothers, Virl and Tom, took tap lessons and came home to teach the rest of us. This started a sort of domino effect where each of us would take lessons at something, and share what we learned with the rest of the family. Obviously, my niche ended up being the drums, and performing my drum solo on this tour was almost surreal. I also thought about my brother Jimmy who looks after all of us, and made sure the whole 50th Anniversary celebration was set in motion. What a flood of memories – past and present! I'll never forget any of it!

Above: Jay and his drums! I believe this was at the former KOLOB Recording Studio at The Riviera Apartments in Provo, Utah in 1974.

Below: Jay in 1977 on the *Osmond Family Christmas Show*.

The Brunson Brothers and Jay Osmond
Tis The Season
2008

Notes:

- "Tis the Season" CD and DVD-CD combinations can now be found on Amazon.

Donny
Osmond

The Donny Osmond Album
SE-4782

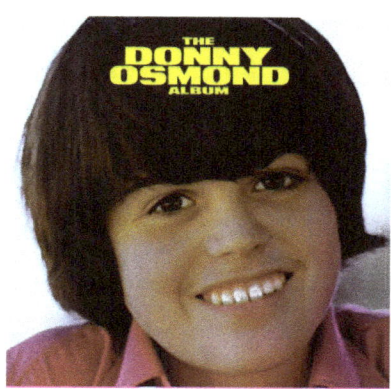

Track Listings:
Sweet and Innocent / I'm Your Puppet / Hey Little Girl / Don't Say No / So Shy / Lollipops, Lace, and Lipstick / Flirtin' / Burning Bridges / Time To Ride / Wake Up Little Susie

Production Information:
Produced and Arranged by: Rick Hall
Recorded at: Fame Recording Studio, "Home of the Muscle Shoals Sound," Muscle Shoals, Alabama and Independent Recorders, Studio City, California
Engineers: Rick Hall, Jerry Masters, Ron Malo

String Arrangements: Pete Carpenter
Horn Arrangements: Rick Hall and Harrison Calloway, Jr.
Sweet and Innocent Strings and Woodwinds arranged by Jimmy Haskell
Vocal Supervision: Earl Brown
Art Direction: Saul Saget

Singles released from this album:
Sweet and Innocent / Flirtin' - 2065 059 (Canada) (Polydor)
Sweet and Innocent / Flirtin' - 2006042 (Australia)
Sweet and Innocent / Flirtin' - 2006042 (New Zealand)

The following releases were issued with a picture sleeve:
Sweet and Innocent / Flirtin' - K 14227 (US)
Sweet and Innocent / Flirtin' - 20 06 042 (Spain)
Sweet and Innocent / Flirtin' - 2006042 (Germany)

LP Data:
Billboard Chart Debut: July 10, 1971
Highest Chart Position: 13
# of Weeks on Chart: 37

Notes:

- This album was originally released on LP, cassette, 8-Track and reel tape formats on June 5, 1971.
- This album was awarded a gold record for sales in excess of 500,000 copies on December 13, 1971
- Sheet music was marketed for this album.

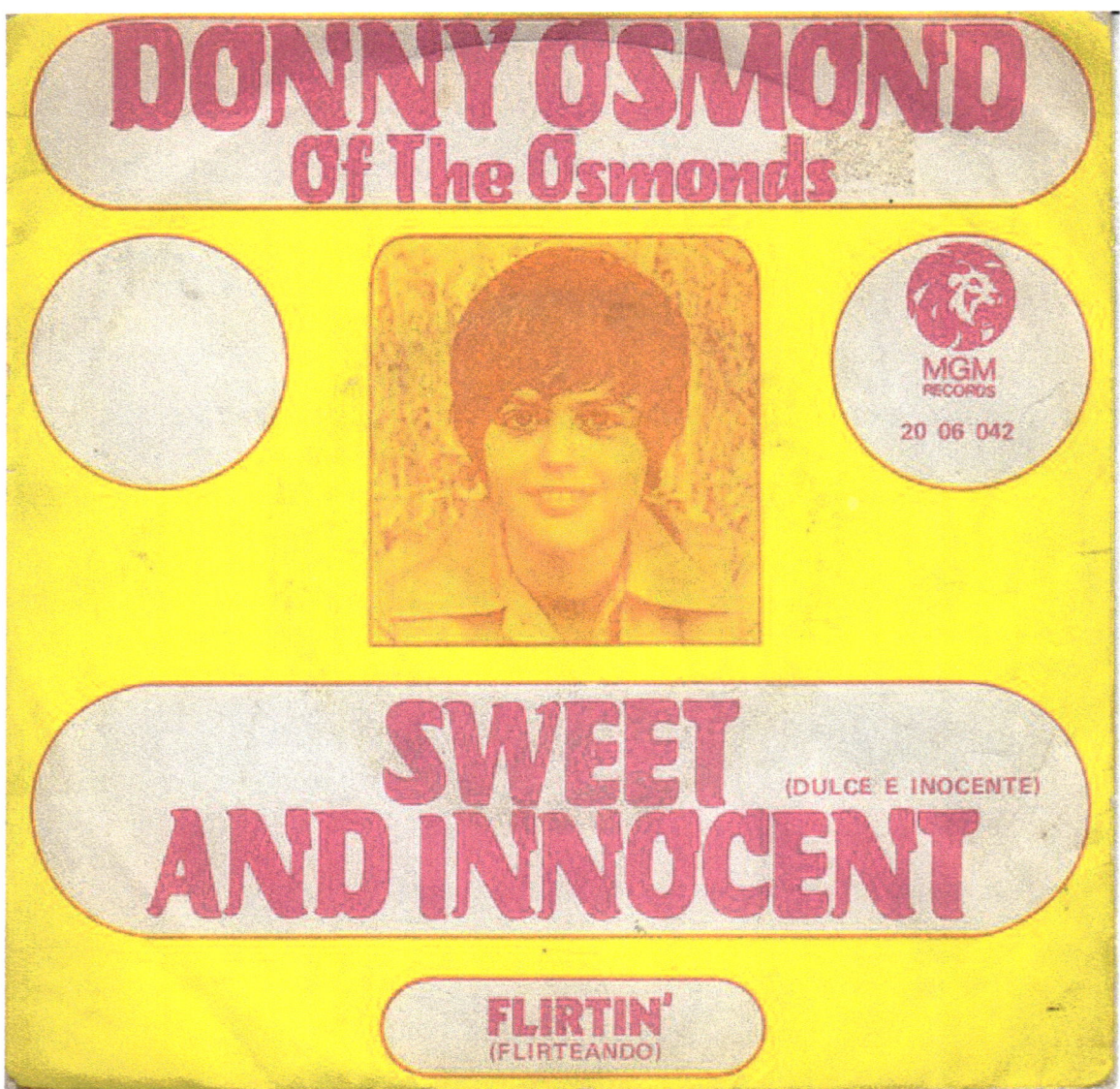

The Spanish picture sleeve for *Sweet & Innocent*.

To You With Love, Donny
SE-4797

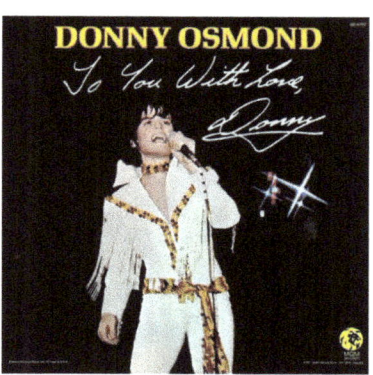

Track Listings:
I Knew You When / Little Bit / Go Away Little Girl / Hey, Little Johnny / Sit Down, I Think I Love You / A Little Bit Me, A Little Bit You / Do You Want Me (We Can Make It Together) / Bye Bye Love / I'm Into Something Good / Standing In The Need of Love

Production Information:
Produced by Alan Osmond and Michael Lloyd
Music recorded at Fame Recording Studios, Muscle Shoals, Alabama.
Vocals overdubbed at: MGM Recording Studios, Hollywood, California
Strings overdubbed at: Independent Recorders, Studio City, California
Recording Engineer: Rick Hall, Mickey Buckins, and Jack Hunt

String Arranger: Peter Carpenter
Horn Arrangers: Dale Quillen and Ronnie Eades
Vocal Arrangers: The Osmonds and Earl Brown

Liner Photography: Emerson - Loew

Singles released from this album:
Go Away Little Girl / The Wild Rover - K-14285 (US)
Go Away Little Girl / The Wild Rover - K-14285 (Jamaica)
Go Away Little Girl / The Wild Rover - 2162 008 (Brazil)
Go Away Little Girl / The Wild Rover - 2065 081 (Canada) (Polydor)
Go Away Little Girl / The Wild Rover - 2006 271 (Australia)
Go Away Little Girl / The Wild Rover - 2006 271 (UK)
A-side is Donny singing Go Away Little Girl in German.
Vete Lejos Chiquilla (Go Away Little Girl) / Un Poquito (Little Bit) - 2006 099 Mexico
Hey Girl / I Knew You When - K14322 (US)
Hey Girl / I Knew You When - 2065 095 (Canada) Polydor
Hey Girl / I Knew You When - 2006 087 (UK)
Hey Girl / I Knew You When - 2006087 (Peru)
Hey Girl / I Knew You When - 2006 087 (Australia)

The following releases were issued with a picture sleeve:
Go Away Little Girl / The Wild Rover - CD-1008 (Japan) (PS)
Go Away Little Girl / The Wild Rover - 2006 271 (Germany) (PS)
Go Away Little Girl / The Wild Rover - S 53 636 (Yugoslavia) (PS)

Bleib' Bei Mir, Little Girl / A Little Bit Me, A Little Bit You - 2006 089 (Germany) (PS)
Hey Girl / I Knew You When - 2006 087 (Germany) (PS)
Hey Girl / I Knew You When - 2006 087 (Netherlands) (PS)

LP Data:
Billboard Chart Debut: Nov 6, 1971
Highest Chart Position: 12
# of Weeks on Chart: 33

- This album was originally released on LP, cassette, 8-Track and reel tape formats on October 11, 1971.
- This album was awarded a gold record for sales in excess of 500,000 copies on January 26, 1972.
- Sheet music was marketed for this album.

The German picture sleeve for *Go Away Little Girl*. Sung in German!

Portrait of Donny
SE-4820

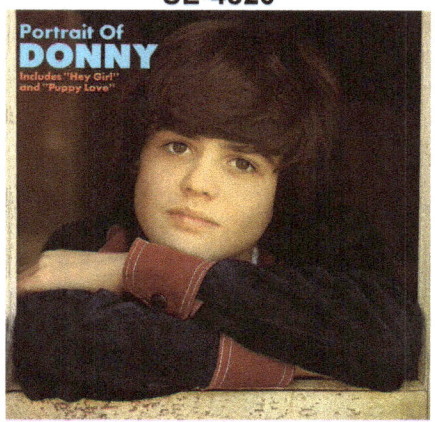

Track Listings:
Puppy Love / Hey Girl / Going, Going, Gone (To Somebody Else) / I've Got Plans For You / Promise Me / Let My People Go / All I Have To Do Is Dream / Hey There, Lonely Girl / Big Man / Love Me / This Guy's In Love With You

Production Information:
Puppy Love / I've Got Plans For You
Produced by: Mike Curb and Don Costa
Arranged by: Don Costa

Hey Girl / All I Have To Do Is Dream / Hey There, Lonely Girl / Big Man
Produced by: Rick Hall
Arranged by: Pete Carpenter

Going, Going Gone (To Somebody Else) / Promise Me
Produced by: Alan Osmond and Michael Lloyd
Arranged by: Tommy Oliver

Love Me
Produced by: Alan Osmond and Michael Lloyd
Arranged by: Merrill Osmond

This Guy's In Love With You
Produced by: Alan Osmond and Michael Lloyd
Arranged by: Tommy Oliver

Let My People Go
Produced by: Mike Curb and Ray Ruff

Photography by: Emerson / Loew
Art Direction: Derek Church

Singles released from this album:
Puppy Love / Let My People Go - K 14367 (US)
Puppy Love / Let My People Go - 2006-104 (UK)

Puppy Love / Let My People Go - 2006 111 (Lebanon)
Puppy Love / Let My People Go - 2006 104 (Brazil)
Puppy Love / Let My People Go - PS-199 (South Africa)
Puppy Love / Let My People Go - 2065 108 (Canada) (Polydor)
Puppy Love / Let My People Go - 2006127 (Greece)
Puppy Love / Let My People Go - 2006 104 (Austria)
Puppy Love / Let My People Go - 711 (Venezuela)
Puppy Love / Let My People Go - 2006 104 (Scandinavia)
Puppy Love / Let My People Go - 2006 104 (New Zealand) (Polydor)
Puppy Love / Let My People Go - 2006 104 (Turkey)
Puppy Love / Let My People Go - 2006 104 (Peru)
Puppy Love / Let My People Go - 2006 104 (Australia)

The following releases were issued with a picture sleeve:
Puppy Love / Let My People Go - 2006 104 (Belgium)
Puppy Love / Let My People Go - 20 06 104 (Spain)
Puppy Love / Let My People Go - 2006 104 (Portugal)
Puppy Love / Let My People Go - 2006 104 (Germany)
Puppy Love / Too Young - 2006 167 (France)

Notes:

- This album was originally released on LP, cassette and 8-Track tape formats on May 27, 1972.
- This album was awarded a gold record for sales in excess of 500,000 copies on December 30, 1972.
- Sheet music was marketed for this album.
- This album came with three black and white 8x10 glossy photos of Donny.

LP Data:
Billboard Chart Debut: May 27, 1972
Highest Chart Position: #6
# of Weeks on Chart: 36

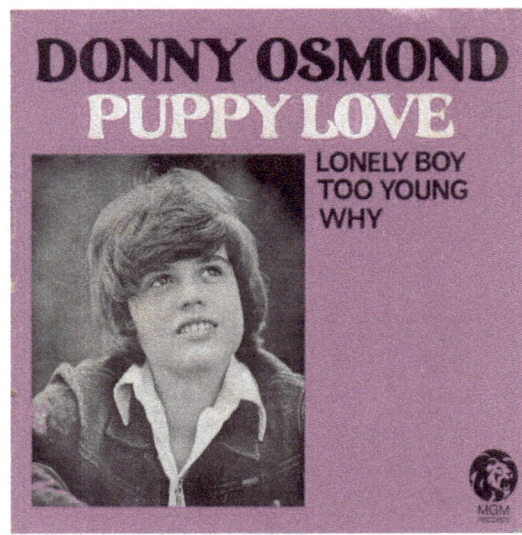

A Belgium EP picture sleeve

Too Young
SE-4854

Track Listings:
Donna / Too Young / Pretty Blue Eyes / To Run Away / A Teenager In Love / Lonely Boy / Why / Run To Him / Take Good Care of My Baby / Last of the Red Hot Lovers

Production Information:
Produced by: Mike Curb and Don Costa
Recorded at MGM Recording Studios, Hollywood, CA
Engineer: Ed Greene

Singles released from this album:
Too Young / Love Me - 2006 113 (UK)
Too Young / Love Me - 2006 113 (Australia)
Too Young / Love Me - K 14407 (US)
Too Young / Love Me - 2065 133 (Canada) (Polydor)
Too Young / Love Me - 2065133 (Lebanon)
Why / Lonely Boy - 2006-119 (UK)
Why / Lonely Boy - 2006-119 (New Zealand)
Why / Lonely Boy - 2006-119 (Australia)
Why / Lonely Boy - K 14424 (US)
Why / Lonely Boy - 2065-143 (Canada) (Polydor)
Why / Lonely Boy - K-14424 (Guatemala)

The following releases were issued with a picture sleeve:
Too Young / Love Me - 2006 113 (Germany)
Too Young / Love Me - 2006 113 (Belgium)
Why / Lonely Boy - 2006-119 (France)
Lonely Boy / Why - 2006-119 (Belgium)
A Teenager In Love / Why - 2006 124 (Germany)

LP Data:
Billboard Chart Debut: July 22, 1972
Highest Chart Position: #11
# of Weeks on Chart: 30

Notes:

- This album was originally released on LP, cassette and 8-Track tape formats on July 15, 1972.
- This album was awarded a gold record for sales in excess of 500,000 copies on January 24, 1973.
- Sheet music marketed for this album.

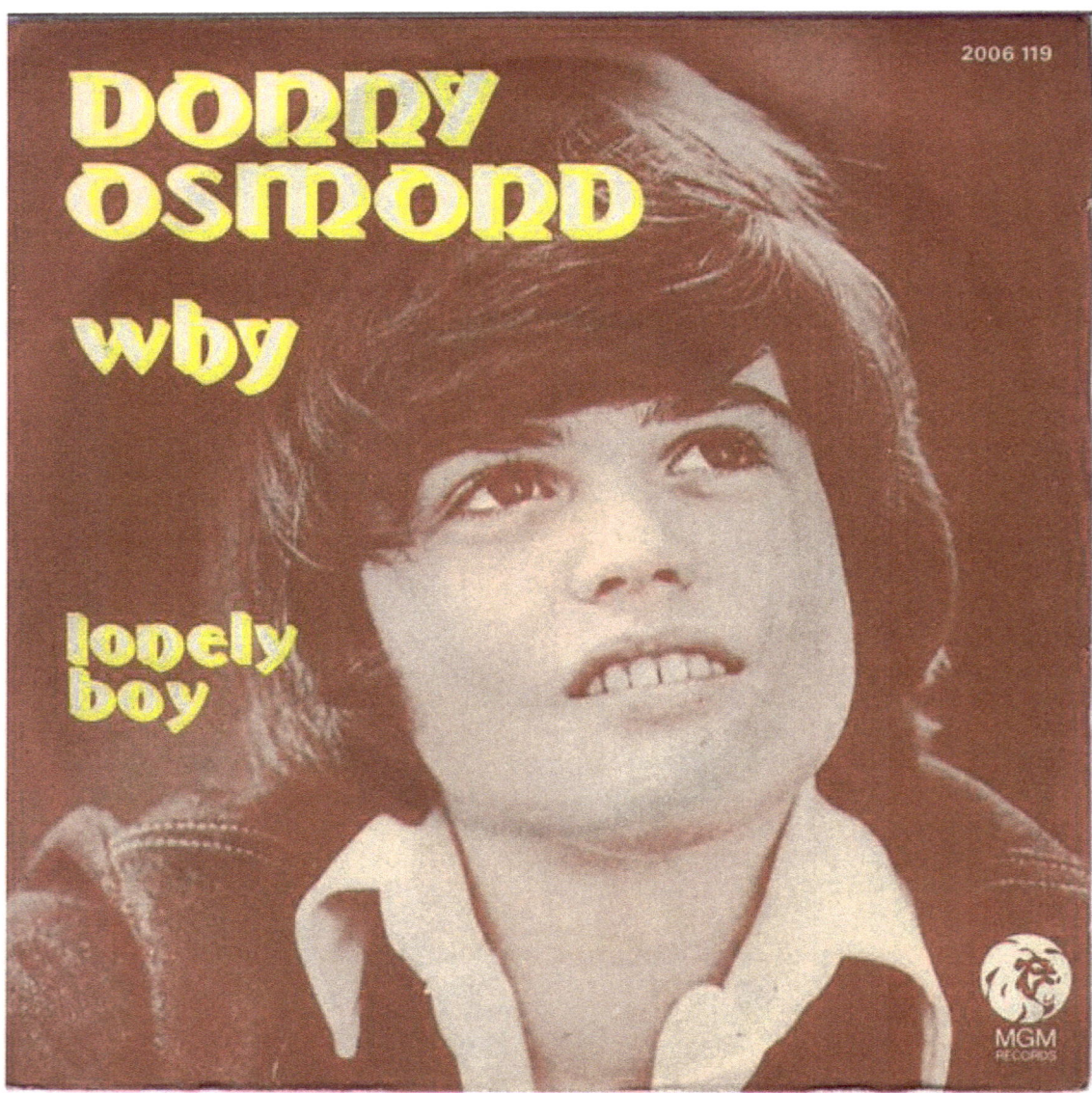

The French picture sleeve for *Why*.

My Best To You
SE 4872

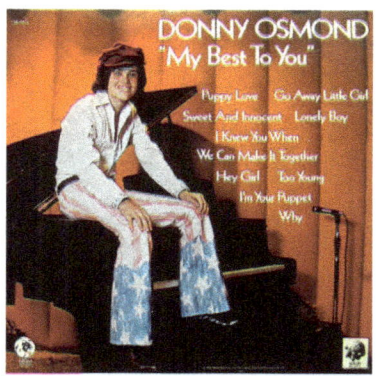

Track Listings:
Sweet and Innocent / Go Away Little Girl / I'm Your Puppet / Hey Girl / I Knew You When / Puppy Love / Too Young / Why / Lonely Boy / We Can Make It Together (Do You Want Me?)

Production Information:
Produced by: Rick Hall
Recorded at: Fame Recording Studios, Muscle Shoals, Alabama, MGM Recording and Independent Recorders, Hollywood, Ca.
Engineers: Rick Hall and Ed Greene.
Recorded: November 10, 1970 – April 17, 1972.

Singles Released From This Album:
All!

Notes:

- This album was originally released on LP, cassette and 8-Track tape formats on December 9, 1972
- This album was awarded a gold record for sales in excess of 500,000 copies on September 14, 1973
- Donny's clothes designed by Male

Alone Together
SE-4886

Track Listings:
Life Is Just What You Make It / The Twelfth of Never / Sunshine Rose / Do You Want Me? / It's Hard To Say Goodbye / Young Love / Who Can I Turn To (When Nobody Needs Me) / Other Side of Me / Tears on My Pillow / It Takes A Lot of Love

Production Information:
Life Is Just What You Make It / Do You Want Me / It's Hard To Say Goodbye / It Takes A Lot of Love
Produced by: Alan Osmond
Arranged by: Tommy Oliver

The Twelfth of Never / Young Love
Produced by: Mike Curb and Don Costa
Arranged by: Don Costa

Sunshine Rose / Who Can I Turn (When Nobody Needs Me) / Other Side of Me / Tears On My Pillow
Produced by: Michael Lloyd and Alan Osmond

Recorded at MGM Recording Studios, Hollywood, CA
Engineer: Ed Greene and Michael Lloyd

Arranged by: Tommy Oliver, except where noted.

Photography: Emerson-Loew

Singles released from this album:
The Twelfth of Never / Life Is Just What We Make It - K 14503 (Canada)
The Twelfth of Never / Life Is Just What We Make It - 2006 199 (Scandinavia)
The Twelfth of Never / Life Is Just What We Make It - 2006 199 (UK)
The Twelfth of Never / Life Is Just What We Make It - 20 06 199 (Ireland)
The Twelfth of Never / Life Is Just What We Make It - 2006 199 (New Zealand)
The Twelfth of Never / Life Is Just What We Make It - K 14503 (Jamaica)
Young Love / A Million To One - K 14583 (US)
Young Love / A Million To One - K 14583 (Canada)

Young Love / A Million To One - K 14583 (Jamaica)
Young Love / A Million To One - 2006 300 (Scandinavia)
Young Love / A Million To One - 2006 300 (Ireland)
Young Love / A Million To One - 2006 300 (Australia)
Amor Joven (Young Love) / lagrimas en mi almohada (Tears On My Pillow) MGM304 (New Zealand)
Amor Joven (Young Love) / lagrimas en mi almohada (Tears On My Pillow) MGM317 (Mexico)

The following releases were issued with a picture sleeve:
The Twelfth of Never / Life Is Just What We Make It - K 14503 (US)
The Twelfth of Never / Life Is Just What We Make It - 2006 199 (Germany)
The Twelfth of Never / Life Is Just What We Make It - 2006 199 (France)
The Twelfth of Never / Life Is Just What We Make It - PS 246 (South Africa)
The Twelfth of Never / Life Is Just What We Make It - 2006 199 (Australia)
The Twelfth of Never / Life Is Just What We Make It - DM-1242 (Japan)
The Twelfth of Never / Life Is Just What We Make It - 20 06 199 (Spain)
The Twelfth of Never / Life Is Just What We Make It - 2006 199 (Netherlands)
The Twelfth of Never / Life Is Just What We Make It - 2006 199 (Belgium)
The Twelfth of Never / Life Is Just What We Make It - S 53 687 (Yugoslavia)
Young Love / A Million To One - 2006 300 (Belgium)
Young Love / A Million To One - 2006 300 (Germany)
Young Love / A Million To One - 2006 300 (France)
Young Love / A Million To One - 2006 300 (UK)
Young Love / A Million To One - 2006 300 (Portugal)
Young Love / A Million To One - DM-1246 (Japan)

Billboard Chart Debut: March 24, 1973
Highest Chart Position: 26
# of Weeks on Chart: 29

Notes:

- Sheet music marketed for this album and whole album songbook.
- This album was originally released on LP, cassette and 8-Track tape formats on March 17, 1973.

Though the cover photo remains the same in most countries there are some slight differences to the cover of this album from different countries. In the U.S., the cover has a black and white photo insert that can be removed from the album. There is a cut-out easel on the back of the insert to stand it up such as on a night table or desk. The album from Japan and Germany does not have the insert, but the Japanese cover features the black and white photo insert as the main cover.

A Time for Us
SE-4930

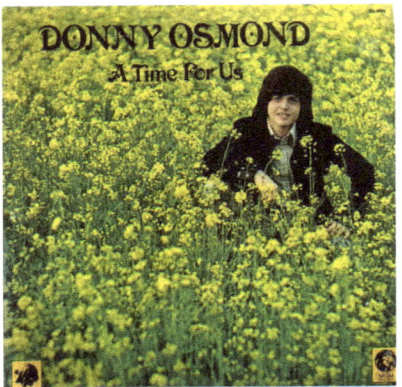

Track Listings:
A Time For Us / Hawaiian Wedding Song (Features Marie Osmond) / When I Fall In Love / Are You Lonesome Tonight / I Believe / Guess Who / Young And In Love / A Million to One / A Boy Is Waiting / Unchained Melody

Production Notes:
Produced by Mike Curb and Don Costa
Recorded at MGM Recording Studios, Hollywood, CA
Engineered by: Humberto Gatica and Wayne Osmond

Arranged by Don Costa

Art Direction: Saul Saget
Cover Photography: Tyler Thornton
Liner Photography: William R. Eastabrook

Singles released from this album:
Are You Lonesome Tonight / When I Fall In Love - K 14677 (US)
Are You Lonesome Tonight / When I Fall In Love - K 14677 (Canada)
Are You Lonesome Tonight / When I Fall In Love - 2006 365 (Australia)
Are You Lonesome Tonight / When I Fall In Love - 2006 365 (Guatemala)
Are You Lonesome Tonight / When I Fall In Love - 2006 365 (New Zealand)
Are You Lonesome Tonight / When I Fall In Love - 2006 365 (Scandinavia)
A Time For Us / Guess Who - 2006 393 (Australia)
A Time For Us / Guess Who - 2006 393 (Ireland)

The following releases were issued with a picture sleeve:
Are You Lonesome Tonight / When I Fall In Love - 2006 365 (France)
Are You Lonesome Tonight / When I Fall In Love - 2006 365 (Netherlands)
Are You Lonesome Tonight / When I Fall In Love - 2006 365 (UK)
Are You Lonesome Tonight / When I Fall In Love - 2006 365 (Germany)
Are You Lonesome Tonight / When I Fall In Love - 2006 365 (Spain)
Are You Lonesome Tonight / When I Fall In Love - 2006 365 (Belgium)
Are You Lonesome Tonight / When I Fall In Love - DM-1250 (Japan)
Are You Lonesome Tonight / When I Fall In Love - AS 264 (Italy)

Are You Lonesome Tonight / When I Fall In Love - S - 53732 (Yugoslavia)
A Time For Us / Guess Who - 2006 393 (France)
A Time For Us / Guess Who - 2006 393 (Belgium)
A Time for Us / Hawaiian Wedding Song - DM1255 (Japan)
Hawaiian Wedding Song / A Boy Is Waiting - 2006 434 (Netherlands)

LP Data:
Billboard Chart Debut: Dec 8, 1973
Highest Chart Position: 58
# of Weeks on Chart: 13

Notes:

- Sheet music marketed for this release
- This album was originally released on LP, cassette and 8-Track tape formats on November 1973 (U.K.), December 8, 1973 (U.S.)
- .This album was awarded a gold record for sales in excess of 500,000 copies on January 1, 1974.

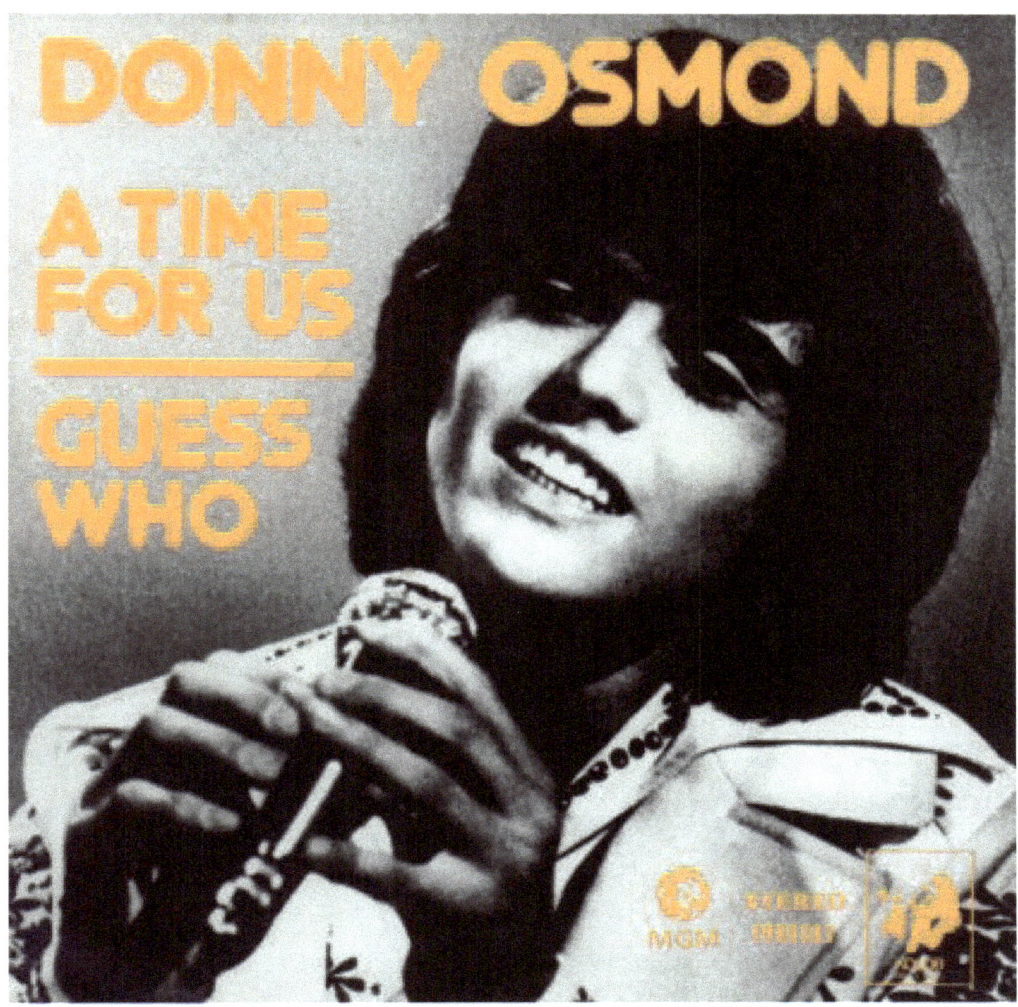

The Belgium picture sleeve for *A Time For Us*.

Donny
M3G- 4978

Track Listings:
I'm So Lonesome I Could Cry / What's He Doing In My World / If Someone Ever Breaks Your Heart / Sixteen Candles / Where Did All the Good Times Go / Mona Lisa / This Time / I'm Dyin' / Ours / I Have A Dream

Production Information:
Produced by: Mike Curb and Don Costa for Mike Curb Productions
Executive Producers: The Osmonds
Recorded at: MGM Recording Studios, Hollywood, CA
Engineer: Ed Greene
Assistant Engineer: Umberto Garcia

I'm So Lonesome I Could Cry
Arranged by: Ralph Ferraro
What's He Doing In My World / If Someone Ever Breaks Your Heart / Sixteen Candles / Where Did All the Good Times Go / Mona Lisa / Ours / I Have A Dream
Arranged by: Don Costa

This Time / I'm Dyin'
Produced by: Michael Lloyd and Alan Osmond
Arranged by: Tommy Oliver
Executive Producers: The Osmonds
Recorded at: Kolob Recording Studios, Provo Utah
Engineered by: Wayne Osmond

Design: Rod Dyer, Inc.
Photography: Len Correa
Art Direction: Sheri Leverich
Wardrobe Design: Bill Belew

Singles released from this album:
¿Donde Fueron Los Buenos Tiempos? (Where Did All The Good Times Go) / Monalisa (Mona Lisa) - MGM 487 (Mexico)
Where Did All The Good Times Go / I'm Dyin' - 2006 468 (New Zealand)

Where Did All The Good Times Go / I'm Dyin' - 2006 468 (Australia)
I Have A Dream / I'm Dyin' - 2006 491 (New Zealand)
I Have A Dream / I'm Dyin' - 2006 491 (UK)
I Have A Dream / I'm Dyin' - 2006 491 (Australia)
I Have A Dream / I'm Dyin' - M 14781 (US)
I Have A Dream / I'm Dyin' - M14781 (Canada)

The following releases were issued with a picture sleeve:
Where Did All The Good Times Go / I'm Dyin' - 2006 468 (France)
Where Did All The Good Times Go / I'm Dyin' - 2006 468 (UK)
Where Did All The Good Times Go / I'm Dyin' - 2006 468 (Netherlands)
Where Did All The Good Times Go / I'm Dyin' - 2006 468 (Germany)
Where Did All The Good Times Go / I'm Dyin' - 2006 468 (Belgium)
I Have A Dream / I'm Dyin' - 2006 491 (Belgium)
I Have A Dream / I'm Dyin' - S 53 874 (Yugoslavia)
I Have A Dream / I'm Dyin' - 2006 491 (Germany)
I Have A Dream / I'm Dyin' - 2006 491 (Netherlands)

LP Data:
Billboard Chart Debut: Dec 7, 1974
Highest Chart Position: 57
# of Weeks on Chart: 17

Notes:
- This album was originally released on LP, cassette and 8-Track tape formats on December 7, 1974.

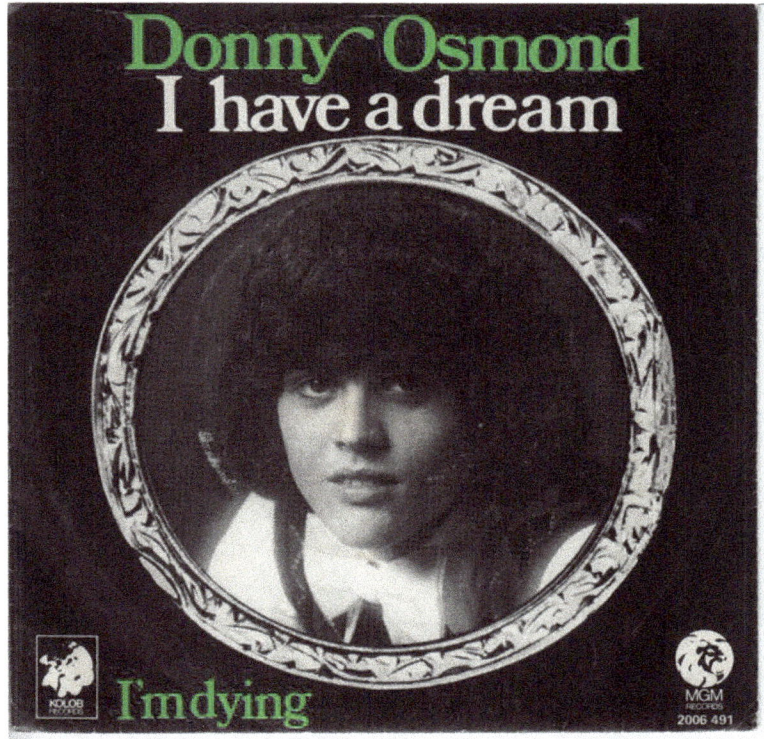

The Belgium picture sleeve for *I Have A Dream*.

Disco Train
PD-1-6067

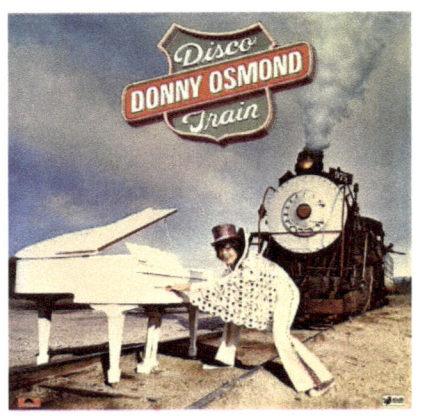

Track Listings:
C'mon Marianne / Old Man Auctioneer / Swingin' City Gal / I Follow The Music (Disco Donny) (Recorded August 21, 1975) / Don't Need No Money / I Can't Put My Finger On It (Recorded August 25, 1975) / Disco Train / Reachin' For The Feelin' (Recorded August 25, 1975) / I Got Your Lovin' / Disco Dancin' (Recorded August 21, 1975) / Never Gonna Let You Go (Recorded August 25, 1975)

Production Information:
C'mon Marianne / Never Gonna Let You Go
Produced by Mike Curb
Executive Producers: The Osmonds
Associate Producer: Jerry Styner
Arranged by: Al Capps

Old Man Auctioneer / I Follow The Music (Disco Donny) / Don't Need No Money / I Can't Put My Finger On It / Disco Train / Reachin' For the Feelin' / I Got Your Lovin' / Disco Dancin'
Produced by Mike Curb
Executive Producers: The Osmonds
Associate Producer: Jerry Styner
Arranged by: Jerry Styner

Swingin' City Gal
Produced by: Alan, Wayne, and Merrill Osmond
Arranged by: John Rosenburg

Recorded at KOLOB Recording Studios, Los Angeles, CA and Provo, Utah
Engineers: Ed Green and Humberto Gatica

Musicians:
Jay Graydon, Jerry Styner, James Gordon, Wilton Felder, Don Randi, Lee Ritenour, Josephine Dapar, Robert Ross, Ann Bartold, William Collette, Alan O. Estes, Dick Hyde, Brian Childers, A.D. Bristois, Dalton Smith, Charles Loper, William Green, William Perkins

Singles released from this album:
C'mon Marianne / Old Man Auctioneer - 2066 688 (Ireland) (June 1976)
C'mon Marianne / Old Man Auctioneer - 2066 688 (New Zealand)
C'mon Marianne / Old Man Auctioneer - 2066 676 (Australia)
Vamos Marianne (C'mon Marianne) / Viejo Rematador (Old Man Auctioneer) - 2066 688 (Uruguay)
C'mon Marianne / Old Man Auctioneer - PD 14320 (US)
C'mon Marianne / Old Man Auctioneer - PD 14320 (Canada)

The following releases were issued with a picture sleeve:
C'mon Marianne / Old Man Auctioneer - 2066 688 (UK)
C'mon Marianne / Old Man Auctioneer - 2066 688 (Germany)
C'mon Marianne / Old Man Auctioneer - 2066 688 (Belgium)
C'mon Marianne / Old Man Auctioneer - DPQ6010 (Japan)

Notes:

- Sheet music was marketed with this release.
- This album was originally released on LP, cassette and 8-Track tape formats on August 21, 1976.

Songs recorded for this album, but not released:
You Betcha (Recorded August 21, 1975)
Dancin' Man (Recorded August 25, 1975)

The Japanese picture sleeve for *C'mon Marianne.*

Donald Clark Osmond
PD-1-6109

Track Listings:
I Can't Stand It / The More I Live, The More I Love / Fly Into The Wind / You Are the Music In My Life / I Haven't Had A Heartache All Day / You Got Me Dangling On A String / I'm Sorry / Oh, It Must Be Love / I Discovered You, You Discovered Me / You'll Be Glad

Production Information:
A Holland, Cozier, Holland Production
Produced by: Brian Holland for Kolob Productions
Executive Producer: Edward J. Holland
Recorded at: Kolob Recording Studios, Provo Utah
Studio Masters, Los Angeles, CA
Wally Heider #4, Los Angeles, CA
Recording Engineers: L.T. Horn, Peter Granet, Don Blake
Tape editing: L.T. Horn
Mixing Engineers: Lawrence T. Horn for Supertec Sound Services and B.V. Holland

I Can't Stand It / The More I Live (The More I Love) / You Are The Music In My Life / You Got Me Dangling on A String / Oh, It Must Be Love / You'll Be Glad / I Haven't Had A Heartache All Day / I Discovered You, You Discovered Me Arranged by: McKinley Jackson
Fly Into The Wind / I'm Sorry Arranged by: Jimmie Haskell

Strings and Horns arranged by Jimmie Haskell

Album Coordinators: Richard J. Davis and L.T. Horn
Production Coordinators: Richard J. Davis and Willie Davis

Musicians:
Keyboards: John Barnes, Ronnie Coleman
Drums: James Gadson, Ed Greene
Conga: Eddie "Bongo" Brown, Paulinho Dacosta, Ollie Brown
Percussion: Bob Zimmit, Gary Coleman
Guitars: Ben Benay, Lee Ritenour, Greg Poree, Thom Rotella, Mitch Holder
Bass: Tony Newton
Synthesizer: Dan Wyman for Sound Arts, John Barnes

Background Vocalists: Maxine Willard, Julia Tillman, Pat Henderson, Adrienne Williams
Vocal Arrangements by: Brian Holland

Art Direction: Mike Doud (AGI)
Design: Marilyn Romen
Back Cover Photos: Jimmy Osmond
Cover Photo Tinting: Larry Dupont

Singles released from this album:
You've Got Me Dangling On A String / I'm Sorry - PD 14417 (US)

Notes:
- This album was originally released on LP, cassette and 8-Track tape formats on August 6, 1977

Promotional ad for *Donald Clark Osmond* as seen in Billboard.

Donny Osmond
V2469 (UK Version)

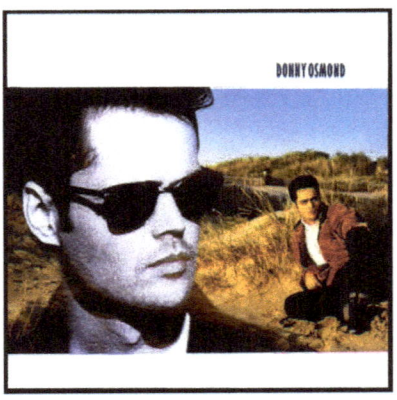

Track Listings:
Soldier of Love / If It's Love That You Want / Sacred Emotion / Inner Rhythm / Faces In The Mirror / My Secret Touch / I'm In It For Love / Groove / Only Heaven Knows / Hold On

Production Information:
Soldier of Love / If It's Love That You Want / Sacred Emotion / Inner Rhythm / Faces In The Mirror / I'm In It For Love / Hold On
Produced by: Carl Sturken and Evan Rogers

Groove / Only Heaven Knows
Produced by: George Acogny

My Secret Touch
Produced by: George Acogny, Donny Osmond, and Evan Rogers

Recorded at: The Real World, Bath England
The Town House, London, England
Music Grinder, Los Angeles, CA
Unique Recording Studios, New York, NY
Gnome Sound, New York
The Sandbox, Fairfield, CT

Additional Recording at:
MCA Los Angeles, CA & London, England
Surrey Sound, England
Front Page Recorders, Orange Co., CA
Engineers: Darroll Gustamachio (Appears courtesy of Visual Sound Design Inc.), Acar Key, Dave Botrill, Rod Beale
Additional Engineers: Matt Noble, Mike Harlow, Quinn Batson, Matt Hathaway, Steve Heinke

Mastered at: The Townhouse by: Tony Cousins

Evan Rogers appears courtesy of Capital Records
Michael Brekker appears courtesy of MCA / Impulse
Lorelei McBroom appears courtesy of Capitol

Cindy Mizelle appears courtesy of CBS

Photography: Dean Freeman
Design: Stylorouge

Management: Ged Doherty / Renegade Artists Management

Thanks to:
Larry Samuels and Frank Foster with Atari/Hybrid Arts, Jim Byron for the Roland gear, Mark Fleisher, Bill Waite, Chad Murdock, and my Nightstar staff, Frank Rand, Paul Rodwell, Gema Caufield, Amanda Doherty, John Reid, and Brenda Chandler.

Special thanks to:
Martin Serene, Richard Griffiths, and everyone at Virgin Records for being so committed and dedicated.

My very special thanks to: my friends Peter Gabriel, Ged Doherty, Simon Draper, and Willie Richardson for making it happen.

This album is dedicated to my family, Debbie, Donald, Jeremy, and Brandon. I love you.

Perception vs. Reality is deceiving!

Don "O" smond logo appears courtesy of Nightstar, Inc.

The following 7" singles were issued with a picture sleeve:
I'm In It For Love / Keep Me Hummin' - Virgin - 109 387 (Europe)
I'm In It For Love / Keep Me Hummin' - Virgin - VSP994 (UK)
I'm In It For Love / Keep Me Hummin' - VIN - 45242 (Italy)
I'm In It For Love / Keep Me Hummin' - VIN - 009947 (France)
Groove / Heaven Only Knows - VS 1016 (UK)

The following 12" singles were issued with a picture sleeve:
I'm In It For Love / Keep Me Hummin' / What Am I Here For (Instru) - Virgin 609 387 (Germany)
I'm In It For Love / Keep Me Hummin' / What Am I Here For (Instru) - Virgin 609 387 (UK)
I'm In It For Love / Keep Me Hummin' / What Am I Here For (Instru) - VG 2094Z (Greece)
I'm In It For Love / Keep Me Hummin' / What Am I Here For (Instru) - VG 2094Z (Australasia)
Groove (Club Mix) / Only Heaven Knows (Alternate Mix) VST1016 (UK)
Groove (Club Mix) / Only Heaven Knows (Extended Mix) F-609 584 (Spain)

Cassette single released from this album:
VSC99412 / Track Listing:
A1 - I'm In It For Love (Full Mix) / A2 - Keep Me Hummin' / A3 - What Am I Here For (Instrumental)
B1 - I'm In It For Love (Full Mix) / B2 - Keep Me Hummin' / B3 - What Am I Here For (Instrumental)

Notes:

- Sheet music marketed for this release.

CD Maxi-Singles Released from this album:
CDEP 5 / Track List
1 - I'm In It For Love
2 - Keep Me Hummin'
3 - What I Am Here For (Instrumental)
4 - I'm In It For Love (Full Mix)

CDEP 15 / Track List
1 - Groove (Club Mix)
2 - Only Heaven Knows (Alternate Mix)
3 - I'm In It For Love (Radio Remix)

Notes:

- Sheet music marketed for this release.
- This album was released on CD, LP and cassette tape on July 21, 1988.

The UK 12" single for *I'm In It For Love.*

Donny Osmond
C1-92354 (US Version)

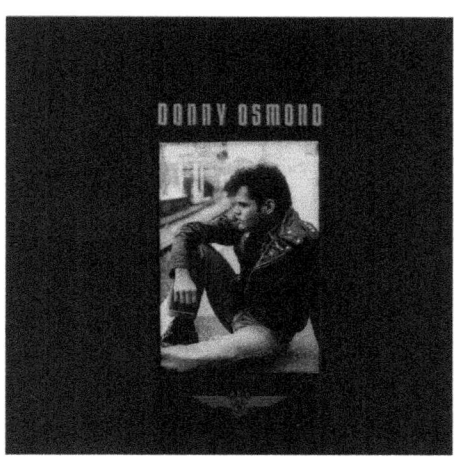

Track Listings:
Soldier of Love / If It's Love That You Want / Sacred Emotion / Inner Rhythm / Faces In The Mirror / My Secret Touch / I'll Be Good To You / Groove / Only Heaven Knows / Hold On

Production Information:
Soldier of Love / If It's Love That You Want / Sacred Emotion / Inner Rhythm Faces In The Mirror / I'm In It For Love / Hold On
Produced by: Carl Sturken and Evan Rogers

Groove / Only Heaven Knows
Produced by: George Acogny

My Secret Touch
Produced by: George Acogny, Donny Osmond, and Evan Rogers

Recorded at: The Real World, Bath, England
The Town House, London, England
Music Grinder, Los Angeles, Ca
Unique Recording Studios, New York, NY
Gnome Sound, New York, NY
The Sandbox, Fairfield, CT

Additional Recording at
MCA Studios, Los Angeles, CA & London, England
Surrey Sound, England
Front Page Recorders, Orange Co., CA

Engineers: Darroll Gustamachio (Appears courtesy of Visual Sound Design Inc.), Acar Key, Dave Botrill, Rod Beale

Additional Engineers: Matt Noble, Mike Harlow, Quinn Batson, Matt Hathaway, Steve Heinke

Mastered at the Townhouse by: Tony Cousins

Evan Rogers appears courtesy of Capital Records
Michael Brekker appears courtesy of MCA / Impulse
Lorelei McBroom appears courtesy of Capitol
Cindy Mizelle appears courtesy of CBS
Photography: Dean Freeman
Design: Stylorouge
Management: Ged Doherty / Renegade Artists Management

Thanks to:
Larry Samuels and Frank Foster with Atari/Hybrid Arts, Jim Byron for the Roland gear, Mark Fleisher, Bill Waite, Chad Murdock, and my Nightstar staff, Frank Rand, Paul Rodwell, Gema Caufield, Amanda Doherty, John Reid, and Brenda Chandler.

Special thanks to:
Martin Serene, Richard Griffiths, and everyone at Virgin Records for being so committed and dedicated.

My very special thanks to:
My friends Peter Gabriel, Ged Doherty, Simon Draper, and Willie Richardson for making it happen.

This album is dedicated to: my family, Debbie, Donald, Jeremy, and Brandon. I love you.

Perception vs. Reality is deceiving!

Don "O" smond logo appears courtesy of Nightstar, Inc.

The following 7" singles were issued with a picture sleeve:
Soldier of Love / Time Can't Erase - VSX 1094 (UK) (7" boxed set with postcards and badges)
Soldier of Love / Time Can't Erase - VS 1094 (UK)
Soldier of Love / Time Can't Erase - 111 784 (Germany)
Soldier of Love / Time Can't Erase - 90459 (France)
Soldier of Love / Time Can't Erase - 112 405 (Europe)
Soldier of Love / My Secret Touch - B-44369 (Canada)
Soldier of Love / My Secret Touch - B-44369 (US)
If It's Love That You Want / Come Down - VSP 1140 (UK) (w/ Poster)
Sacred Emotion / Groove - B-44379 (US)
Sacred Emotion / Sacred Emotion (Spanish Version) - 7PRO-79858 (US)
Sacred Emotion / Groove - VS 1211 (UK)
Hold On (7" Radio Version) / Only Heaven Knows - B-44423 (Canada)

The following 12" singles were issued with a picture sleeve:
Soldier Of Love / Soldier Of Love (Dub Mix) / Time Can't Erase - 611 784-213 (Europe)
Soldier Of Love /Soldier Of Love (Dub Mix) / Time Can't Erase - VST 1094 (UK)
Soldier Of Love /Soldier Of Love (Dub Mix) / Time Can't Erase - 612 405 (Germany)
Soldier Of Love /Soldier Of Love (Dub Mix) / Time Can't Erase - VSTY 1094 (UK)
If It's Love That You Want (Extended Remix) / If It's Love That You Want (7" Remix) / Come Down - VST 1140 (UK)
If It's Love That You Want (Extended Remix) / If It's Love That You Want - VST 1140 (Australia)

The following 12" singles were issued without a picture sleeve:
Soldier Of Love / Soldier Of Love (Dub Mix) / Time Can't Erase - VST 1094 (Australia)
If It's Love That You Want / If It's Love That You Want - VS 1140 (Australia)
Hold On (12" Club Mix) / Hold On (Perc-a-pella) / Hold On (Extended Mix) / Hold On (Instrumental) / Hold On (7" Version) - V-15505

CD Maxi singles released from this album:
Soldier Of Love / Groove / Soldier Of Love (Twelve Inch Version) / Time Can't Erase - VSCD 1094 (UK)

Mini CD singles released from this album:
Soldier Of Love / I'm In It For Love - VJD-10213 (Japan)

If It's Love That You Want (7" Remix) / Come Down / If It's Love That You Want (Extended Remix) / Soldier Of Love (7" Remix) - VSCD 1140 (UK)

Cassette single released from this album:
Soldier Of Love / My Secret Touch / Soldier Of Love / My Secret Touch - 4JM-44369 (US)
Sacred Emotion / Groove - 4JM-44379 (US)
Hold On (7" Radio Version) / Only Heaven Knows / Hold On (7" Radio Version) / Only Heaven Knows - 4JM-44423 (US)

Notes:

- Sheet music marketed for this album.
- This album was released on CD, LP and cassette tape on April 25, 1989.

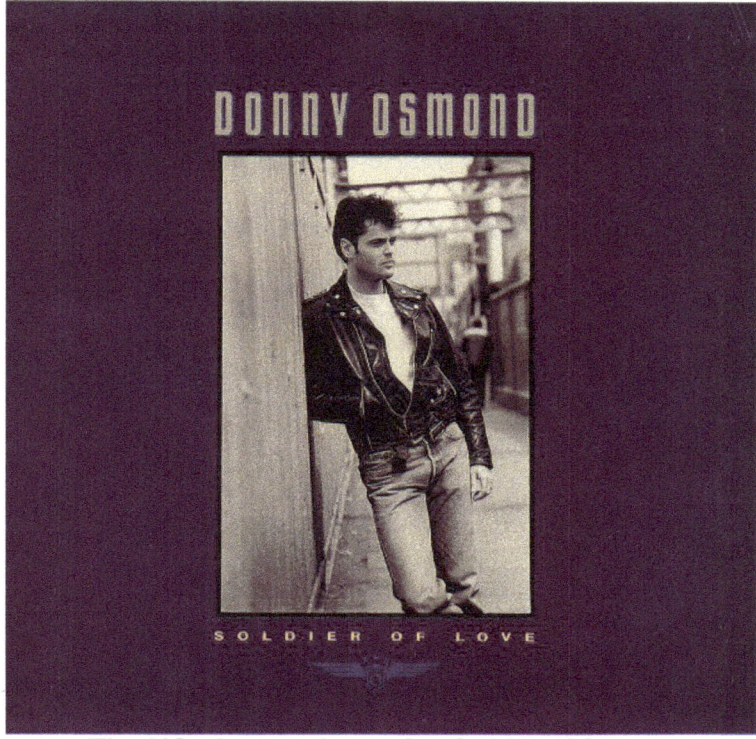

The US picture sleeve for *Soldier Of Love*.

Eyes Don't Lie
C1-94051

Track Listings:
My Love Is A Fire / Eyes Don't Lie / Love Will Survive / Sure Lookin' / Private Affair / Take Another Try (At Love) / Make It Last Forever / Never Too Late For Love / Just Between You and Me / Before It's Too Late

Production Information:
Produced by: Carl Sturken, Even Rogers, David Gamson, Ric Wake
Executive Producer: Donny Osmond
Recorded at: The Loft Recording Studio
Mastered by: Stephen Marcussen at Precision Lacquer, L.A.

Strings:
Leader: Jeremy Lubbock
Contractor: Jule Chaikin
Violins: Bruce Dukov / Debra Price / Arnold Belnick / Isabelle Daskoff / Joel DeRovin / Henry Ferber / Reg Hill / Brian Leonard / Gordon Marron / Don Palmer / Haim Shtrum / Bob Sushel / Mari Tsumura / Shari Zippert
Cello: Fred Seykora / Ron Cooper / Larry Corbett / Ernie Ehrnhardt / Dennis Karmazyn / Suzie Katayama
Viola: Sam Bog Ossian / Ken Burward-Hoy / Myra Kirshenbaum / Dan Neufeld

Art Direction: Tommy Steele and Jeffery Fey
Design: Jeffery Fey
Photographer: Wayne Maser
Hair: Andi Anderson

The following 7" singles were issued with a picture sleeve:
My Love Is A Fire (Edit) / Before It's Too Late - CL 600 (UK)
My Love Is A Fire (Edit) / Before It's Too Late - Cap. 016 20 4169 7 (Germany)

The following 12" singles were issued with a picture sleeve:
My Love Is A Fire (D.J. Pierre's In-Da-House Mix) / My Love Is A Fire (D.J. Pierre's House Instrumental Mix) / My Love Is A Fire (Da-House Radio Mix) - V-15642 (US)

My Love Is A Fire (D.J. Pierre's In-Da-House Mix) / My Love Is A Fire (D.J. Pierre's House Instrumental UK Edit) / My Love Is A Fire (Da-House Radio Version) - 12CL 600 (UK)

Sure Lookin' (Radio Remix) / Sure Lookin' (LP Version) / Sure Lookin' (Soul To Jack R&B Mix) / Sure Lookin' (Sho'Housin Club Mix) / Sure Lookin' (Soul To Jack Instrumental) / Sure Lookin' (Sho'Housin Instrumental) - Cap.5666 (US)

Sure Lookin' (Sho' Housin' Club Mix) / Sure Lookin' (Sho' Housin' Instrumental) / Sure Lookin' (Radio Remix) Sure Lookin' (Soul To Jack R&B Mix) / Sure Lookin' (Soul To Jack Instrumental) - V-15666 (US)

CD singles released from this album:
My Love Is A Fire (Edit) / My Love Is A Fire (D.J. Pierre's In-Da-House Mix) / My Love Is A Fire (D.J. Pierre's In-Da-House Instrumental Mix)/ My Love Is A Fire (Da-House Radio Version) - Cap.560-20 4186 2 (Europe)

My Love Is A Fire (Edit) / My Love Is A Fire (D.J. Pierre's In Da-House Mix) / Eyes Don't Lie / My Love Is A Fire (Da-House Radio Version) - Cap.20 4169 2 (UK)

Cassette singles released from this album:
My Love Is A Fire (Edit) / Eyes Don't Lie / My Love Is A Fire (Remix) / My Love Is A Fire (Edit) / Eyes Don't Lie / My Love Is A Fire (Remix) - 4JM-44634 (US)

Love Will Survive / Just Between You And Me / Love Will Survive / Just Between You And Me - 4JM-44707 (US)

Notes:

- This album was released on CD, LP and cassette tape on October 30, 1990
- Sheet music marketed for this album.

The UK 12" single for *Sure Lookin'*.

Christmas at Home
7001-2

Track Listings:
Angels We Have Heard on High / God Rest Ye Merry Gentlemen / I've Been Looking For Christmas / After December Slips Away / The Most Wonderful Time of the Year / Baby, What You Goin' To Be / Deck the Halls / Hark The Herald Angels Sing / I'll Be Home For Christmas / Who Took The Merry Out of Christmas / Oh, Holy Night / Divine / Soldier's King / The Kid In Me / My Grown-Up Christmas List / Mary Did You Know? / Come, To The Manger

Production Information:
Produced and Arranged by: Darrell Brown
Co-Produced by: Donny Osmond

Recorded at: Tejas Recording Studios, Franklin, TN
Engineer: David Leonard
Additional Recording: Recording Arts, The Bonus Room, Chameleon Sound, Quad Recording Studios, Maddening Studios, and Record Lab
Additional recording Engineers: Brian Scheuble, Patrick Kelly, David Schober, Donny Osmond, Darrell Brown and Don Osmond, Jr., Brad Burke, Jim Scheffler

Mixed by: David Leonard at Maddening Studios, Provo, UT
Mastered by: Dave Collins at A&M Mastering, Los Angeles, CA

Except "After December Slips Away" and "Oh, Holy Night / Divine"
Recorded at Schnee Studio, N. Hollywood, CA
Engineer: Brian Scheuble
"Come To The Manger"
Recorded at Record Lab, Provo, UT
Engineer: Cliff Maag

"Come To The Manger" Mixed by Cliff Maag and Donny Osmond at Record Lab, Provo Utah

"God Rest Ye Merry Gentlemen", Mixed by Donny Osmond

Musicians:
Drums: Chad Cromwell, Curt Bisquera
Bass: Michael Rhodes, Bob Glaub, Craig Poole
Guitar: Kenny Greenberg, Kevin Dukes, and Rich Dixon
B3, Wurlitzer, Rhodes, & Piano: Dennis Matkosky
Synths: Jai Winding, Darrell Brown and Dennis Matkosky
Percussion: Eric Darkin, Kevin Ricard, David Osmond and Don Osmond, Jr.

Lead and harmony Vocals: Donny Osmond
Vocal Arrangements: Darrell Brown and Donny Osmond
Background Vocals: Beth Neilsen Chapman / Bonnie Keen / Marke Kibble / Sherrie Kibble, Deborah Lippman, Marty McCall and David Robertson

Special Guests Vocalist: Debbie Osmond / Don Osmond Jr., Jeremy Osmond / Brandon Osmond and Christopher Osmond

Violins: David Davidson, Pam Sixfin, David Angel
Viola: Jim Grosjean
Cello: Anthony Lamarchino
Arco Bass: Craig Nelson
Strings Arranged and Conducted by: John Darnall

Horns: Mark Douthit, Chris McDonald, Mike Haynes, and Jeff Bailey
Horn Arrangements: Chris McDonald
Flugelhorn solo on "I'll Be Home For Christmas": George Tidwell
Sax solos on Who Took the Merry Out of Christmas and "I've Been Looking For Christmas: Mark Douthit
Flute on "My Grown Up Christmas List": Leslie Hall Matkosky
SKA Guitar on "Deck the Halls / Hark The Herald Angels Sing": Jeremy Osmond
Piano on "Come To The Manger": Darrell Brown

Copyists: Ebnerhard Ramm and Ric Demonico
Nightstar Assistant: Pat Dresbach
Art Direction and Design by: Dina Barnes
Photography by: Matthew Barnes, Nashville, TN
Styling by: Lynn Bugai, LA
Hair and Makeup by: Michelle Hyde, Provo, Utah

CD singles from this album:
I've Been looking For Christmas / The Echo Of Your Whisper - (Promo CD only)

Notes:
- 1997 Nightstar Records
- Album re-issued by: Legacy/Epic E2K 65830 in 1998.

This is the Moment
440 013 052-2

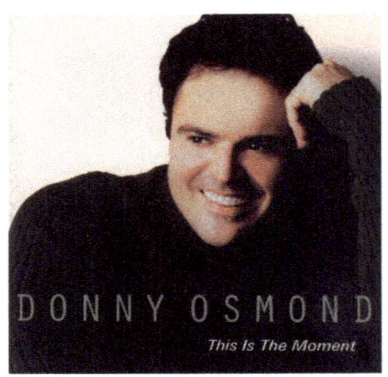

Track Listing:
Seasons Of Love / This Is The Moment / Luck Be A Lady / Our Kind Of Love / It's Possible / At The Edge Of The World / Not While I'm Around (with Vanessa Williams) / Solla Sollew / No Matter What / Immortality / I Know The Truth / You've Got A Friend In Me (with Rosie O'Donnell) / Give My Regards To Broadway

*The UK track listing included these additional selections:

Puppy Love / Too Young / Young Love / The Twelfth Of Never / Why / When I Fall In Love

Production Information:
Produced by: Phil Ramone

Singles from this album:

Seasons Of Love / It's Possible - Decca - DONNY1 (UK) (Promo CD Only / Not for sale)

Seasons Of Love (Radio Remix) / Luck Be A Lady / Seasons Of Love (Original Version) - PCD 20011 (Europe) (Promo CD Only / Not for sale)

Notes:

- This album was released on CD and cassette tape on February 6, 2001.
- *2 Disc UK set released March 1, 2001.

Somewhere in Time
066 530-2

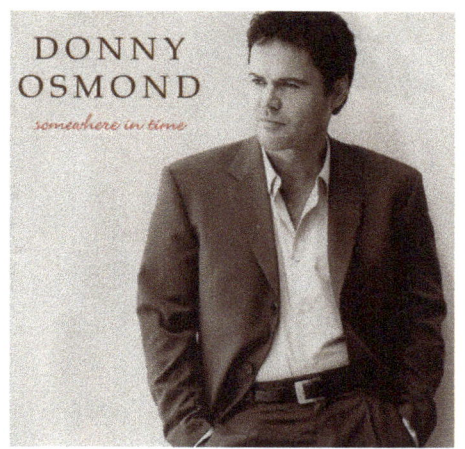

Track Listing:
Without You / I Can't Go For That / All Out Of Love / Could It Be I'm Falling In Love / Don't Dream It's Over / After The Love Has Gone / Would I Lie To You / I'm Not In Love / Puppy Love / Happy Together / Don't Give Up On Us Baby / No One Has To Be Alone

The UK track listing included these selections:

Could It Be I'm Falling In Love / Without You / All Out Of Love / I Can't Go For That / After The Love Has Gone / Would I Lie To You / I'm Not In Love / Don't Dream It's Over / I Wish / Don't Give Up On Us Baby / Crazy Horses / Puppy Love

Notes:

- This album was released on CD on October 29, 2002.

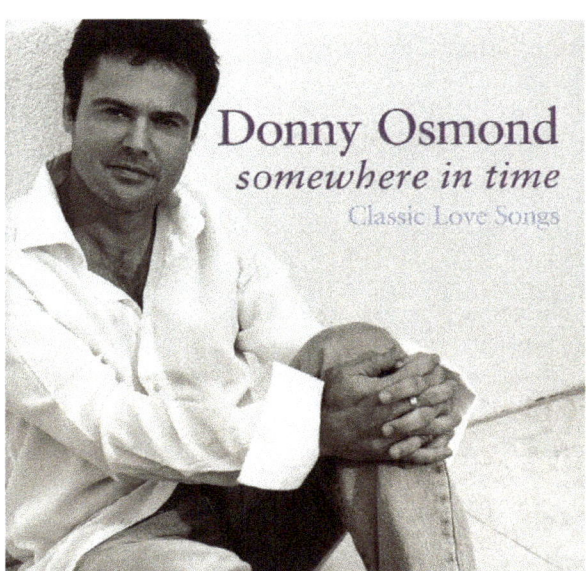

The UK edition with different cover design released December 2, 2002.

What I Meant To Say
B0003737-02

Track Listing:
What I Meant To Say / Breeze On By / Keep Her In Mind / One Dream / In It For Love / Right Here Waiting / My Perfect Rhyme / Shoulda' Known Better / Whenever You're In Trouble / Insecurity / This Guy's In Love With You / Broken Man

The UK track listing included these selections:

Breeze On By (Album Version) / Keep Her In Mind / In It For Love / I Wanna Know What Love Is / My Perfect Rhyme / Faith / What I Meant To Say / Whenever You're In Trouble / Shoulda' Known Better / Broken Man / This Guy's In Love With You / Insecurity / One Dream / Christmas Time

Production Information:
Produced by: Donny Osmond
Co-Producers: The True North Music Company
Recorded at: True North Studios, Cheshire, England and
Maddening Studios, Provo, Utah
Engineers: Donny Osmond / Ryan Carline / Robbie Adams
Horn and Flute arrangements: Eliot Kennedy, Steve Beighton
String arrangements: Gary Barlow

Photography By - Jeff Katz

Singles released from this album:
Breeze On By (Radio Edit) / Right Here Waiting / Breeze On By - 9863140 (UK & Europe)

CD single released from this album:
Keep Her In Mind (Radio Edit) / Whenever You're In Trouble / Just The Way You Are
Bonus CD Video: Whenever You're In Trouble (Director – Phil Griffin) - Decca-9880282 (UK)

Notes:
- Released: January 11, 2005 (US)

Love Songs Of The 1970's
B0008863-10 / May 5, 2007

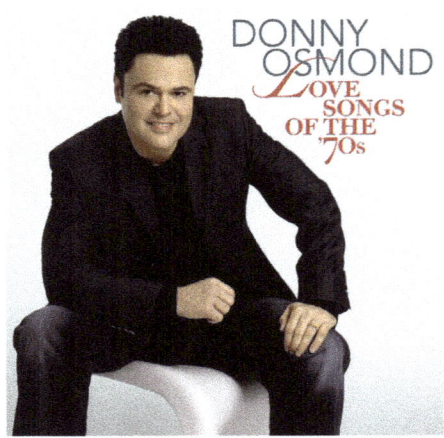

Track Listing:
I Can See Clearly Now / Sometimes When We Touch / Let's Stay Together / Laughter In The Rain / When I Need You / How Long / Mandy / You Are So Beautiful / Will It Go Round In Circles / How Deep Is Your Love / Alone Again (Naturally) / If

DVD - Exclusive Live Rehearsal Footage
Breeze On By / Broken Man / What I Meant To Say / Sacred Emotion / Young Love / Behind The Scenes Look At The Making Of Love Songs Of The '70s

The UK track listing included these selections:

I Can See Clearly Now / Sometimes When We Touch / Let's Stay Together / Laughter In The Rain / Oh Girl / When I Need You / How Long / Mandy / How Deep Is Your Love / Will It Go Round In Circles / Alone Again (Naturally) / You Are So Beautiful

Production Information:
Producers: Michael Mangini and Donny Osmond
Executive-Producer: Eric Gardner
Recorded at: Chung King Studios and Mojo Studios
Engineer, Mixed By: Howie Beno
Engineer [Assistant]: Adam Pallin, Andy Marcinkowski
Mastered By: Chris Gehringer
Mixed by: Michael Mangini
Mastered at: Sterling Sound

Musicians:
Alto Saxophone: Dave Mann, Ken Gioffre
Baritone Saxophone: Tom Timko
Tenor Saxophone: John Scarpulla
Bass: Neil Jason
Guitar: John McCurry
Drums: Caesar Griffin
Piano, Organ: Raymond Angry
Trombone: Ozzie Melendez

Trumpet: Don Harris
Cello: Alan Stepansky, Eileen Moon, Elizabeth Dyson, Jeanne Leblanc
Viola: Nick Cords, Becky Young, Shmuel Katz, Vivek Kamath
Violin: Ann Lehmann, Duoming Ba, Liz Lim, Eva Burmeister, Katherine Fong, Kuan Cheng Lu, Laura Seaton, Mateusz Wolski, Matt Lehmann, Peter Winograd, Rob Shaw, Sandra Park, Sein Ryu, Sharon Yamada, Suzanne Ornstein, Tom Carney.
Backing Vocals – Donny Osmond and Honey Larochelle

Love Songs Of The '70s Promotional Poster

The Entertainer
2 Disc Set (CD/DVD)

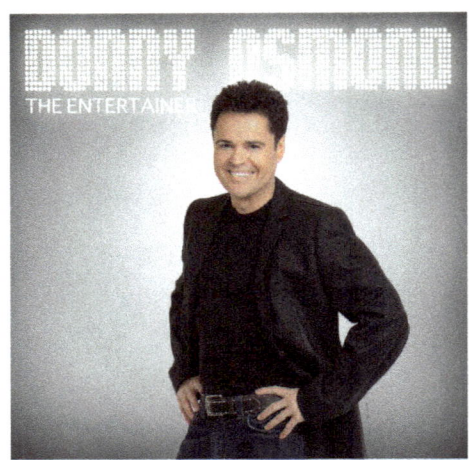

Track Listing:
I Can't Go For That / In It For Love / Seasons Of Love / Laughter In The Rain / Breeze On By / When I Fall In Love / Luck Be A Lady / Could It Be I'm Falling In Love / If / Don't Dream It's Over / Sometimes When We Touch / The Twelfth Of Never / Crazy Horses / Any Dream Will Do / Puppy Love / It's Possible / This Is The Moment / Luck Be A Lady / Not While I'm Around (With Vanessa Williams) / Seasons Of Love / Solla Sollew / Our Kind Of Love / I Know The Truth / Any Place I Hang My Hat Is Home (Featuring Vanessa Williams) / At The Edge Of The World / No Matter What / Puppy Love / Immortality / This Is The Moment (Reprise)

Notes:

- Released: May 4, 2010

Soundtrack Of My Life
US Release: B0022310-02

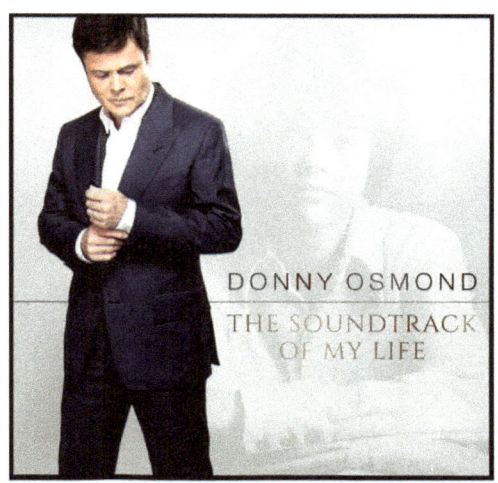

Track Listing:
My Cherie Amour / Ben / Peg / The Gift Of Love / Could She Be Mine / I've Got You Under My Skin / Baby Love / Moon River / Your Song / The Long And Winding Road / Don't Give Up / Survivor

The UK Deluxe Edition included these extra selections:
Broken Wings / I Who Have Nothing / Nothing Compares 2 U

Production Information:
Produced by: Eliot Kennedy, James Jayawardena

Notes:

- European release date: November 10, 2014 / European Release: 3795151
- US release date: January 13, 2015

One Night Only!
DONNYGZ101CD

Track Listing:
Celebration / Puppy Love / Let's Stay Together / Long Haired Lover From Liverpool / Sacred Emotion / Any Dream Will Do / Breeze On By / The Long And Winding Road / Could She Be Mine / My Love Is A Fire / Peg / Private Affair / I'll Make A Man Out Of You / Soldier Of Love / Moon River / Young Love / 12th Of Never / When I Fall In Love / Love Me For A Reason / Whenever You're In Trouble / Close Every Door / Survivor / Crazy Horses / This Is The Moment

Production Information:
Recorded at: Birmingham NEC in February 2017.

Notes:

- Released on: October 27, 2017
- A deluxe box set celebrating Donny Osmond's February 2017 performance at the Birmingham NEC. CD package was signed & numbered. Limited to 1000 copies.
- Released on special edition purple double vinyl LP set. Catalog # DONNYGZ103LP. Limited to 300 copies with the first 100 autographed. The LP quickly sold out.
- Moon River, Young Love, 12th Of Never, and When I Fall In Love were originally performed at this show and were included on the CD / DVD but were omitted from the vinyl release due to lack of space.

Marie
Osmond

Paper Roses
SE-4910 - 1973

Track Listings:
Paper Roses / Louisiana Bayou / Everything Is Beautiful / You're The Only World I Know / Fool No. 1 / Least of All You / Sweet Dreams / Too Many Rivers / It's Such a Pretty World Today / True Love Lasts Forever

Production Notes:
Arranged and produced by: Sonny James
Executive Producer: Don Ovens
Recorded at: Columbia Recording Studios, Studio B, Nashville, TN
Engineers: Charlie Tallent and Stan Hutto
String Arrangements: Cam Mullins
Vocal Accompaniment: The Jordanaires & The Hershel Wiggington Singers

Cover Photography: James London
Art Direction: Saul Saget

Notes:

Singles Released From This Album:
Paper Roses / Least of All You - 2006 315 (Ireland)
Paper Roses / Least of All You - 2006 315 (UK)
Paper Roses / Least of All You - 2006 315 (Australia)
Paper Roses / Least of All You - K 14609 (Canada)
Paper Roses / Least of All You - 2006 315 (New Zealand)
Paper Roses / Least of All You - 2006 315 (Turkey)
Paper Roses - R-0496 (Poland) (6", 45 RPM, Single Sided, Picture Card)

The following releases were issued with a picture sleeve:
Paper Roses / Least of All You - 2006 315 (Netherlands)
Paper Roses / Least of All You - K 14609 (US)
Paper Roses / Least of All You - S-53.725 (Yugoslavia)
Paper Roses / Least of All You - 2006 315 (France)

Paper Roses / Least of All You - 2006 315 (Scandinavia)
Paper Roses / Least of All You - DM1248 (Japan)
Paper Roses / Least of All You - 2006 315 (Germany)

LP Data:
Billboard Chart Debut: Sept 22, 1973
Highest Chart Position: #1 on Nov. 16, 1973
# of Weeks on Chart: 19
Billboard Chart: Top Country LP's

Songbook / sheet music marketed with this release:
Paper Roses Folio
Whole Album Songbook (Sweet Dreams does not appear due to copyright restrictions)

Notes:

- This album was originally released on LP, cassette and 8-Track tape formats on September 22, 1973.
- This album was awarded a gold record for sales in excess of 500,000 copies on December 7, 1973.

Trivia:

- "Paper Roses" has been adopted by fans of the Scottish football team *Kilmarnock F.C.* as the club's anthem and is played at major games throughout the season.
- Marie Osmond became the first female country singer to have a #1 hit with her debut single since Connie Smith with "Once a Day" in 1964.

The Japanese picture sleeve for *Paper Roses*.

In My Little Corner of the World
M3G-4944

Track Listings:
In My Little Corner of the World / Big Hurts Can Come (From Little White Lies) / Invisible Tears / I Love You So Much It Hurts / Everybody's Somebody's Fool / True Love's A Blessing / I Love You Because / It's Just the Other Way Around / Crazy Arms / Singing The Blues

Production Information:
Arranged and produced by: Sonny James In conjunction with Mike Curb Productions
Executive Producer: Don Ovens
Recorded at: Columbia Recording Studios, Studio B, Nashville, TN and
Jack Clement Studios, Nashville, TN
Engineers: Charlie Tallent and Stan Hutto
Vocal Accompaniment: The Jordanaires & Nashville Edition
String Arrangements: Cam Mullins

Singles Released From This Album:
In My Little Corner Of The World / It's Just The Other Way Around - K 14694 (US)
In My Little Corner Of The World / It's Just The Other Way Around - K 14694 (Canada)
In My Little Corner Of The World / It's Just The Other Way Around - 2006 429 (UK)
In My Little Corner Of The World / It's Just The Other Way Around - 2006 429 (Australia)

The following releases were issued with a picture sleeve:
In My Little Corner Of The World / It's Just The Other Way Around - DM-1254 (Japan)
In My Little Corner Of The World / It's Just The Other Way Around - 2006 429 (Germany)
In My Little Corner Of The World / It's Just The Other Way Around - 2006 429 (Belgium)

LP Data:
Billboard Chart Debut: July 6, 1974
Highest Chart Position: 10 on August 23, 1974
# of Weeks on Chart: 18
Billboard Chart: Top Country LP's

Notes:

- This album was originally released on LP, cassette and 8-Track tape formats on July 20, 1974.
- Sheet music marketed with this release

The UK / German album cover for *In My Little Corner Of The World*.

Who's Sorry Now
M3G-4979

Track Listings:
Who's Sorry Now / Anytime / This I Promise You / Love Letters In The Sand / Making Believe / The Things I Tell My Pillow / Among My Souvenirs / Jealous Heart / Clinging Vine / It's The Little Things

Production Information:
Arranged and produced by: Sonny James in conjunction with Mike Curb Productions
Associate Producer: Don Ovens
Executive Producer: The Osmonds
Recorded at: Jack Clement Studios, Nashville, TN
Engineer: Ron Reynolds
Assistant Engineers: Steve Hodge and Charlie Tallent

String Arrangements: Cam Mullins

Vocal Accompaniment: The Jordanaires & Studio Singers

Photography: Albert McKenzie Watson
Design: John & Barbara Casado
Art Direction: Sheri Leverich

Singles Released From This Album:
Who's Sorry Now / This I Promise You - M 14786 (US)
Who's Sorry Now / This I Promise You - M 14786 (Canada)
Who's Sorry Now / This I Promise You - 2006496 (Peru)
Who's Sorry Now / This I Promise You - 2006 496 (New Zealand)

The following releases were issued with a picture sleeve:
Who's Sorry Now / This I Promise You - 2006 496 (Belgium)
Who's Sorry Now / This I Promise You - 2006 496 (Netherlands)
Who's Sorry Now / This I Promise You - 2006 496 (Germany)
Who's Sorry Now / This I Promise You - 2006 496 (UK)
Who's Sorry Now / This I Promise You - DM-1265 (Japan)

Notes:

- This album was originally released on LP, cassette and 8-Track tape formats on March 8, 1975.
- Sheet music marketed for this release

The German picture sleeve for *Who's Sorry Now.*

This Is The Way That I Feel
PD-1-6099

Track Listings:
This is the Way That I Feel / Play The Music Loud / Didn't I Love You Boy / Please Tell Him That I Said Hello / Miss You Nights / Where Did Our Love Go / Cry Baby Cry / You're My Superman (You're My Everything) / All He Did Was Tell Me Lies / Run To Me

Production Information:
A Kolob Production
Produced by: Rick Hall for Fame Productions
Executive Producers: The Osmonds
Recorded at: Fame Recording Studios, Muscle Shoals, Alabama
Devonshire Studios, North Hollywood, CA
Kolob Recording Studios, Provo, UT
Recording Engineers: Rick Hall, Don Daily, Ron Malo, Wayne Osmond, Donny Osmond

Musicians:
Keyboards: Randy McCormick / Tim Henson
Drums and Percussion: Roger Clark / Jimmy Evans
Guitars: Travis Wammack / Ken Bell / Pete Carr / Larry Byron
Bass: Bob Wray / Jerry Bridges
Horns: ("Muscle Shoal Horns") Harrison Calloway / Harvey Thompson / Ronnie Eades / Charles Rose
Strings: Sid Sharp Strings
String Sessions conducted by: Lee Holdridge and Jimmie Haskell
Horn Arrangements: Harrison Calloway
Background Vocals: Rhodes, Chalmers, and Rhodes
Except on Run to Me - Background Vocals: The Osmonds

This Is The Way That I Feel / Miss You Nights / You're My Superman (You're My Everything)
String Arrangements by: Lee Holdridge
Run To Me
String Arrangements by: Lee Holdridge
Didn't I Love You Boy / Please Tell Him That I Said Hello
String Arrangements by: Jimmie Haskell
Play The Music Loud / Cry Baby Cry
String Arrangements by: Lee Holdridge and Mark Snow
Where Did Our Love Go
String Arrangements by: Andrew Belling

Art Direction: Mike Doud
Photography: Gary Heery

Singles Released From This Album:
This Is The Way That I Feel / Play The Music Loud - PD 14385 (Canada)
This Is The Way That I Feel / Play The Music Loud - 2066 793 (UK)
This Is The Way That I Feel / Play The Music Loud - 2066 793 (Scandinavia)
This Is The Way That I Feel / Play The Music Loud - PD 14385 (Promo, Seafare Fun Days / 95 KJR / Coca Cola / Pay 'N Save)

Please Tell Him That I Said Hello / Cry, Baby, Cry - PD-14405 (US)
Please Tell Him That I Said Hello / Cry, Baby, Cry - PD-14405 (Canada)

The following releases were issued with a picture sleeve:
This Is The Way That I Feel / Play The Music Loud - (PD-14385) (US)
This Is The Way That I Feel / Play The Music Loud - 2066 793 (Belgium)
This Is The Way That I Feel / Play The Music Loud - 2066 793 (Germany)
This Is The Way That I Feel / Play The Music Loud - DPQ-6053 (Japan)
This Is The Way That I Feel / Play The Music Loud - 2066 793 (Spain)
This Is The Way That I Feel / Play The Music Loud - 2066 793 (Belgium)
This Is The Way That I Feel / Play The Music Loud - 2066 793 (France)
This Is The Way That I Feel / Play The Music Loud - 2066 793 (Scandinavia)

Notes:

- This album was originally released on LP, cassette and 8-Track tape formats on April 9, 1977. Recorded Fall - Winter 1976.
- Sheet music marketed for this release.

The Japanese picture sleeve for *This Is The Way That I Feel.*

It's The Falling In Love
(Unreleased Marie Album)
Polydor 1979

Known Track Listing:
It's The Falling In Love / (You're Gonna) Get Me To Heaven / LA Song / Tenderly / Cryin' / I'm A Woman

Production Information:
Produced By: Denny Crocket and Ike Egan
Recorded at: Osmond Entertainment Center, Orem, Utah and
KOLOB Studios, Provo, Utah

Singles released from this album:
(You're Gonna) Get Me To Heaven / LA Song POSP-147 - 1980 (UK only)

Notes:

- Album design: Jimmy Osmond Graphics.

The UK Only 1980 Release Of *(You're Gonna) Get Me To Heaven.*

Back to Believin' Again
(Unreleased Marie Album)
Elektra 1983

Known Track List
Back to Believin' Again / I've Got A Bad Case Of You / You Still Get The Best Of Me
I'm Learnin' / Look Who's Getting Over Who

This album was to be released as what was known as a "Mini LP" which contained only 8 tracks - 4 per side. But just prior to completion Elektra announced it was pulling out of the country market. Warner was given the contract options but decided to cancel the contracts with Marie at this time along with Mel Tillis and Nancy Sinatra.

Who's Counting
RCA/Regard 1984
(Unreleased Marie Album)

Known Track Listing:
Who's Counting / Our Song

Produced By: Tom Collins
Recorded at Woodland Sound Studios, Nashville, TN
Engineer: Les Ladd

The 1984 green promotional only single for *Who's Counting.*

There's No Stopping Your Heart
ST-12414

Track Listings:
There's No Stopping Your Heart / Needing a Night Like This / Read My Lips / The Best of You / I'll Be Faithful To You / Meet Me In Montana (with Dan Seals) / That Old Devil Moon / Love Will Find Its Way To You / Until I Fall In Love Again / Blue Sky Shinin'

Production Information:
Produced by: Paul Worley
"Meet Me In Montana" Produced by: Paul Worley and Kyle Lebning

Recorded at: Audio Media Recorders, Nashville, TN
Engineers: Marshall Morgan and Kyle Lebning
Additional Engineering by: Hollis Halford, Paul Worley
Assisted by: Robbie Rose

Sound Stage Studios, Nashville, TN
Engineer: Eric Prestidge
Assisted by: Lee Groitszeb

The Bennett House, Nashville, TN
Engineer: Gene Eichelberger
Assisted by: Don Cobb

"Until I Fall In Love Again" and "That Old Devil Moon"
Mixed by Marshall Morgan at Audio Media
"Read My Lips," "Love Will Find Its Way To You" and "There's No Stopping Your Heart"
Mixed by: Eric Prestidge at Soundstage Studios
"Meet Me In Montana," "Needing A Night Like This," "Blue Sky Shinin'," "I'll Be Faithful To You" and "The Best of You"
Mixed by: Gene Eichelberger and Don Cobb at the Bennett House

Special Thanks to: Jim Foreclosing / Dick Whitehouse / Lynn Shutls / Terry Choate / Paul Lovelace / Norma Jean Owen / Kyle Lebning / Dan Seals / Karl Engemann

Mastered at: Masterfonics by: Glenn Meadows

Musicians:
Drums: Eddie Bayers / Barry Beckett
Bass: Joe Osborn / Michael Rhodes
Keyboards: Dennis Burnside / Barry Beckett
Synthesizer: David Innis
Acoustic Guitar: Paul Worley / Steve Gibson Larry Byrom
Electric Guitar: Steve Gibson / Kenny Mims / Paul Worley
Fiddle and Mandolin: Mark O'Connor
Steel Guitar: Sonny Garrish
Percussion: Tom Roady
Strings arranged by: Bergen White
Played by The Nashville String Machine

Background Vocals: Bergen White / Lisa Silver / Dianne Tidwell / Jessica Boucher (courtesy of Warner Bros, Inc.) / Doug Clements / Bruce Dees / Marsha Woods / Paul Worley / Dennis Wilson / Paula Ward

Art Direction: Roy Kobara
Design: John O'Brien
Photography: Dick Zimmerman

Singles released from this album:
Until I Fall in Love Again / I Don't Want To Go Too Far - B-5445 (US)
Until I Fall in Love Again / I Don't Want To Go Too Far - B-5445 (Canada)
Meet Me In Montana (with Dan Seals) / What Do Lonely People Do - B-5478 (Canada)
Meet Me In Montana (with Dan Seals) / Meet Me In Montana (with Dan Seals) P-B-5478 (US) (Promotional single - Stereo / Mono)
Puedes Detener Tu Corazon (There's No Stopping Your Heart) / Lee Mis Labios (Read My Lips) - 121-0053 (Ecuador) (Both songs sung in English)
Read My Lips / That Old Devil Moon - B-5563 (Canada)

The following releases were issued with a picture sleeve:
Until I Fall in Love Again / I Don't Want To Go Too Far - B-5445 (UK)
Meet Me In Montana* (with Dan Seals) / What Do Lonely People Do - B-5478 (US)
*Peaked at #1 on 10/11/1985 (US)
There's No Stopping Your Heart* / Blue Sky Shinin' - B-5521 (US)
*Peaked at #1 on 2/21/1986 (US)
There's No Stopping Your Heart / Love Will Find Its Way To You - CL 390 (UK)
Read My Lips / That Old Devil Moon - B-5563 (US)

Notes:

- This album was originally released on LP, CD, cassette and 8-Track tape formats in August 1985.
- Songs recorded for this album but released as B sides only:
  "I Don't Want to Go To Far" and "What Do Lonely People Do"
- Sheet music marketed for this release.

I Only Wanted You
ST-12516

Track Listings:
Cry Just A Little / I Only Wanted You / You're Still New To Me (with Paul Davis) / Making Magic / I Know the Feeling / Your Love Carries Me Away / We're Gonna Need A Love Song / New Love / More Than Dancing / Everybody's Crazy 'bout My Baby

Production Information:
Produced by: Paul Worley
Recorded at: Treasure Isle Studios, Nashville, TN and Audio Media, Nashville, TN
Engineer: Marshall Morgan
Assistant engineers: by Bob Wright and Hollis Halford
Mixed by Ed Seay
Assisted by Tom Harding and Tom Durr

Musicians:
Drums: Eddie Bayers / James Stroud
Percussion: Tom Roady
Bass: Michael Rhodes / Tom Robb
Acoustic Guitars: Larry Byrom / Paul Worley
Electric Guitars: Steve Gibson / Paul Worley except for Kenny Mims on "Your Love Carries Me Away"
Piano: Dennis Burnside
Synthesizers: David Innis / Mike Lawler
Steel Guitar: Tom "The Swede" Choate
Saxophone: Jim Horn

Background Vocals: Jessica Boucher / Dennis Wilson / Thom Flora / Lisa Silver / Diane Tidwell, Paul Davis / Paul Worley / Kathie Baillie / Michael Brook / Alan LeBoeuf

Strings: The "A" Strings
String Arrangements: Dennis Burnside

Special thanks to three Paul's: Worley, Davis, and "Cupcake"

Art Direction: Roy Kohara
Design: John O'Brien
Photography: Charles Bush

Singles released from this album:
Cry Just A Little / More Than Dancing - B-44044
Cry Just A Little / Cry Just A Little - P-B-44044 (US) (Radio Station Promotional copy - Stereo / Mono)
I Only Wanted You / I Only Wanted You - P-B-5663 (US) (Radio Station Promotional copy - Stereo / Mono)
Everybody's Crazy 'Bout My Baby / Making Magic - B-5703 (US)
Everybody's Crazy 'Bout My Baby / Everybody's Crazy 'Bout My Baby P- B-5703 (US) (Radio Station Promotional copy - Stereo / Mono)

The following releases were issued with a picture sleeve:
You're Still New To Me* (with Paul Davis) / New Love B-5613 (US)
*Peaked at #1 on 11/21/1986 (US)
I Only Wanted You / We're Gonna Need A Love Song - B-5663 (US)

LP Data:
Highest Chart Position: 19 on Oct. 17, 1986

Notes:

- This album was originally released on LP, CD cassette and 8-Track tape formats in September 1986
- Songs recorded for this album but not released: "He Talks to Me." Promotional cassette copies are thought to exists with I Only wanted You / He Talks To Me.

The US picture sleeve for *I Only Wanted You*.

All In Love
CI-48968

Track Listings:
I'm In Love and He's In Dallas / Raining Tears / My Home Town Boy / Baby's Blue Eyes
Lonely As the Night Is Long / 99% of the Time / Somebody Else's Moon / Sweet Life (with Paul Davis) / All In Love / Without A Trace

Production Information:
Produced by: Paul Worley / Ed Seay
Recorded at: Treasure Isle Recorders
Engineer: Ed Seay
Mixed by: Ed Seay at Digital Recorders
Assisted by: Mike Poole
"Lonely As the Night Is Long"
Recorded by Marshall Morgan at Audio Media Recorders
"My Hometown Boy," "All In Love" and "Somebody Else's Moon"
Recorded at Nightingale Studio
Engineer: Joe Bogan
Assisted by Gary Paczosa
Assistant Engineers: Clarke Schleicher, Mike Poole and Tom Harding
Additional Engineering by: Tom Harding, Clarke Schleicher, Mike Poole

Mastered at Georgetown Masters by: Denny Purcell

Musicians:
Drums: Eddie Bayers / Mark Hammond / Martin Parker / James Stroud / Steve Turner
Bass: Mike Brignardello / Michael Rhodes / Tom Robb / Joe Osborn
Lead Guitar: Larry Byrom / Steve Gibson / Jon Goin / Paul Worley
Acoustic Guitar: Larry Byrom / Greg Galbreath / Paul Worley
Piano and Synth: Dennis Burnside / Mitch Humpheries / David Innis / Matt Rollins
Fiddle and Mandolin: Mark O'Conner
Steel: Paul Franklin
Strings Arranged by Bergen White
Strings by Nashville String Machine

Background Vocals:
Jessica Boucher / Jana King / Diane Vanette / Lisa Silver . Marie Osmond / Dennis Wilson / Michael Black

Production Coordination: Sharon Eaves

Art Direction / Design: Tommy Steele and Benjamin Cziller
Photography: Aaron Rapoport
Paul Davis appears courtesy of EMI – Manhattan Records

Singles released from this album:
Without A Trace / Baby's Blue Eyes - B-44176 (US)
Without A Trace / Baby's Blue Eyes - B-44176 (Canada)
Without A Trace / Without A Trace - P-B-44176 (US) (Radio Station Promotional copy - Stereo / Mono)
Sweet Life (with Paul Davis) / Somebody Else's Moon - B-44215
Sweet Life (with Paul Davis) / Sweet Life (with Paul Davis) - P- B-44215 (US) (Radio Station Promotional copy - Stereo / Mono)
I'm In Love and He's In Dallas / My Hometown Boy - B-44269 (US)
I'm In Love and He's In Dallas / I'm In Love and He's In Dallas - P-B-44269 (US) (Radio Station Promotional copy - Stereo / Mono)

LP Data:
Highest Chart Position: 29 on Aug. 19, 1988

Notes:

- This album was originally released on LP, CD and cassette tape in July 1988.

The promo single for *Sweet Life* with Paul Davis

Steppin' Stone
C1-91781

Track Listings:
What Would You Do About You (If You Were Me) / Slowly But Surely / What's In It For Me / Steppin' Stone / What's A Little Love Between Friends / If You Think About It Call Me / Help Me Get Over You / A Too Blue Moon / Love Speaks Louder Than Words / Let Me Be The First

Production Information:
Produced by: Jerry Crutchfield
Recorded at: Music Mill Studios, Nashville, TN and Ominsound Studios, Nashville, TN
Recording Engineers: Jim Cotton and Scott Hendricks
Assistant Recording Engineers: Paul Goldberg and Carry Summers
Overdubbed at: Javelina Recording Studios, Nashville, TN and House of David. Nashville, TN
Engineers: Chris Hammond, Warren Peterson and Lynn Peterzell
Assistant Engineers: Robert Charles, Tom Hitchcock and Carry Summers
Remixed at: The Castle Recording Studios, Nashville, TN
Remix Engineer: Scott Hendricks
Assistant Remix Engineer: Mark Nevers

Mastered at: Master Mix Studios, Nashville, TN
Mastering Engineer: Hank Williams

Musicians:
Keyboards: David Briggs / Mitch Humphries / Matt Rollings
Drums: Clyde Brooks / Larry Londin
Acoustic Guitar: Mark Casstevens
Steel Guitar: Steve Fishell / Sonny Garrish
Acoustic and Electric Guitar: Steve Gibson
Percussion and Harmonica: Terry McMillan
Electric Guitar: Brent Rowan
Bass: Bob Wray
Background Vocals: Jessica Boucher / Carol Chase / Greg Gordon / Paul Overstreet* / Dennis Wilson / Curtis Young
Paul Overstreet appears courtesy of RCA Records
Make-up: Bob Ryan
Hair: Gail Rowell

Art Director: Tommy Steele
Designer: Peter Grant
Photo by: Bruno Goget
Reprinted by permission of Redbook Magazine © 1989 by the Hearst Corporation

There are so many people to thank…
To Jerry Crutchfield – This has been the most enjoyable album I have worked on and I know it's because of you. Thanks Jerry.

To the engineers, musicians, publishers, and especially to all the writers – Thank you so much. You're the greatest!

To my manager, Karl Engemann (Man of Destiny) – For all the years of dedication and devotion. Thank you.

And a special thank you to Capitol Records – I love you all! – Marie

Singles released from this album:
Steppin' Stone / What Would You Do About You (If You Were Me) - B-44412 (US)
Steppin' Stone / Steppin' Stone P-B-44412 (US) (Radio Station Promotional copy - Stereo / Mono)
Slowly But Surely / What Would You Do About You (If You Were Me) - B-44468 (US)
Slowly But Surely /Slowly But Surely - 7PRO-79808 (US) (Radio Station Promotional copy - Stereo / Mono)
Let Me Be the First / What's A Little Love between Friends - B-44505 (US)
Let Me Be the First / Let Me Be the First - P-B-44505 (US) (Radio Station Promotional copy - Stereo / Mono)

CD Singles Released From This Album:
Steppin' Stone - DPRO-79719 (US) (CD Promotional Copy / Not For Sale)
Slowly But Surely - DPRO-79809 (US) (CD Promotional Copy / Not For Sale)

Cassette Singles Released From This Album:
Stepping Stones / What Would You Do About You (If You Were Me) - 4JM-44412 (US)

Notes:

- This album was originally released on LP, CD and cassette tape formats on September 12, 1989.

The Best Of Marie Osmond
D2-77263

Track Listing:
Paper Roses / There's No Stoppin' Your Heart / Meet Me In Montana (Duet with Dan Seals) / Everybody's Crazy 'Bout My Baby / Like A Hurricane / Think With Your Heart / Read My Lips / I Only Wanted You / You're Still New To Me (Duet with Paul Davis) / I'll Be Faithful To You

Production Information:
Producer – James Stroud (tracks: 5, 6), Kyle Lehning (tracks: 3), Paul Worley (tracks: 2, 3, 4, 7, 8, 9, 10), Sonny James (track: 1)

Notes:

- Released: September 25, 1990
- This album was originally released on CD and Cassette tape formats.
- Track 1 (Paper Roses) is a 1990 re-recording using the same producer, studio and as many of the original musicians who played on the original 1973 recording 17 years earlier.
- Title in Germany: **The Best Of Marie Osmond - American Superstars.**

Also released in Japan with modified cover art.

True Love (Never Goes Away)
(Unreleased Marie Album)
D-77542 - Curb 1992

Known Track Listing:
True Love Never Goes Away / What Kind of Man (Walks on a Woman) / The Loft / Baby, It's Tonight

Production Information:
Produced by: James Stroud

CD Singles released from this album:
True Love (Never Goes Away) (1992) (Promo Only)
What Kind Of Man (Walks on a Woman) (1994) (Promo Only)

Cass-singles released from this album:
A1 What Kind Of Man (Walks on a Woman) (1995)
B1 The Loft (1:06 preview only) B2 Baby, It's Tonight (1:06 preview only)

Cass-single and promotional CD of *What Kind Of Man (Walks On A Woman)*.

Magic Of Christmas
HF-1001

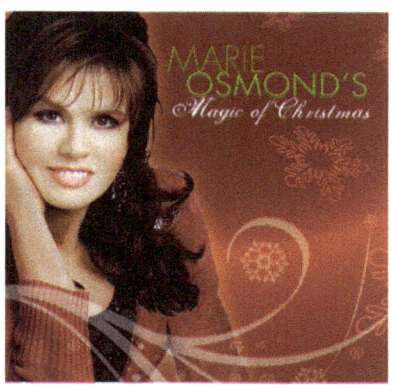

Track Listing:
The Christmas Song / When Christmas Comes This Year (with Donny Osmond) / Angels We Have Heard on High / Away in a Manger / Season of Seasons (with Stephen Craig) / Christmas Lullaby / The Gift of Love (with Paul Engemann) / Hark! the Herald Angels Sing / O Come All Ye Faithful / The Locket (with The Osmond Brothers) / Christmas in the Country / It's Christmas Once Again (with Jimmy Osmond) / O Holy Night / The Secret of Christmas / The Lord's Prayer / True Love / Santa Claus is Coming to Town (with Merrill Osmond)

Album Data:

Highest Christian (Billboard) Chart Position: 4
# of Weeks on Chart: 7
Peak Date: November 30, 2007

Notes:
- Reissued in 2008 through Genius Entertainment (#HF-1003) with slightly altered cover art and bonus tracks: White Christmas / Sleigh Ride / Have Yourself A Merry Little Christmas / It's Beginning To Look A Lot Like Christmas / Pine Cones And Holly Berries / My Favorite Things
- Songs dropped from 2008 reissue: Season of the Season / The Gift of Love
- A bonus CD with the additional tracks above was marketed through QVC upon original 2007 release with the title "Stocking Stuffer."

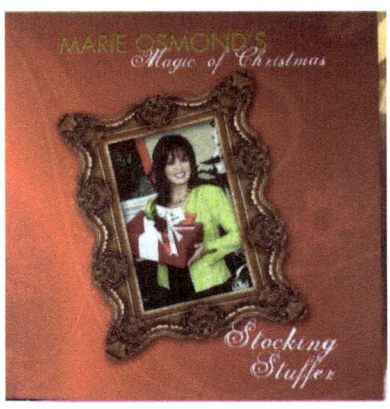

I Can Do This
OE2010-81

Track Listing:
How Great Thou Art / I Can Only Imagine / Pie Jesu / Now Thank We All Our God / World Without Walls / Tell Me to Breathe / I Need Thee Every Hour / Ave Verum Corpus / I Can Do This / Lead, Kindly Light / Be Still My Soul / Bless This House / Gift to Be Simple / Tender Mercies / The Only One

Production Information:
Produced and arranged by Jerry Williams
Recorded at: Smecky Music Studios in Prague, Czech Republic and Rite Tune Studios

Singles released from this album:
Pie Jesu (Digital Download Only)

Notes:

Christian Chart Debut: November 27, 2010
Highest Christian Chart Position: 5
# of Weeks on Christian Charts: 1

- Original Release: November 16, 2010
- Reissued on January 12, 2016.
- All proceeds of this album were donated to Children's Miracle Network Hospitals.

Music Is Medicine
AOMR-1419-1

Track Listing:
Music Is Medicine / Unbreak This Break Up / Give Me a Good Song (with SisQo) / Getting Better All the Time (with Olivia Newton-John) / Baby You're Crazy / I'd Love to Be Your Last / Love This Tough (with John Rich) / Then There's You (with Alex Boye) / Wild & Sweet / I'll Find You

Production Information:
Produced by Jason Deere
Production Assistants: Jeremy Barron and Brad Hull
Recorded at: Soundstage Studios, Nashville, TN and Westwood Studios, Nashville, TN
Audio Mix House and Studios at The Palms in Las Vegas, NV
Engineers: Jim Cooley / Jason Deere / Jason "JP" Patterson / Josh Connolly / David Axelrod / Mike Clute and Brady Tilow
Mastered by: Silvio Richetto at The Living Room Studios in Aventura, FL.

Musicians:
Bass: David LaBruyere and Lee Hendricks
Keyboard: Dave Cohen and David Dorn
Drums: Evan Hutchins and Miles McPherson
Electric Guitars: Justin Ostrander and Adam Shoenfeld
Acoustic, Banjo, Mandolin, Electric Guitar: Ilya Toshinskiy
Background vocals: Jason Deere, Cheaza Figueroa, Rachael Lauren, Tasha Layton, Justin Richards, Silvio Richetto, Russel Terrell, Briana Tyson

Photography: Bill Livingston and Jeff katz
Album Design: Paul Kruegar
Hair and Makeup: Kim Goodwin

Songs recorded for this album but not released:
More You (With Diamond Rio)
Got Me Cuz He Gets Me

Singles released from this album:
Music Is Medicine (Digital download only)
Baby, You're Crazy (Digital download only)

Notes:

- The album entered the Billboard Top Country Albums chart at #10 on May 7, 2016.
- Originally released on CD and digital download on April 15, 2016. On November 18, 2016 an autographed limited edition "Crystal Clear" vinyl LP was offered by Amazon and by November 22, 2016 had quickly sold out.
- On March 27, 2016 a video for the song "Then There's You" was released on the internet video site Vevo and it received almost 200,000 views in less than 48 hours.
- On April 13, 2016 the video for the title track Music is Medicine was released also on Vevo and was filmed with patients from Children's Miracle Network Hospitals.

An on-line promotional card for the new album.

THE PHOTO GALLERY

Total

Hysteria!

They Could Not Get Enough Of The Osmonds

SPECIAL OFFER

1. NEW FROM DONNY

Life Size Head To Toe 24" x 60" Full Color Poster
$2.25

2. OSMOND BROTHERS MOTHER'S COOK BOOK

A collection of Mrs. Osmond's thoughts and recipes. Durable Vinyl Binder
$5.00

3. "SWEET DREAMS" PILLOWCASE

Something You Don't have to share with anyone. Your very own "Sweet Dreams" pillowcase from Donny Osmond. 100% COTTON
$2.25

4. THE OSMONDS IN CONCERT

Osmond's in Concert Picture Book. 24 pages – Candid Shots – Autographed Pin-ups. Full Color Cover and Center Spread
$2.25

5. OSMONDS GOLD SONG BOOK — 88 PAGES

8 PAGES FULL COLOR. OVER 50 PICTURES – 25 SONGS. Includes: One Bad Apple, Go Away Little Girl, Puppy Love, Down By The Lazy River, Hold Her Tight. And Many Others Just Released! Collector's Item
$3.25

6. JOIN THE O'SHIRT* CROWD
*It's really a T-shirt, but with the Osmond insignia on it – We call it an O-Shirt for fun. Chest Measurements: 30-32, 34-36, 38-40, 42-44. 100% COTTON

$3.25

7. IT'S A PUZZLE, IT'S A PORTRAIT, IT'S DONNY!

Giant jigsaw. Is a Color portrait of Donny with his autograph.
$3.00

8. OSMOND SWEAT SHIRT

Tropic blue with blue and red lettering. 50% Creslan – 50% Cotton. Chest Measurement: 30-32, 34-36, 38-40, 42-44
$5.00

Arriving… somewhere. Travel is a big part of the performers life.

The Gold Records and Trophies Kept Coming!

A Loving Musical Family

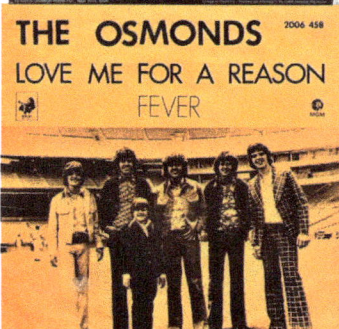

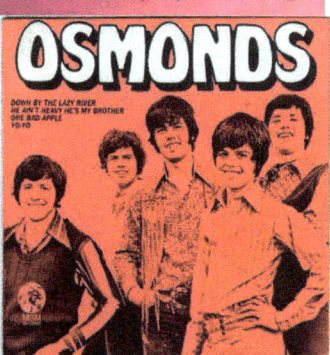

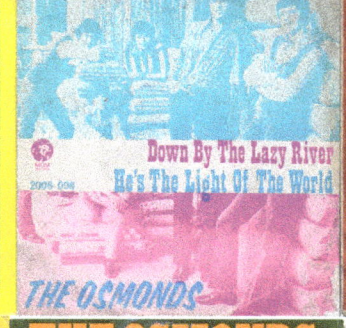

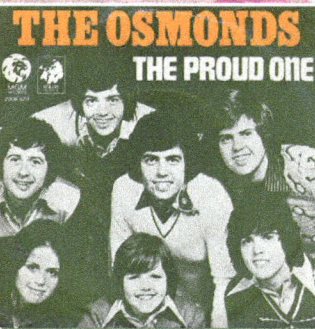

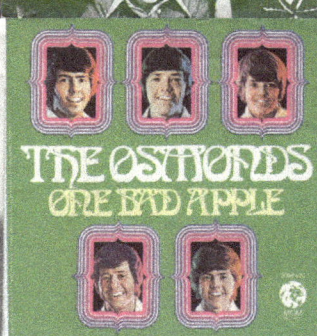

Hey Girl
I Knew You When
I Am Your Puppet
Burning Bridges
DONNY OSMOND
"SWEET AND INNOCENT"
DONNY OSMOND
OF THE OSMONDS
GO AWAY LITTLE GIRL
HEY GIRL
BURNING BRIDGES
Donny Osmond
TOO YOUNG
PUPPY LOVE
LOVE ME
GO AWAY LITTLE GIRL
DONNY OSMOND
PUPPY LOVE
LONELY BOY
TOO YOUNG
WHY
DONNY OSMOND
why
lonely boy
DONNY OSMOND
A TIME FOR US
GUESS WHO
DONNY OSMOND
a time for us
guess who
DONNY OSMOND
I HAVE A DREAM
I'm Dyin'
DONNY OSMOND
Of The Osmonds
SWEET AND INNOCENT
Flirtin'
BLEIB' BEI MIR, LITTLE GIRL
DONNY OSMOND
M-G-M
DONNY OSMOND
Young love
A million to one
Donny Osmond
Young Love
A Million To One
Donny Osmond
A MILLION TO ONE
Young Love
DONNY OSMOND - "The Twelfth Of Never"
"Life Is Just What You Make It"

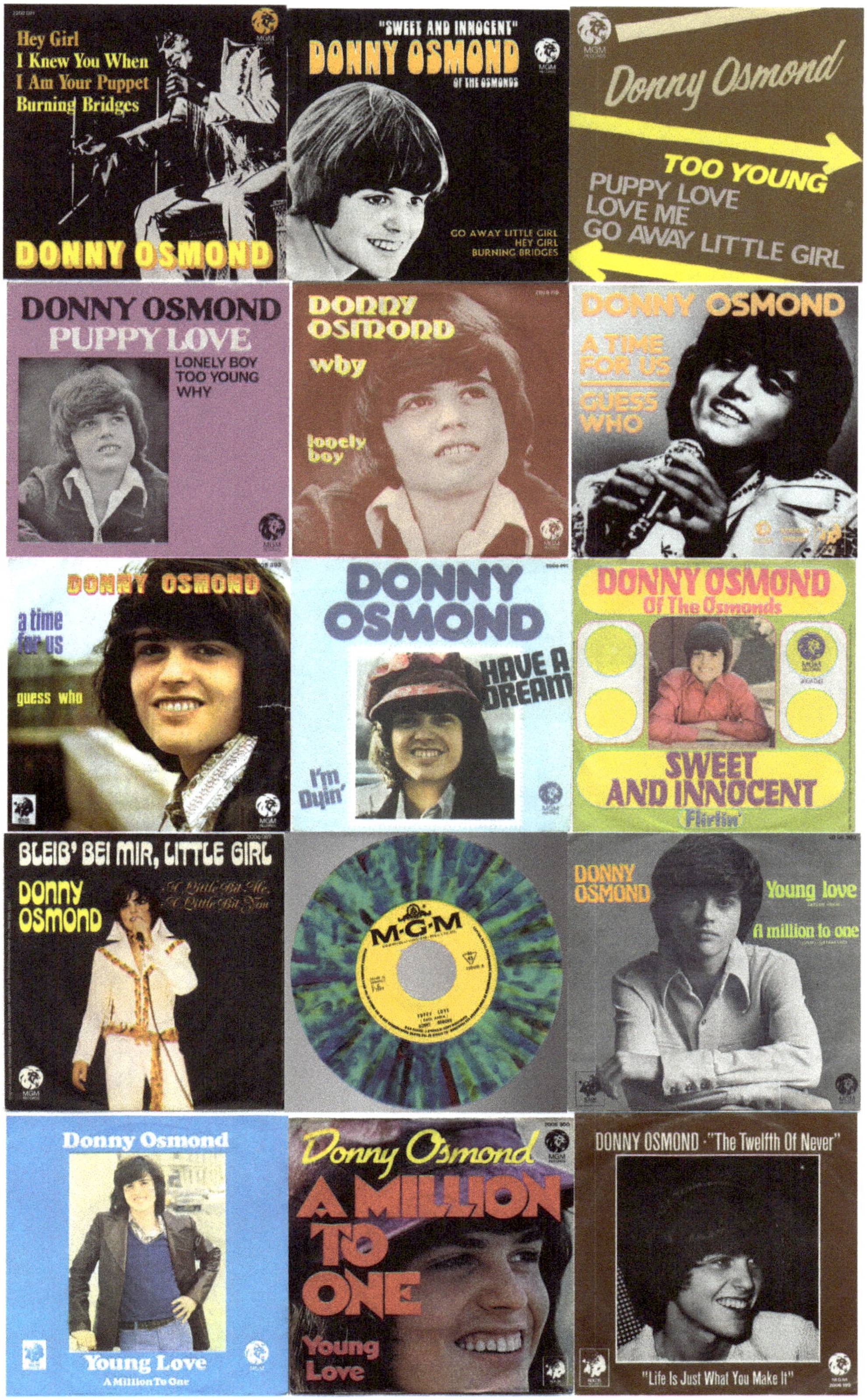

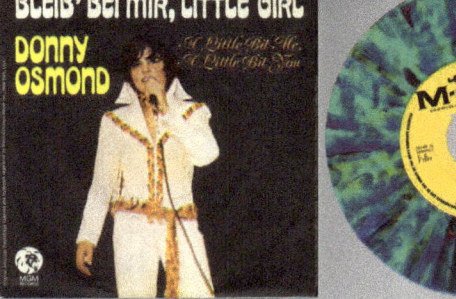

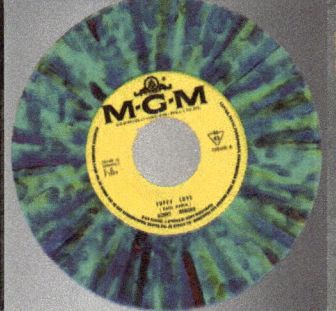

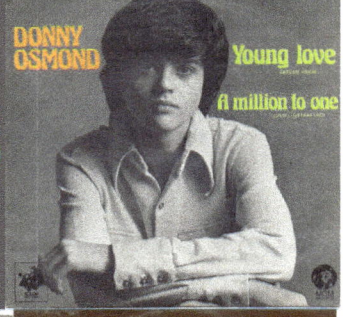

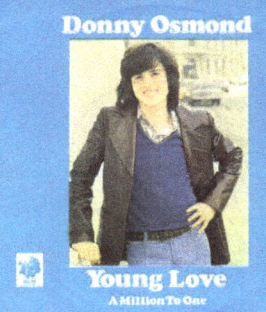

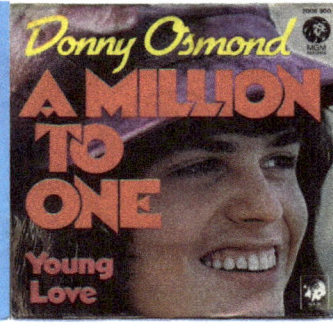

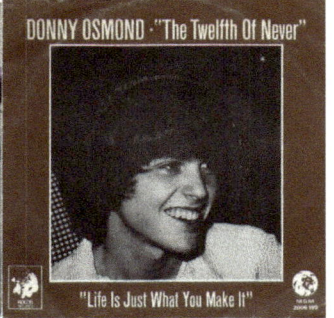

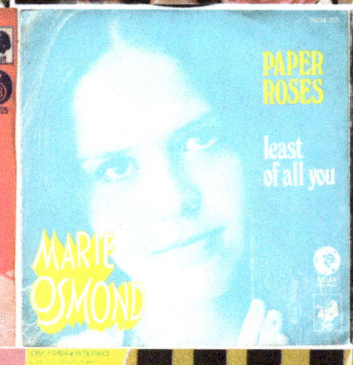
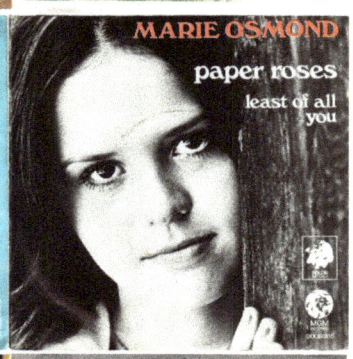

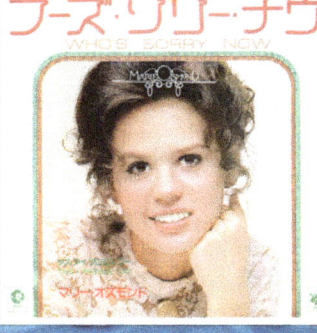

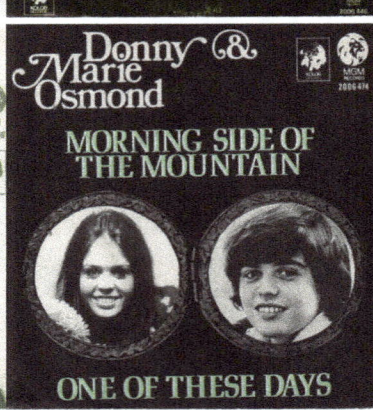

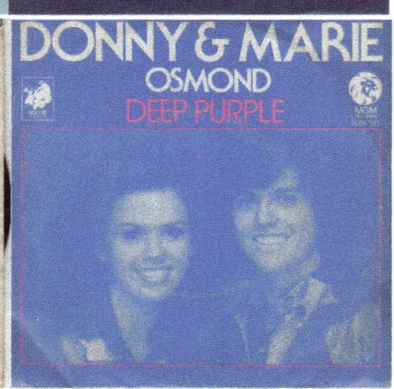

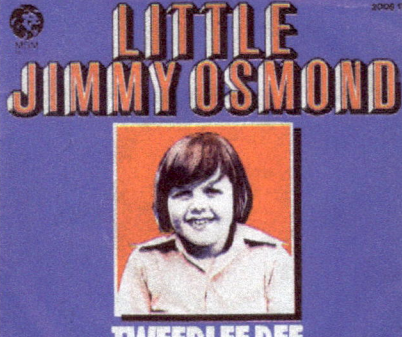

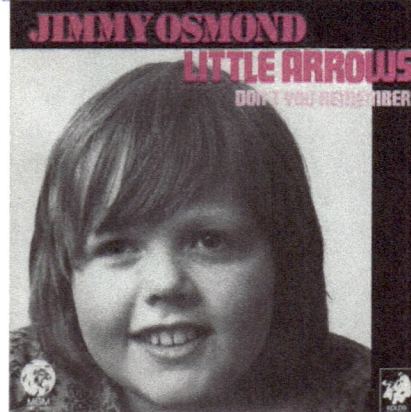
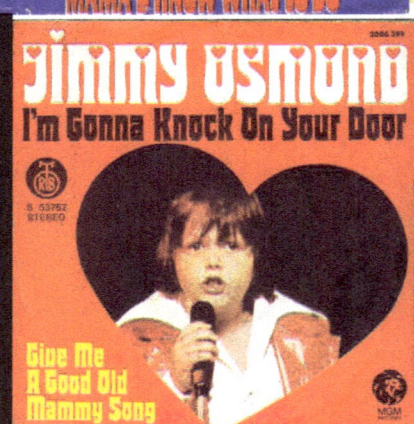

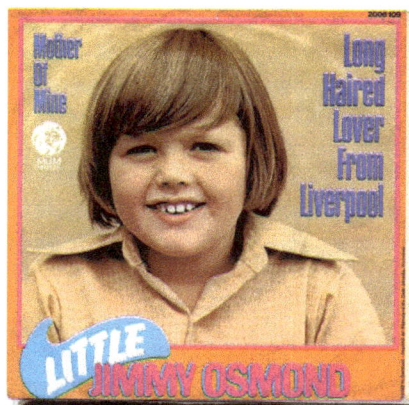

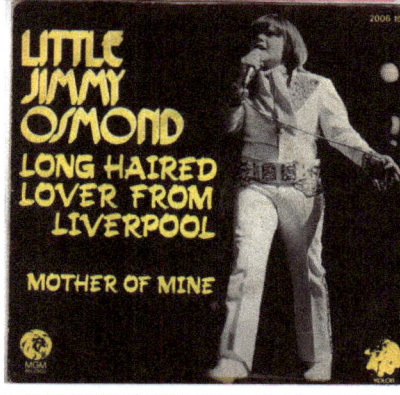
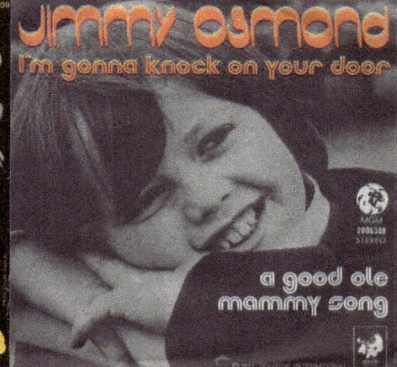

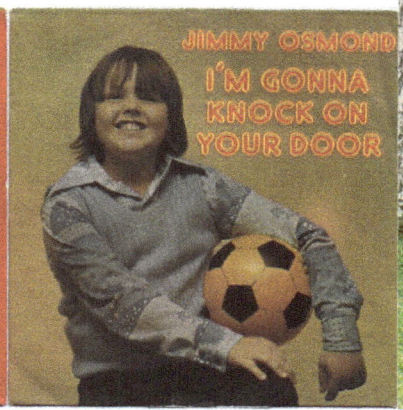

Donny and Marie in KOLOB Studios in 1974 with Mike Curb. Photos: Virl Osmond

Donny and Marie in KOLOB Studios in 1974 with Mike Curb. Photos: Virl Osmond

1984 Postcard from WIXX 101!

Donny and Marie in Concert at the Alameda County Fair in 1984. Photo: Daniel Selby

I stayed in touch with a few of the Ice Vanities / Ice Angels through the years!

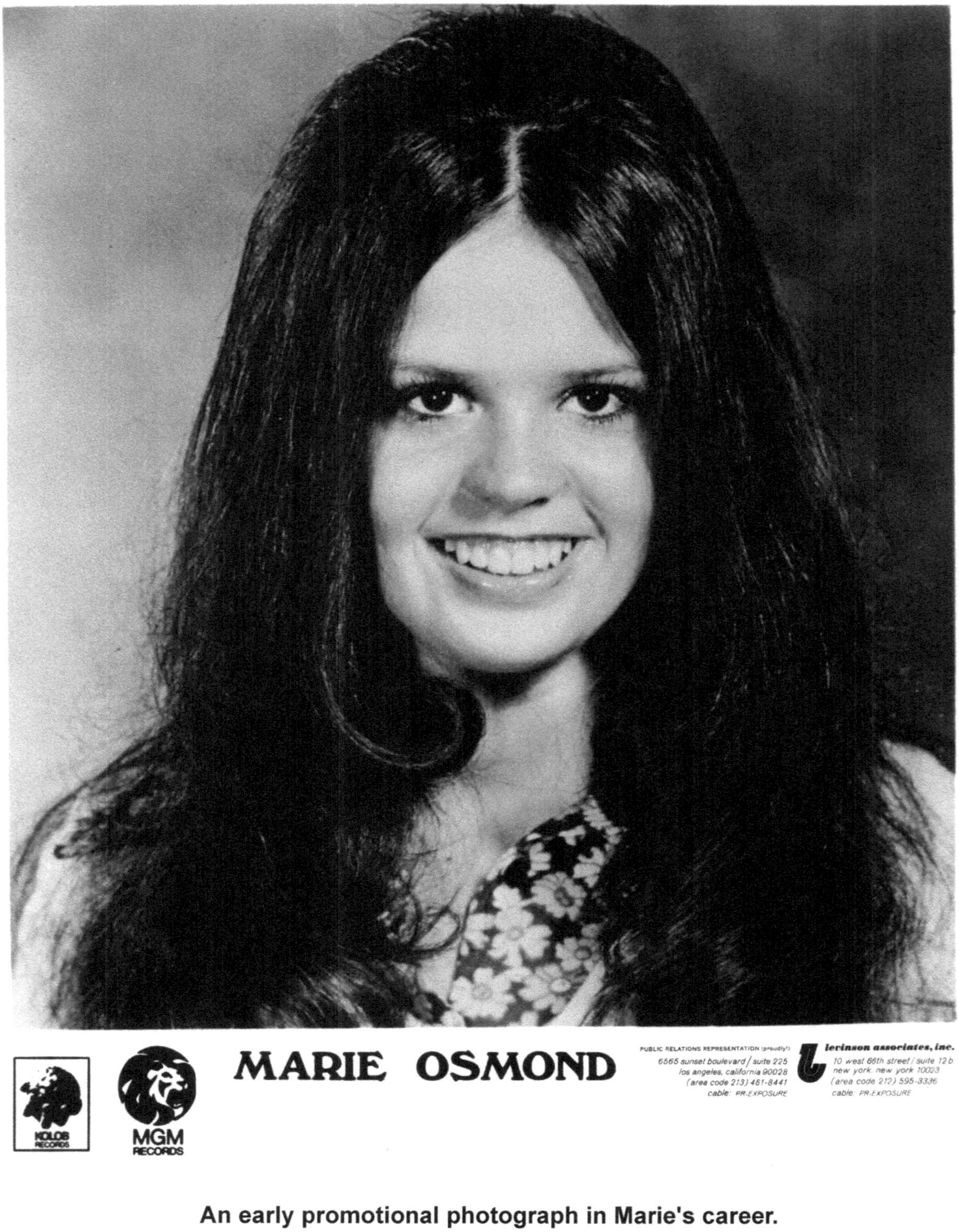

MARIE OSMOND
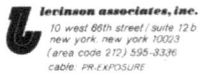

An early promotional photograph in Marie's career.
A beautiful person both inside and out.

MARIE OSMOND   **SONNY JAMES**

At the former KOLOB Recording Studio at The Riviera Apartments in Provo, Utah , 1975.

To me Marie was the epitome of class, grace, beauty, talent and style. *Totally incomparable.* That has not changed even today. Marie in 1977.

Marie in concert at Chabot College, Hayward, CA in 1986. Photos: Daniel Selby

Here I am looking over the Hand Print wall at Osmond Studios in 1978!

Donny and Marie with Mike Curb 1978. New Season Gold Album Award.

The brothers were in harmony in voice and apparel!

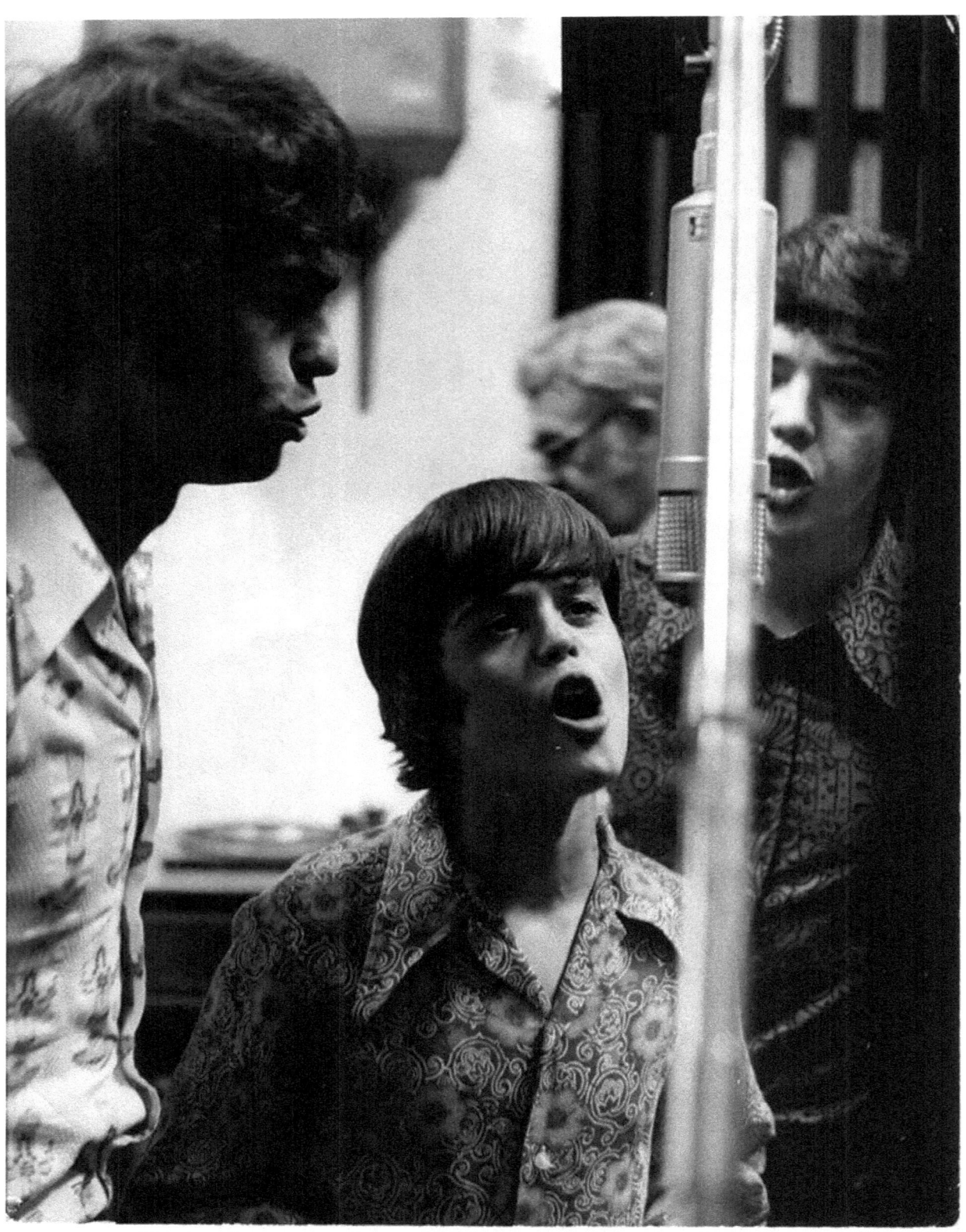
**The brothers recording at FAME Recording Studios in Alabama.
1971**

**The brothers near the top of their game!
1975**

I would laugh hysterically at what went on on The Donny & Marie Show. Friday was my favorite day of the week since they would be on that night! It was good TV!

As a singer and performer Marie was always miles ahead of her time as far as style and content. She answered to no one.

JULY 1985 RELEASE

CUSTOMER _____
ADDRESS _____
CITY _____

MARIE OSMOND
THERE'S NO STOPPING YOUR HEART
ST-12414
4XT-12414
898

Multi-faceted entertainer Marie Osmond brings her recording career full blossom with the release of *There's No Stopping Your Heart* which features the premiere single, a duet with Dan Seals, entitled "Meet Me In Montana." With this release, producer Paul Worley has created a new country sound and style for the seasoned performer. Tracks such as "Until I Fall In Love Again," "Love Will Find It's Way To You," as well as the title track, demonstrate Marie's strong vocal delivery and distinctive style. Marie is no stranger to the recording industry. When she was just thirteen her first single "Paper Roses," attained gold status within a few short weeks after its release and prompted two nominations by the National Academy of Recording Arts and Sciences for "Best Vocal Performance," and "Best Artist" of 1973. A duet with brother Donny, "I'm Leaving It All Up To You," struck gold a year later. *There's No Stopping Your Heart* is destined to secure Marie a place at the top of the Country charts where she belongs.

THE SONGS:
Side One:
THERE'S NO STOPPING YOUR HEART • NEEDING A NIGHT LIKE THIS • READ MY LIPS • THE BEST OF YOU • I'LL BE FAITHFUL TO YOU

Side Two:
MEET ME IN MONTANA • THAT OLD DEVIL MOON • LOVE WILL FIND IT'S WAY TO YOU • UNTIL I FALL IN LOVE AGAIN • BLUE SKY SHININ'

Configurations: Order
Album — **ST-12414**   _____ QTY.
Bar Code No. 7777-12414-1

Cassette — **4XT-12414** _____ QTY.
Bar Code No. 7777-12414-4

Marie Osmond Capitol Records July 1985 Sales Solicitation Sheet

Donny & Marie **Osmond**

I'm Leaving It All Up To You
M3G-4968

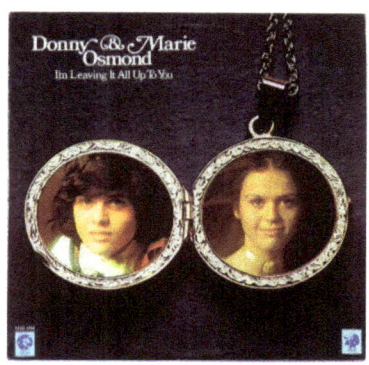

Track Listings:
I'm Leaving It All Up To You / Take Me Back Again / A Day Late and a Dollar Short / Everything Good Reminds Me Of You / Gone / Morning Side of the Mountain / True Love / It Takes Two / The Umbrella Song / Let It Be Me

Production Information:
I'm Leaving It All Up To You / Take Me Back Again / Gone / Let It Be Me
Produced by: Mike Curb
Executive Producers: The Osmonds
Arranged by: Tommy Oliver

A Day Late and a Dollar Short
Produced by: Mike Curb
Executive Producers: The Osmonds
Arranged by: Lyle Ritz

Everything Good Reminds Me Of You / The Umbrella Song
Produced by: Mike Curb
Executive Producers: The Osmonds
Arranged by: Jimmy Haskell

Morning Side of The Mountain / True Love / It Takes Two
Produced by: Mike Curb
Executive Producers: The Osmonds
Arranged by: H.B. Barnum

Music recorded at: MGM Recording Studios, Los Angeles, CA
Vocals overdubbed at: Kolob Recording Studios, Provo, Utah
Engineer: Ed Greene
Additional Engineering: Wayne Osmond
Additional Mixing: Michael Lloyd

Musicians:
Jay Graydon, Olivia Page, Edward Green, Ronald L. Brown, Joe L. Clayton, Tommy Vig, Don Peake, Sylvester L. Rivers.

Wardrobe Designed by: Bill Belew
Photography by: Leandro Correa, Rod Dyer, Inc.
Album designed by: Michael Wiseltier / Kameny Associates, Inc.

Singles released from this album:
I'm Leaving It All Up To You / The Umbrella Song - M 14735 (US / Canada / Guatemala)
I'm Leaving It All Up To You / The Umbrella Song - 2006 446 (Ireland)
I'm Leaving It All Up To You / The Umbrella Song - 2006 446 (UK)
I'm Leaving It All Up To You / The Umbrella Song - 2006 446 (Australia)
Morning Side Of The Mountain / One of These Days - M 14765 (US)
Morning Side Of The Mountain / One of These Days - 2006 474 (Ireland)
Morning Side Of The Mountain / One of These Days - 2006 474 (UK)
Morning Side Of The Mountain / One of These Days - 2006 474 (Uruguay)
Amanecer En la Montaña (Morning Side Of The Mountain) / Amor Verdadero (True Love) - 2006 486 (Mexico)

The following releases were issued with a picture sleeve:
I'm Leaving It All Up To You / The Umbrella Song - 2006 446 (Spain)
I'm Leaving It All Up To You / The Umbrella Song - 2006 446 (France)
I'm Leaving It All Up To You / The Umbrella Song - 2006 446 (Turkey)
I'm Leaving It All Up To You / The Umbrella Song - 2006 446 (Germany)
I'm Leaving It All Up To You / The Umbrella Song - 2006 446 (Belgium)
I'm Leaving It All Up To You / The Umbrella Song - 2006 446 (Austria)
I'm Leaving It All Up To You / The Umbrella Song - 2006 446 (Switzerland)
I'm Leaving It All Up To You / The Umbrella Song - 2006 446 (Yugoslavia)
I'm Leaving It All Up To You / The Umbrella Song - 2006 446 (Netherlands)
I'm Leaving It All Up To You / The Umbrella Song - DM-1256 (Japan)
Morning Side Of The Mountain / One of These Days - 2006 474 (Germany)
Morning Side Of The Mountain / One of These Days - 2006 474 (Austria)
Morning Side Of The Mountain / One of These Days - 2006 474 (Belgium)
Morning Side Of The Mountain / One of These Days - DM-1262 (Japan)
Morning Side Of The Mountain / One of These Days - 2006 474 (Yugoslavia)

LP Data:
Billboard Chart Debut: Sept 7, 1974
Highest Chart Position: 35
# of Weeks on Chart: 32
Billboard Chart: Top Selling LPs

Notes:
- There are two known mixes with alternate verses of "A Day Late and A Dollar Short."
- This album was issued with a different cover in Spain.
- Sheet music marketed for this album.
- This album was originally released on LP, cassette and 8-Track tape formats on July 6, 1974.
- This album was awarded a gold record for sales in excess of 500,000 copies on February 21, 1975.

Make The World Go Away
M3G-4996

Track Listings:
Make The World Go Away / It's All In The Game / Together / When Somebody Cares For You / When You're Young And In Love / I Will / One of These Days / Jigsaw (Recorded on November 12, 1974) / Living On My Suspicion / Mama Didn't Lie

Production Information:
Make The World Go Away / When Somebody Cares For You / I Will
Produced by: Mike Curb
Executive Producers: The Osmonds
Arranged by: Tommy Oliver

It's All In The Game / Together / Jigsaw / Mama Didn't Lie
Produced by: Mike Curb
Executive Producers: The Osmonds
Arranged by: Gene Page

When You're Young and In Love
Produced by: Mike Curb and Don Costa
Executive Producers: The Osmonds
Arranged by: Don Costa

One of These Days / Living On My Suspicion
Produced by: Alan Osmond and Michael Lloyd
Executive Producers: The Osmonds

Music recorded at: MGM Recording Studios, Los Angeles, California
Vocals overdubbed at: Kolob Recording Studios, Provo Utah
Engineered by: Umberto Gatica, Ed Greene, and Steve Hodge
Director of Engineering: Ed Greene

Musicians:
Jay Graydon, Olivia Page, Edward Green, Ronald L. Brown, Joe L. Clayton, Tommy Vig, Don Peake, Sylvester L. Rivers.

Photography: Albert Mckenzie Watson
Art Direction: Sheri Leverich

Singles released from this album:
Make The World Go Away / Living On My Suspicion - M 14807 (US / Canada)
Make The World Go Away / Living On My Suspicion - 2006 523 (New Zealand)
Make The World Go Away / Living On My Suspicion - 2006 523 (Australia)
Make The World Go Away / Living On My Suspicion - 2006 523 (Ireland)
Make The World Go Away / Living On My Suspicion - 2006 523 (UK)
Make The World Go Away / Living On My Suspicion - 2006 523 (Austria)

The following releases were issued with a picture sleeve:
Make The World Go Away / Living On My Suspicion - 2006 523 (Belgium)
Make The World Go Away / Living On My Suspicion - 2006 523 (France)
Make The World Go Away / Living On My Suspicion - 2006 523 (Germany)
Make The World Go Away / Living On My Suspicion - 2006 523 (Netherlands)

Notes:

- Sheet music marketed for this album.
- This album was originally released on LP, cassette and 8-Track tape formats on June 28, 1975.

The German picture sleeve for *Make The World Go Away*.

Featuring Songs From Their Television Show
PD-1-6068

Track Listings:
+C'mon Marianne / +Butterfly / +A Little Bit Country, A Little Bit Rock 'N Roll / +Dandelion / *Deep Purple / +"A" My Name Is Alice / Sunshine Lady / #Take Me Back Again / +Weeping Willow / #It Takes Two / +May Tomorrow Be A Perfect Day
© #1974 *1975 +1976 MGM/Polydor

Production Information:
Produced by: Mike Curb
Executive Producers: The Osmonds
Recorded, overdubbed and remixed at: Kolob Recording Studios, Provo, Utah
Engineers: Humberto Gatica / Wayne Osmond / Donny Osmond

Musicians:
Jay Graydon, Michael Lloyd, John D'Andrea, Steve Olitzky, Ben Benay, James Hughart, Ron Krasinski, Dan Sawyer, Reginald Powell, Shaun Duffey Harris

Photography by: George Hurrell and Ralph Nelson
Cover designed and prepared by: Virl Osmond and AGI/Hollywood

Singles released from this album:

Donny:
C'mon Marianne / Old Man Auctioneer - 2066 688 (Ireland)
C'mon Marianne / Old Man Auctioneer - 2066 688 (New Zealand)
C'mon Marianne / Old Man Auctioneer - 2066 676 (Australia)
Vamos Marianne (C'mon Marianne) / Viejo Rematador (Old Man Auctioneer) - 2066 688 (Uruguay)
C'mon Marianne / Old Man Auctioneer - PD 14320 (US)
C'mon Marianne / Old Man Auctioneer - PD 14320 (Canada)

Marie:
"A" My Name Is Alice / Weeping Willow - PD 14333 (US)
"A" My Name Is Alice / Weeping Willow - 2066 697 (New Zealand)

The following releases were issued with a picture sleeve:
C'mon Marianne / Old Man Auctioneer - 2066 688 (UK)
C'mon Marianne / Old Man Auctioneer - 2066 688 (Germany)
C'mon Marianne / Old Man Auctioneer - 2066 688 (Belgium)

Notes:

- This album was originally released on LP, cassette and 8-Track tape formats on April 3, 1976.
- This album was awarded a gold record for sales in excess of 500,000 copies on December 23, 1976.
- The title of this album in the UK is "Deep Purple."

The back jacket for *Featuring Songs From Their Television Show / Deep Purple* album

New Season
PD-1-6083

Track Listings:
Ain't Nothing Like The Real Thing / Anytime Sunshine / It's All Been Said Before / Which Way You Goin' Billy (Recorded June 1, 1976) / Show Me / You Broke My Heart / Now We're Together / Hold Me, Thrill Me, Kiss Me (Recorded May 27, 1976) / Sing / We Got Love

Production Information:
Produced by: Mike Curb and Michael Lloyd
Except "Sing" Produced by: Alan Osmond and Michael Lloyd
Executive Producers: The Osmond Brothers
Recorded at: Kolob Recording Studios, Los Angeles, CA, and Provo, Utah, 1976.
Engineered by: Humberto Gatica, Wayne Osmond, and Michael Lloyd

Musicians:
Jay Graydon, Michael Lloyd, John D'Andrea, Steve Olitzky, Ben Benay, James Hughart, Ron Krasinski, John Morell, Ray Pohlman, William A. Mays, James B. Gordon, Alwin W. Casey, John P. Guerin, Shaun Duffey Harris

Arranged by: Johdn D'Andrea and Michael Lloyd
Art Direction: Beverly Parker
Design: William Naegels

Singles released from this album:
Ain't Nothing Like The Real Thing / Sing - PD 14363 (US / Canada)
Ain't Nothing Like The Real Thing / Sing - 2006 756 (UK)

The following releases were issued with a picture sleeve:
Ain't Nothing Like The Real Thing / Sing - DPQ 6037 (Japan)
Ain't Nothing Like The Real Thing / Sing - 2066 756 (Germany)
Ain't Nothing Like The Real Thing / Sing - S 53990 (Yugoslavia)

Notes:

- This album was originally released on LP, cassette and 8-Track tape formats on November 27, 1976.
- This album was awarded a gold record for sales in excess of 500,000 copies on January 12, 1978.
- Sheet music marketed for this album
- **Songs recorded for this album but not released:**
  Sugar Candy (Recorded May 27, 1976)
  Can't Help Falling In Love (Recorded June 1, 1976)
  Can't Stop Loving You (Recorded June 2, 1976)
  She's Got You (Recorded June 2, 1976)
  Don't You Love It (Recorded July 22, 1976)

The German picture sleeve for *"Ain't Nothing Like The Real Thing."*

Winning Combination
PD-1-6127

Track Listings:
Winning Combination / Best of Me / Baby, I'm Sold On You / Sure Would Be Nice / Angel Love (Heaven is Where You Are) / Oh, Sweet Lovin' / I Want To Give You My Everything / (You're My) Soul and Inspiration / I Can't Do Without You / You Remind Me / I Want To Be In Your World

Production Information:
Winning Combination / Best of Me / Baby, I'm Sold On You / I Can't Do Without You / I Want To Be In Your World
Produced by: Brian Holland for Kolob Productions
Executive Producer: Edward J. Holland
Arranged by: McKinley Jackson
A Holland, Dozier, Holland Production

Sure Would Be Nice / Oh, Sweet Lovin' / You Remind Me
Produced by: Brian Holland for Kolob Productions
Executive Producer: Edward J. Holland
Arranged by: Jimmie Haskell
A Holland, Dozier, Holland Production

Angel Love (Heaven Is Where You Are)
Produced by: Brian Holland for Kolob Productions
Executive Producer: Edward J. Holland
Arranged by: McKinley Jackson and Jimmie Haskell
A Holland, Dozier, Holland Production

I Want To Give You My Everything / (You're My) Soul and Inspiration
Produced by: Mike Curb and Michael Lloyd For Mike Curb Productions and Kolob Productions
Arranged by: John D'Andrea

Recorded at: Kolob Recording Studios, Provo Utah
Wally Heider Studios, Los Angeles, CA
Whitney Recorders, Los Angeles, CA
Studio Masters, Los Angeles, CA
Recording Engineers: Biff Dawes, Don Blake, Frank Kejmar, Humberto Gatica
Mixing Engineers: Brian Holland, L.T. Horn and Humberto Gatica
Director of Recording: L.T. Horn for Supertec Sound Services
Disc Mastering: Bob MacLeod, Artisan Sound Recorders

Background vocal arrangements: Maxine Willard
Backgrounds vocals: Maxine Willard, Julia Tillman, Patricia Henderson, Adrienne Williams
Album Coordinator: Richard J. Davis
Production Coordinators: McKinley Jackson and Darnell Grays
Art Direction: Mike Doud, AGI
Design: Philip Chiang
Photography: Jim McCrary

Singles released from this album:
You're My Soul and Inspiration / Now We're Together - PD 14439 (US / Canada)
You're My Soul and Inspiration / Now We're Together - 2066 879 (UK)
You're My Soul and Inspiration / Now We're Together - 2066 879 (New Zealand)
(Tu Eres) Mi Alma E Inspiración ((You're My) Soul And Inspiration) / Ahora Estamos Juntos (Now We're Together) - 2066 879 (Guatemala) (Both songs sung in English)
Baby, I'm Sold On You / Sure Would Be Nice - PD-14456 (US)

The following releases were issued with a picture sleeve:
You're My Soul and Inspiration / Now We're Together - 2066 879 (Germany)
You're My Soul and Inspiration / Now We're Together - DPQ-6076 (Japan)
You're My Soul and Inspiration / Now We're Together - 2066 879 (Germany)
Baby, I'm Sold On You / Sure Would Be Nice - 2066 905 (France)

Notes:

- Sheet music marketed for this album.
- This album was originally released on LP, cassette and 8-Track tape formats on December 17, 1977.

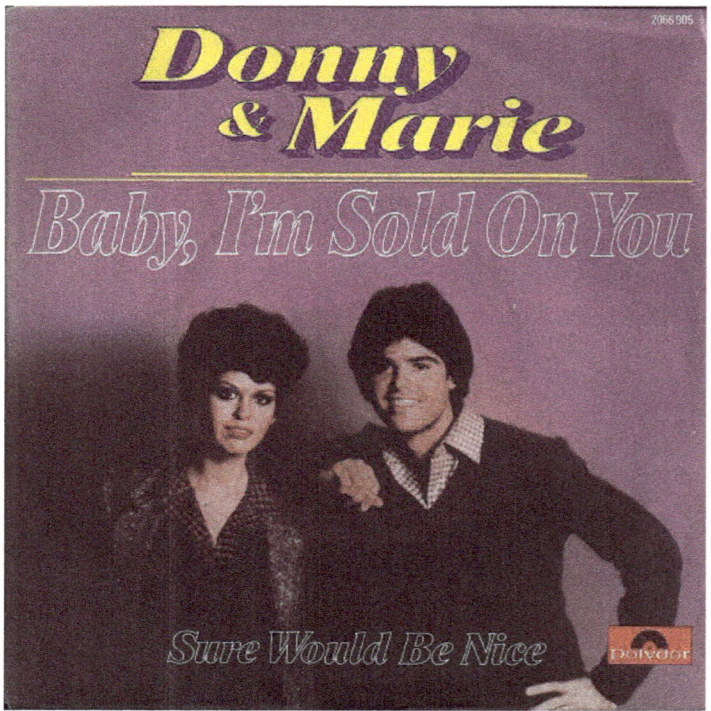

The French picture sleeve for *Baby, I'm Sold On You*.

Calpis Presents Donny & Marie
CL-1024 - 1978 (Japan)

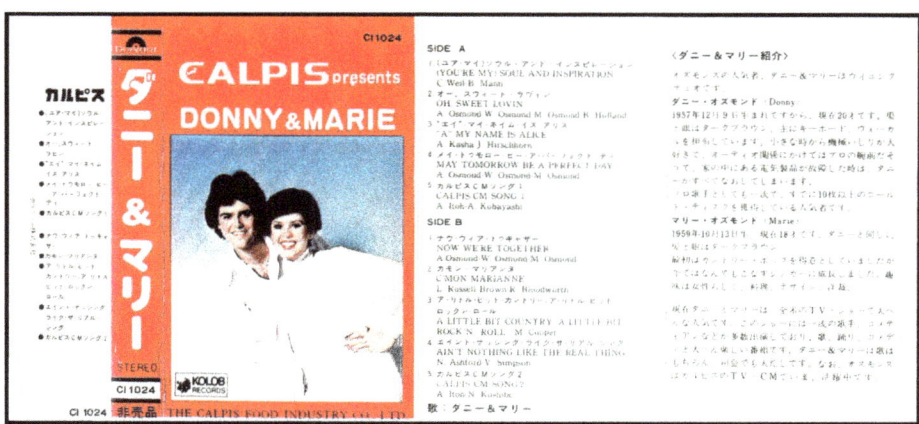

1978 Cassette Tape Insert

Soul and Inspiration / Oh, Sweet Lovin' / "A" My Name is Alice / May Tomorrow Be A Perfect Day / Calpis Commercial Song 1 / Now We're Together / C'mon Marianne / A Little Bit Country, A Little Bit Rock and Roll / Ain't Nothing Like The Real Thing / Calpis Commercial Song 2

From the late 1960's to at least the mid 1970's the Osmond family were spokespeople for a Japanese milk drink called Calpis which is still made today. This album is a compilation of Polydor records material from 1976 and 1977 along with two commercial songs sung in Japanese. This album has been released on LP and cassette tape and being mail order only it is *extremely* hard to find. The cassette and LP contained a short bio on each Osmond.

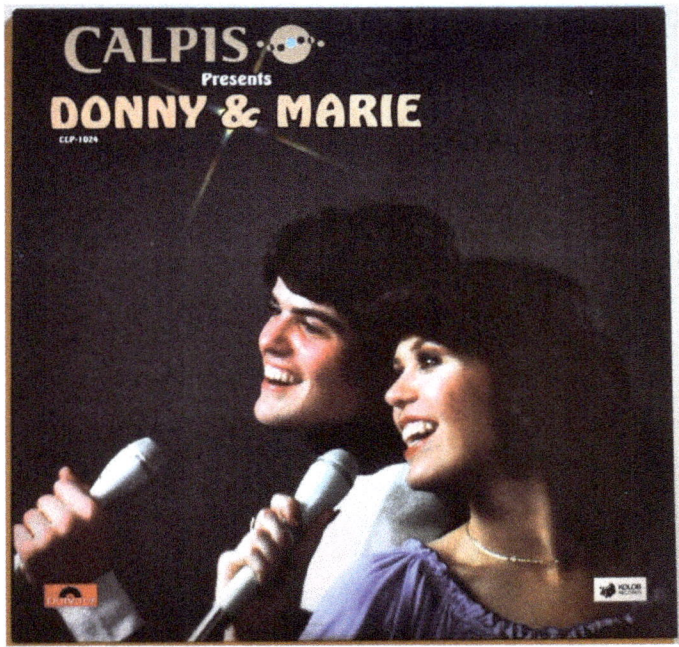

LP cover of Japanese Calpis album

Goin' Coconuts
PD-1-6169

Track Listings:
On The Shelf (Recorded July 14, 1978) / Don't Play With The One Who Loves You (Recorded July 14, 1978) / You Don't Have to Say You Love Me (Recorded July 14, 1978) / Baby, Now That I've Found You / Gimme Some Time (Recorded July 14, 1978 / Re-recorded July 24, 1978) / Let's Fall In Love (Recorded July 14, 1978 / Re-recorded July 24, 1978) / You Bring Me Sunshine / Fallin' In Love Again / Doctor Dancing' / You Never Can Tell / May Tomorrow Be A Perfect Day

Production Information:
A Kolob Production

On The Shelf / Don't Play With the One / You Don't Have To Say You Love Me / Baby, Now That I've Found You / Gimme Some Time / Let's Fall In Love / You Never Can Tell
Produced by: Mike Curb and Michael Lloyd for Mike Curb Productions
Engineered by: Humberto Gatica and Michael Lloyd
Second Engineer: Jim Crosby
Arranged by: John D'Adrea

You Bring Me Sunshine / Fallin' In Love Again / Doctor Dancing' / May Tomorrow Be a Perfect Day
Produced by: the Osmonds
Engineered by Humberto Gatica, Michael Lloyd, Wayne Osmond, Jim Anglesey and Tracy Jorgensen
Arranged by: Denny Crockett and Ike Egan

Recorded and mixed at: Kolob Recording Studios, Provo Utah and Michael Lloyd Studio, Los Angeles, CA
Mastering: Artisan Sound Recorders by Bob MacLeod

Art Direction and Design: David Larkham
Coconut Work: Ed Caraeff Studio
Cover Photo: Stan McBean
Liner Photo: Lee Sporkin

Singles released from this album:
On The Shelf / Certified Honey - PD 14510 (US / Canada)
En La Repisa (On The Shelf) / Dame Tiempo (Gimme Some Time) - 75225 (Ecuador)

The following releases were issued with a picture sleeve:
On The Shelf / Certified Honey - DPQ-6117 (Japan)
On The Shelf / Certified Honey - 2095 015 (France)
On The Shelf (12") - A On The Shelf 4:28 / B On The Shelf 4:28 - Polydor - PRO 054 (US)

Songs recorded for this album but not released:
"Rhythm of the Rain" (Recorded July 14, 1978 / Re-recorded July 24, 1978)
Produced by: Mike Curb and Michael Lloyd for Mike Curb Productions
Engineered by: Humberto Gatica and Michael Lloyd
Second Engineer: Jim Crosby
Arranged by: John D'Adrea

Notes:

- Sheet music marketed for this album.
- This album was originally released on LP, cassette and 8-Track tape formats on October 7, 1978.
- This album was awarded a gold record for sales in excess of 500,000 copies on November 6, 1978.

A promotional ad for the album *Goin' Coconuts* from Billboard Magazine.

Donny & Marie
(Unreleased Album)
Polydor 1979

Track Listing:

Production Information:

Notes:

Singles released from this album:

Donny & Marie Special
PD-1-2391 408

Track Listings:
A Little Bit Country, A Little Bit Rock and Roll / On The Shelf / Morning Side of The Mountain / (You're My) Soul and Inspiration / Ain't Nothing Like The Real Thing / Where Did All The Good Times Go / Paper Roses / Too Young / It Takes Two / I'm Leaving It All Up To You / This Is The Way That I Feel / Puppy Love / The Twelfth of Never / Anytime Sunshine / Butterfly / When I Fall In Love

Production Information:

Produced by: Mike Curb, Michael Lloyd, Don Costa, and Rick Hall

Also available on Polydor Musicassette 3177 408

Art Direction: Paul Lau / The Key Advertising Co. Ltd.

Notes:

- Dedicated to their 1980 Southeast Asia Tour
- Released: June 1980 on LP and cassette tape

Donny & Marie
Decca 0625271094028

Track Listings:
A Beautiful Life / Vegas Love / I Know This Much Is True / You Can Do Anything / I Have You To Thank / My Reflection / The Good Life / The Best Of Me / I Can't Wait / Touch / One Last Goodbye / Better Off Blue / I Swear / We Will Find A Way

Bonus Live Tracks on UK Release:
Puppy Love / Paper Roses (Excerpt) / Crazy Horses / It Takes Two

Production Information:
Produced by: Buddy Cannon
Except "I Have You To Thank"
Produced by Buddy Cannon and Gavin DeGraw
Executive Producers: John Titta & Bill Porricelli

Recorded at: Blackbird Recording Studios Nashville, TN
Engineer: Tony Castle
Additional Recording: Record Lab Recording Studio Provo, UT
Fireside Recording Studio, Nashville, TN
Digital Insight Recording Studios Las Vegas, NV
Westwood Sound Recording Studio Nashville, TN
Additional Engineering: Cliff Maag, Butch Carr, Tim Brennan
Mixed by: Tony Castle at The Tone Dock and Westwood Sound Recording Studio Nashville, TN

Mastered by: Andrew Mendelson Georgetown Masters, Nashville, TN
Mastering Assistants: Daniel Bacigalup and Nathaphol Abhigantaphand

A&R: John Titta
Production Coordinator: Shannon Scott

Photography: Brandon Osmond
Design: Paul Enea, Tovero & Marks Creative
CD Production: Jerome Bunke Digital Force

Musicians:
Bass: Larry Paxton
Electric Guitar: Pat Buchanan
Sythesizer, B-3 Organ: Randy McCormick
Gut String Guitar, Acoustic Guitar: Bobby Terry
Acoustic Guitar: John Willis
Piano, Sythesizer, Wurlitzer: John Hobbs
Electric Guitar: Kenny Greenberg
Drums, Percussion, Drum Programming: Paul Leim
Banjo: Scott Vesta
Mandolin: Dan Tminski
Trumpet: Gil Kaupp
Alto Saxophone: Rob Mader
Tenor Saxophone: Rocco Barbato
Trombone: Nathan Tanouye
Baritone Saxophone: Miguel Rodriguez
Synthesizer: Tony Castle
Acoustic Guitar: Buddy Cannon
Piano: Gavin DeGraw
Piano: Jim "Moose" Brown
Steel Guitar: Sonny Garrish

Background Vocalists: Cindy Richardson Walker / John Wesley Ryles / Don Marrandino
Buddy Cannon / Melonie Cannon / Stephen James / Rachael Lauren / Mekenna Bree
Jerry Williams

Horn Arrangement: Jerry Williams

Don Tyminiski appears courtesy of Rounder Records, Gavin DeGraw appears courtesty of J Records, Melonie Cannon appears courtesy of Rural Rhythm Records.

Singles released from this album:
Vegas Love (Digital download only)

Artist Comments:

Marie Would Like To Thank:
Karl Engemann, Marty Singer, Cliff Maag, Darla Sperry, Jerry Williams, Kim Goodwin, Maria Gomez, Staci Michelle Virga.

My children:
Stephen James & Rachael Lauren for great background vocals along with Mekenna Bree who's like one of my kids.

And, Stephen James - thank you for writing your mom a great single record!

Donny Would Like To Thank:
John Ferriter, Eric Gardner, Eric Weissler, Peter Stoll, Leslie Harker, Amber Hamilton, Sandra Lueras, ALori Slagle.

Everyone at donny.com: Naveen Jain, Deb Wallace, Caroline Mickler, Bryan Kim, Alana Miller, Tara Manasse, Tal Flanchraych.

My son, my photographer - Brandon Osmond - brandonosmondphotography.com

Cliff Maag's magic vocal Maag Triad box! Vocalbooth.com, Gred Ondo, Ben James and everone at Steinberg / Yamaha. Staci Michelle Virga, Tina Salmon, Lynn Robinett.

To my lovely wife Debbie, my children and grandkids....BawPa loves you.

Donny And Marie Would Like To Thank:
On the US side:
John Hecker, John Titta, Buddy Cannon, Daniel Savage, John Ferriter, Chip Lightman and the late Danny Gans, Don Marrandino & Laura Ishum and everyone at Flamingo Las Vegas, George Hadowanetz/Cashman photo.

On The UK Side:
Dickon Stainer, Rebecca Allen, Mark Wilkison Judith Mellor, and Oliver Harrop.

Notes:

- Released: December 15, 2009

A Broadway Christmas
HiFi-2010

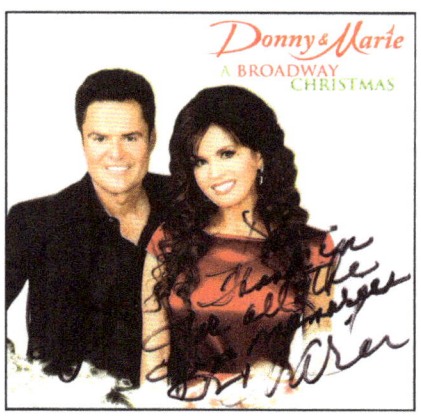

Track Listing:
A Little Bit Country, A Little Bit Rock 'n Roll / Paper Roses / Puppy Love (medley) / When Christmas Comes This Year / Christmas Time / The Locket / It Takes Two

Bonus Tracks:
Donny & Marie*	I Swear
Donny & Marie*	the Best Of Me
Donny & Marie*	I Can't Wait
Donny & Marie*	I Have You To Thank

Tracks 1, 2 and 6 Recorded live at the Flamingo, Las Vegas
Tracks 3 and 5 from Marie Osmond's Magic Of Christmas
Track 4 Courtesy of Universal Classic Group
Tracks 8 through 11 from the album "Donny & Marie" (**MPCA-25742**)

Notes:

- Manufactured to tie-in with their yearly Christmas tours.
- Released October 2010

Donny & Marie
MPCA-25742

Track Listings:
A Beautiful Life / Vegas Love / I Know This Much Is True / You Can Do Anything / I Have You To Thank / My Reflection / The Good Life / The Best Of Me / I Can't Wait / Touch / One Last Goodbye / Better Off Blue / I Swear / We Will Find A Way

Bonus Tracks:
Candle In The Rain
Tell Me To Breathe

Production Information:
Produced by: Buddy Cannon
Except "I Have You To Thank" Produced by Buddy Cannon and Gavin DeGraw
Executive Producers: John Titta & Bill Porricelli
Recorded at: Blackbird Recording Studios, Nashville, TN
Engineer: Tony Castle

Additional Recording: Record Lab Recording Studio Provo, UT
Fireside Recording Studio, Nashville, TN
Digital Insight Recording Studios, Las Vegas, NV
Westwood Sound Recording Studio, Nashville, TN
Engineers: Cliff Maag, Butch Carr, Tim Brennan

Mixed by: Tony Castle at The Tone Dock and Westwood Sound Recording Studio Nashville, TN

Mastered by: Andrew Mendelson at Georgetown Masters, Nashville, TN
Mastering Assistants: Daniel Bacigalup and Nathaphol Abhigantaphand

A&R: John Titta

Production Coordinator: Shannon Scott
Photography: Brandon Osmond
Design: Paul Enea, Tovero & Marks Creative
CD Production: Jerome Bunke Digital Force

Musicians:
Bass: Larry Paxton
Electric Guitar: Pat Buchanan
Sythesizer, B-3 Organ: Randy McCormick
Gut String Guitar, Acoustic Guitar: Bobby Terry
Acoustic Guitar: John Willis
Piano, Sythesizer, Wurlitzer: John Hobbs
Electric Guitar: Kenny Greenberg
Drums, Percussion, Drum Programming: Paul Leim
Banjo: Scott Vesta
Mandolin: Dan Tminski
Trumpet: Gil Kaupp
Alto Saxophone: Rob Mader
Tenor Saxophone: Rocco Barbato
Trombone: Nathan Tanouye
Baritone Saxophone: Miguel Rodriguez
Synthesizer: Tony Castle
Acoustic Guitar: Buddy Cannon
Piano: Gavin DeGraw
Piano: Jim "Moose" Brown
Steel Guitar: Sonny Garrish

Background Vocalists: Cindy Richardson Walker / John Wesley Ryles / Don Marrandino
Buddy Cannon / Melonie Cannon / Stephen James / Rachael Lauren / Mekenna Bree
Jerry Williams

Horn Arrangement: Jerry Williams

Singles released from this album:
The Good Life (Digital download only)
A Beautiful Life (Digital download only)

Donny Would Like To Thank:
Thanks to my wife, my children, and my grandkids.

Also a big thank you to Shane Edwards, Shara Sumnall, and of course to all of the donny.commers for years of loyalty.

Marie Would Like To Thank:
Greg and Darla Sperry: For being the BEST friends I could ever have. You put the locks on everything from my signature to my pantry! Can I pay you something…PLEASE?!?!
Buddy Cannon: Also known as… "Sir Budith." Just think, without this album you wouldn't have known "Belva Burton Flukeyger Hymendinger"…you chicken hater, you! Love ya!
Cliff Maag: I could never have recorded this album without all of the 2-7 am sessions. Oh, and all that CHOCOLATE! Thanks my Derf!

Kim Goodwin: For the laughter and your Vision (LV) in trying to make me look forever "29"! Thank you ever so!!!

To my kids: You inspire me to "keep on, keepin' on"! You've each taught me so much and I love all eight of you eternally. Stephen (Jizzouse), thanks for writing your mom an amazing song on this album and for the great background vocals you and my sweet Rachael sang on "I Can't Wait". You too Mekenna Bree…you're also one of my kids!

And to you, Steve: Thank you my angel, for healing our family. You are the love of my life!

Donny & Marie Would Like To Thank:
John Titta, Buddy Cannon, Rick Mazer, Laura Ishum and everyone at the Flamingo Las Vegas, Alan Nierob and Nicole Perez, Bill Porricelli, Jeff Brady, Doreen D'Agostino, Aan Quasha, Marco Vega, Paul Enea, Bob Morelli, Howie Gabriel, and everyone at Sony.

Don Tyminiski appears courtesy of Rounder Records, Gavin DeGraw appears courtesty of J Records, Melonie Cannon appears courtesy of Rural Rhythm Records.

Notes:

- Released May 3, 2011

- A bonus disc was made available for orders of the above album exclusively through QVC titled: **Donny & Marie Live In Vegas** - MPCA-25772 - May 3, 2011. It consisted of the following tracks: Hits Medley: I'm A Little Bit Country, I'm A Little Bit Rock And Roll - I'm Leaving It All Up To You - Make The World Go Away - Deep Purple - Morning Side Of The Mountain / Paper Roses / Puppy Love / Crazy Horses / It Takes Two / May Tomorrow Be A Perfect Day / It Takes Two (Reprise)

Jimmy
Osmond

Little Jimmy
CD-7028

Track Listings:
Goodbye Mr. Tears / She is Good Lookin' / Moon Was Watching / I Found A Little Happiness / Sha La La / My Little Darling / Put Your Hand in the Hand / Utopia / Peg O' My Heart / Chuk Chuk / Jimmy's the Happy Robbers / Jimmy Lullaby

Production Information:
Recorded in Japan

Singles Released From This Album (All with picture sleeves):
My Little Darling / Peg O' My Heart - CD 62
Chuk Chuk / Jimmy's Lullaby - CD-90
Jimmy's The Happy Robbers / I Found A Little Happiness - CD-103
Put Your Hand In the Hand* / Flirtin'+ - CD-1001
*Jimmy Osmond with Osmond Brothers / +Osmond Brothers
Goodbye Mr. Tears / Utopia - CD-1014-IN
She Is Good Lookin' / Bye Bye Suzanne - CD-1019-IN

Notes:

- Released: April 1972

The Japanese picture sleeve for *Peg O' My Heart*.

Killer Joe
SE-4855

Track Listings:
Killer Joe / Little Girls Are Fun / My Girl / Mama'd Know What To Do / Let Me Be Your Teddy Bear / *Long Haired Lover From Liverpool / If My Dad Were President / Tweedlee Dee / Mother of Mine / Rubber Ball

Production Information:
Produced by: Mike Curb and Don Costa
*Produced by: Perry Botkin, Jr.
Recorded at: MGM Recording Studios, Los Angeles, CA
Engineer: Ed Greene
Arranged by: Don Costa

Cover Photography: Ed Caraeff
Liner Photography: Kenny Lieu

Singles released from this album:
Long Haired Lover From Liverpool / Mother of Mine - 2006-109 (UK)
Long Haired Lover From Liverpool / Mother of Mine - 2006 109 (Australia)
Long Haired Lover From Liverpool / Mother of Mine - K 14376 (US)
Long Haired Lover From Liverpool / If My Dad Were President 2006 109 (Argentina)
Long Haired Lover From Liverpool / Mother of Mine - 2006 109 (Ireland)
Long Haired Lover From Liverpool / Mother of Mine - 2065 111 (Canada) (Polydor)
Long Haired Lover From Liverpool / Mother of Mine - PS240 (South Africa)
Tweedlee Dee/ Mama'd Know What To Do - K 14468 (US / Canada)
Tweedlee Dee/ Mama'd Know What To Do - 2006 175 (Australia)
Tweedlee Dee/ Mama'd Know What To Do - 2006 175 (New Zealand)
Let Me Be Your Teddy Bear / Rubber Ball - 2006 175 (Australia)

The following releases were issued with a picture sleeve:
Long Haired Lover From Liverpool / Mother of Mine - 2006 109 (Belgium)
Killer Joe / Let Me Be Your Teddy bear - 2006 279 (France)
Tweedlee Dee / Killer Joe (Japan)
Killer Joe / Teddy Bear (France)
Tweedlee Dee/ Mama'd Know What To Do - PS-253 (South Africa)
Tweedlee Dee/ Mama'd Know What To Do - 2006 175 (Netherlands)
Tweedlee Dee/ Mama'd Know What To Do - 2006 175 (Belgium)
Tweedlee Dee/ Mama'd Know What To Do - 2006 175 (Portugal)

Tweedlee Dee/ Mama'd Know What To Do - 2006 175 (France)
Long Haired Lover From Liverpool / Mother of Mine - 2006 109 (France)
Long Haired Lover From Liverpool / Mother of Mine - 2006 109 (Netherlands)
Long Haired Lover From Liverpool / Mother of Mine - 2006 109 (Portugal)
Long Haired Lover From Liverpool / Mother of Mine - S 53 676 (Yugoslavia)
Long Haired Lover From Liverpool / Mother of Mine - 2006 109 (Spain)
Long Haired Lover From Liverpool / Mother of Mine - 2006 109 (India)
Tweedlee Dee/ Mama'd Know What To Do - 2006-175 (UK)

Notes:

- Released: November 1972
- Billboard Review: The youngest of the Osmonds proved himself a heavy chart winner earlier this year with his Long-Haired Lover From Liverpool, included in this (US) debut solo package. Along with that hit, he rocks Killer Joe, Tweedlee Dee and Let Me Be Your Teddy Bear for all their worth. His emotion packed sensitive readings of Mama'd Know What To Do and Mother of Mine are truly exceptional for his young years.

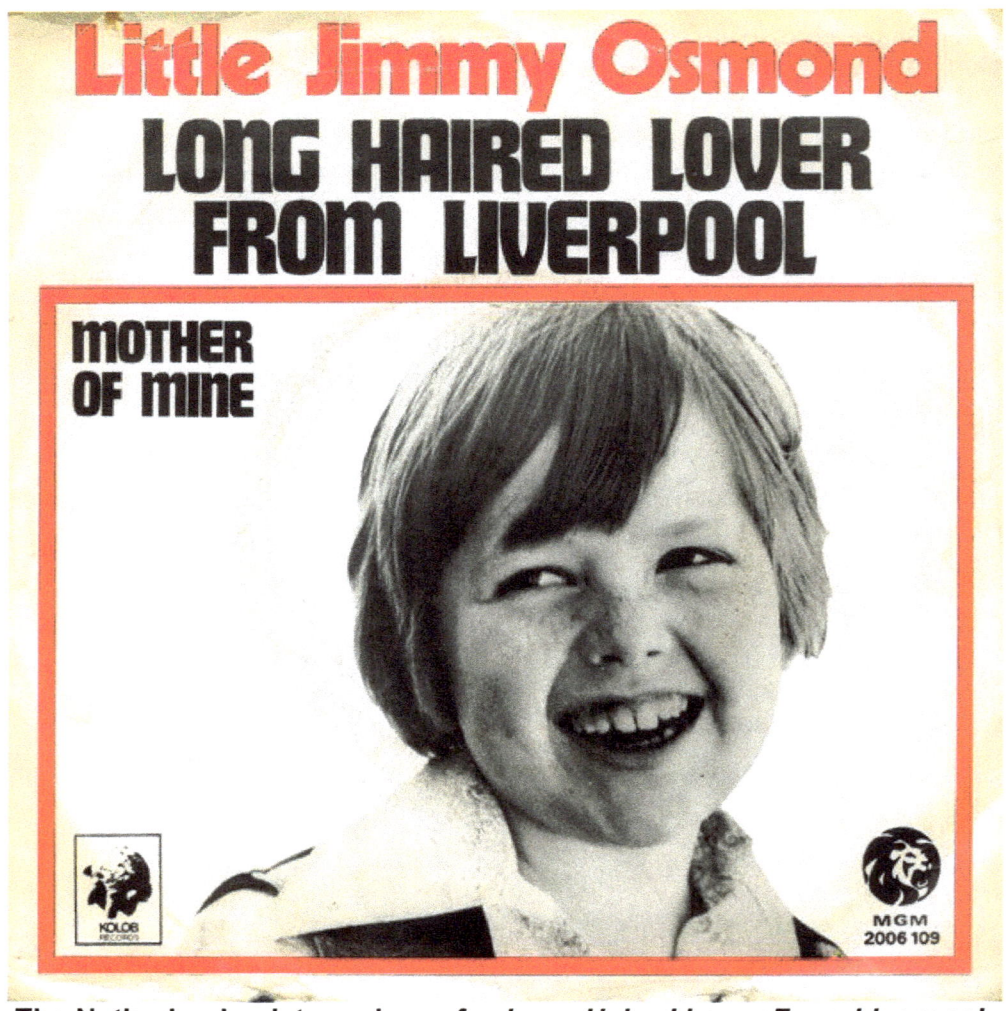

The Netherlands picture sleeve for *Long Haired Lover From Liverpool.*

Little Arrows
M3G-4916

Track Listings:
Little Arrows / I'm Gonna Knock On Your Door / Day O / Tic Tac Toe / Keep Your Eye on the Girlie You Love / The Good Old Bad Old Days / Angry / Purple People Eater / Don't You Remember / Good Ole Mammy Song

Production Information:
A Mike Curb Production
Little Arrows / Tic Tac Toe
Produced by: Mike Curb and Michael Lloyd
Arranged by: Tommy Oliver

Day O / Good Old Bad Old Days / Purple People Eater / I'm Gonna Knock On Your Door / Good Ole Mammy Song
Produced by Mike Curb and Don Costa
Arranged by Don Costa

Don't You Remember
Produced by Michael Lloyd and The Osmonds
Arranged by Tommy Oliver

Keep Your Eye on the Girlie You Love / Angry
Produced by Mike Curb, Michael Lloyd, and The Osmonds
Arranged by Tommy Oliver

Executive Producers: The Osmonds

Music recorded at: MGM Recording Studios, Hollywood CA
Vocals overdubbed at: Kolob Recording Studios, Provo, Utah
Engineered by: Ed Greene, Umberto Gatica, and Donny Osmond

Cover Photography: Leandro Correa
Liner Photography: Albert Mckenzie Watson
Design: Rod Dyer, Inc.

Art Direction: Sheri Leverich

Singles released from this album:
Little Arrows / Don't You Remember - M 14771 (US / Canada)
Little Arrows / Don't You Remember - 2006 478 (Germany)
Little Arrows / Don't You Remember - 2006 478 (UK)
Little Arrows / Don't You Remember - 2006 478 (Netherlands)
Little Arrows / Don't You Remember - 2006 478 (New Zealand)
Little Arrows / Don't You Remember - 2006 478 (France)

The following releases were issued with a picture sleeve:
Little Arrows / Don't You Remember - 2006 478 (Germany)
Little Arrows / Don't You Remember - 2006 478 (Netherlands)
Little Arrows / Don't You Remember - 2006 478 (France)

The German picture sleeve for *Little Arrows.*

Jimmy Osmond
(Unreleased Album)
1979 Polydor

Track Listing:

Production Information:

Notes:

Singles released from this album:

Kimi Wa Pretty
28-3H-46 - (Sony) Japan

Track Listings:
Kimi Wa Pretty / Hot Shot / Uncertain / Kibun Wa Yellow Mellow / After All / Lady Put The Light On Me / Koi No L.D. Call (Ring Ring) / Girl You're Driving Me Crazy / What's He Got / Tokyo Savannah / Got To Have You / Ai No Ashita Ni

Production Information:
Kimi Wa Pretty / Tokyo Savannah / Kibun Wa Yellow Mellow / Ai No Ashita Ni
Produced by: Ikuro Meguro
Arranged by: Toshiyuki Kimori

Uncertain / Hot Shot
Produced by: Donny Osmond and Jimmy Osmond
Arranged by: Walt Gregory

What's He Got / Lady Put The Light On Me / Koi No L.D. Call (Ring Ring) / After All / Girl You're Drivin' Me Crazy / Got To Have You
Arranged and produced by: Ike Egan and Denny Crockett

Executive Producers: Noriko Iida and Yoshio Aoyama

Recording and Mix Engineer: Yuichi Maegima
Recording Engineers: Tracy Joregenson, Martin Anderson
Mix Engineer: Donny Osmond
Production Assistant: Ken Hodges
Recording Management: Aoyama Music Promotion Co. LTD., Nippon Television Music Corporation

Musicians:
Keyboards: Nobuo Kurata / Hiroshi Shibui / Kaxuo Ohtani / Denny Crockett
Bass: Michio Nagaoka / Yasuo Tomikura / Ike Egan
Guitar: Fujimaru Yoshino / Tohru Aoyama / Rich Dixon
Synthesizers: Walt Gregory
Percussion: Nobu Saito / Peccer / Kenny Hodges
Drums: Shuichi "Ponta" Murakami / Hiroshi Ichikawa / Sam Foster / Jay Osmond

Trumpet: Shin Kazuhara / Rick Baptist / Craig Turley
Saxhorn: Jake Concepcion
Trombone: Bryan Hofheins

Background Vocals: Merrill Osmond / Donny Osmond / Jimmy Osmond / Ike Egan / Denny Crockett / Casey D. Rankin / Mike Dann / Kaxuo Ohtani / Michio Nagaoka / Fujimaru Yoshino

Casey D. Rankin courtesy of CBS/Sony Inc. Nobu Saito and Mike Dann courtesy of Canyon Records Co., LTD.

Photography: Kaoru Ijima
Styling: Kumiko Ue
Design: Nobuaki Takahashi

Singles released from this album (all with picture sleeves):
Ring, Ring - 07-5H-77
Kimi Wa Pretty / Tokyo Savannah - 07-5H-93
Livin' In Love / One More Chance - 07-5H-113

Notes:

- This album is sung in half Japanese and half English. The Korean version of this album, You're So Pretty, is all in English; however, there are two songs that are not on the Korean album. This album came with a 12x12 photo as well as a poster and the lyrics printed on the back of the poster.

The Japanese picture sleeve for *Kimi Wa Pretty*.

Siempre Tu
SLEMN 1373 (EMI/Capitol)

Track Listing:
Y No Estas / *Dos En Uno / Mas / Si Pudiera / Siempre Tu / Viva La Vida / +Ontono Y Primavera / Si Volviera A Nacer / Da Un Poco De Amor (Give A Little Love) / Tu Me Haces Falta

*Duet with Yuri
+Duet Pedro Vargas

Production Information:
Produced by: Jose Quintana (tracks: A1-4, B2-4) / Stephen Tavani (tracks: A5, B1,5)
Arranged by: K.C. Porter / Scott V. Smith / Juan Carlos Calderon
Recorded At – George Tobin Studios
Recorded At – Sunset Sound
Recorded At – Image Recording
Recorded At – Peace In The Valley Recording
Recorded At – Osmond Studios
Recorded At – Estudios Lab

Phonographic Copyright (p) – EMI Capitol De Mexico, S.A. De C.V.
Made By – EMI Capitol De Mexico, S.A. De C.V.
Copyright (c) – EMI Capitol De Mexico, S.A. De C.V

Singles released from this album:

+Ontonyo Y Primavera / Tu Me Haces Falta -
+(Duet Pedro Vargas)

Notes:

- Rare 1985 Mexican only 10-track vinyl LP sung in Spanish & featuring duets with Don Pedro Vargas & Yuri

Keep The Fire Burnin'
ADCD001

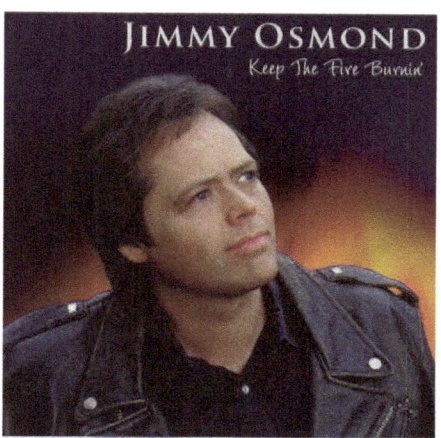

Track Listing:
Keep The Fire Burnin' / I Love To Watch You Shine / Leavin' It Up To You / Within These Walls / This Much I Know Is True / Wrapped Up In You / It Happens In Real Life / Always / How Did You Know / Long Haired Lover From Liverpool

Bonus Track UK Edition: Bring Back The American Dream

Production Information:
Top Of The World Entertainment

Notes:

- Released: February 22, 2001 (UK)
- Re-issued by American Jukebox Limited - AJR200502 - 2005 (UK)
- Re-issued by Osmond Entertainment on July 1, 2016. (US)

Jimmy Osmond's American Jukebox Show
AJR200503

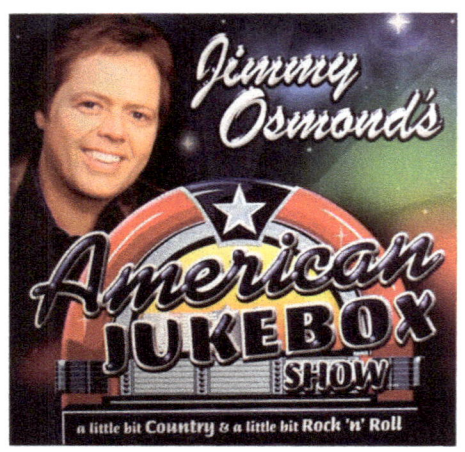

Track Listing:
Dancin' In The Street / 40's And 50's Medley: Dream A Little Dream Of Me - Jukebox Sat. Night - Little Brown Jug - In The Mood - Chattanooga Choo Choo - Jail House Rock - La Bamba - Rock & Roll Is Here To Stay / Country / Rock Medley: A Little Bit Country, A Little Bit Rock N' Roll - Snowbird - Crocodile Rock - 9 To 5 - Heart Of Rock N Roll - Proud Mary - Lil Bit Country & Rock 'N' Roll / Spooky / 60's Medley: My Boyfriend's Back - The Twist - These Boots Are Made For Walkin' - I Get Around - Stop! In The Name Of Love - Oh, Pretty Woman - I Wanna Hold Your Hand - Twist And Shout - Big Girls Don't Cry - Up, Up And Away - Dance To The Music / 70's Medley: Last Dance - Shake Your Groove Thing - That's the Way I Like It - Superstition - Killing Me Softly - Stayin' Alive - ABC - One Bad Apple - YMCA / Tribute Medley: You'll Never Find Another Love Like Mine - Moon River - Can't Take That Away From Me - Come Fly With Me / Rock This Town / Duet Medley: Reunited - Islands In The Stream - Tonight I Celebrate My Love For You - Baby, Come To Me - You Don't Bring Me Flowers - You're The One That I Want - I've Had The Time Of My Life / Have You Ever Really Loved A Woman / 80's And 90's Medley: Thriller - Footloose - R.O.C.K. In The U.S.A. - Missing You - I'm Walkin' On Sunshine - Careless Whispers - Vogue - Man! I Feel Like A Woman - Mambo No. 5 - Livin' la Vida Loca / Osmond Hits Medley: The Proud One - Havin' A Party - Love Me For A Reason - Let Me In - Crazy Horses / Where The Stars & Stripes & The Eagle Flies

Production Information:
Manufactured in the UE by Sounds Good, Ltd.

Notes:

- Released: 2005

Moon River And Me: A Tribute To Andy Williams
OsmondsLP5

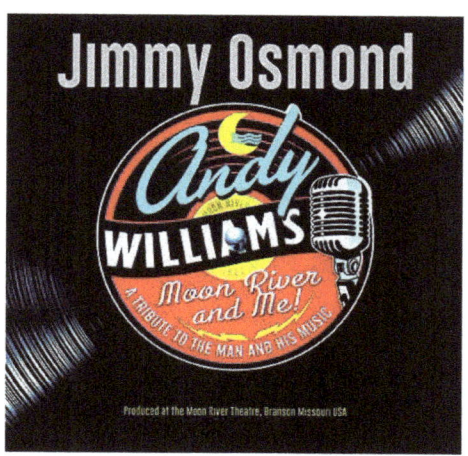

Track Listing:
Charade / Can't Take My Eyes Off You / Alfie / Happy Heart / Any Hits Medley / Moon River / Up, Up And Away / Born Free / Almost There / Maria / Speak Softly, Love (Love Theme From The Godfather) / May Each Day

Production Information:
Vocal Recording / Production / Mixing and Mastering by: Marko G.
Recorded at: MCS Studios, Branson Missouri
Engineer: Stephan John

Musicians:
Piano & Keyboards: Gregg Gray
Bass: Marty Wilhite
Guitar: Gene Puckett
Drums: Pete Generous
Trumpet: Carl Hose
Sax & Flute: Bill Reder

Arranged by: Gregg Gray

Special thanks to: Steve Mason / Jeanette Elton and Jackie Skinner

Design: Monte Baker
Photo: Jim Lersch

Notes:

- Released: June 3, 2016
- Available on CD, LP and Digital download

JIMMY OSMOND'S 70'S JUKEBOX
Osmond Entertainment - 0839868

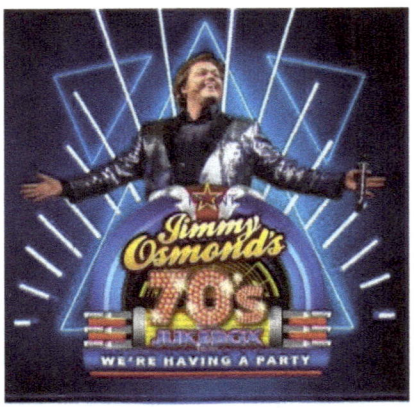

Track Listing:
September / Let's Groove Tonight / That's the Way (I Like It) / Boogie Shoes / Blame It on the Boogie / When I Need You / Sweet Caroline / Hold Me Close / I Think I Love You / Rhinestone Cowboy / Viva Las Vegas / Burning Love / It's Not Unusual / Help Yourself / How Deep Is Your Love / Night Fever / Tragedy / Who Loves You / December 1963 (Oh, What a Night) / Long Haired Lover from Liverpool

Notes:

- Released: September 21, 2018

The Osmond Family

Around The World Live In Concert
M3JB-5012

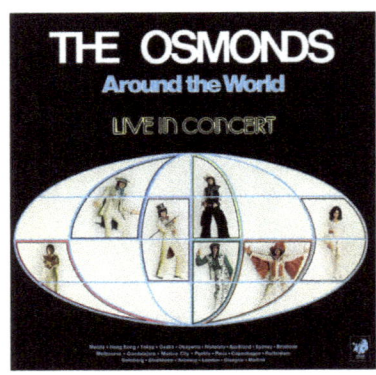

Track Listing:
Introduction / Feelin' All Right / Crazy Horses / Your Mama Don't Dance / Hold Her Tight / Love Me For A Reason / Music Makin' / The Girl I Love / I Can't Get Next To You / Mona Lisa / Donny & Marie Medley: Go Away Little Girl - Puppy Love - It Takes Two - Morningside of the Mountain - I'm Leaving It All Up To You - Paper Roses - Who's Sorry Now - It Takes Two (Reprise) / Make The World Go Away / Some Kind of Wonderful / The Proud One / Jimmy Medley: Long Haired Lover From Liverpool - You Are So Beautiful - Never Can Say Goodbye / Stevie Wonder Medley: Uptight (Everything's Alright) - Higher Ground - Signed, Sealed, Delivered - Superstition - For Once In My Life / Are You Lonesome Tonight / Merrill's Banjo Medley: If You Knew Susie (Like I Know Susie) - One of Those Songs - The World Is Waiting For The Sunrise / 50's Medley: Get a Job - Rock and Roll Is Here To Stay - Jailhouse Rock - At the Hop - Rock Around The Clock - Blueberry Moon - Blue Moon - Lucille - Blue Suede Shoes - Hound Dog - Rock and Roll Is Here To Stay (Reprise) / Down By The Lazy River

Production Information:
Produced by The Osmonds in association with Mike Curb Productions

Guitars and vocals: Alan Osmond
Lead Guitar and Vocals: Wayne Osmond
Bass, Banjo, and Vocals: Merrill Osmond
Drums, Percussion, and Vocals: Jay Osmond
Keyboards, Synthesizer, Hysteria and other electronic paraphernalia to numerous to mention: Donny Osmond
Lead Vocals: Marie Osmond
Congas and Vocals: Jimmy Osmond

The Band:
John Rosenberg / Dan Sawyer / Dennis Parker / Eric Lindemann / Evan Diner / Dana Hughes / John Mitchell

Band Arrangements: John Rosenberg
Cover Concept and Design: Virl Osmond
Art Direction: Sheri Leverich

Engineer: Ed Greene
Sound: Robin Magruder for Showco, Inc.

Master Tapes Mixed and Assembled at: Kolob Recording Studios, Provo Utah

World Tour Stage Manager Masanobo Ono
Costumes: Bill Belew
Special thanks to: Jim Morey

Many thanks to our fans around the world who made this tour possible.

Notes:

- Two album Set
- This album was originally released on LP, cassette and 8-Track tape formats on September 14, 1975.
- Available on CD through Cherry Red Records UK

The Osmond Brothers in 1972

Christmas Album
PD-2-8001

Track Listings:
I'll Be Home For Christmas / Winter Wonderland / Kay Thompson's Jingle Bells / If Santa Were My Daddy / Blue Christmas / Silver Bells / Sleigh Ride / This Christmas Eve / Pine Cones and Holly Berries - It's Beginning To Look A lot Like Christmas / White Christmas / What Are You Doing New Year's Eve / It Never Snows In L.A. / The Christmas Song / A Very Merry Christmas / Caroling Medley / Let It Snow, Let It Snow, Let It Snow / The Christmas Waltz / Old Fashioned Christmas / When He Comes Again / Silent Night

Production Information:
Produced by: Don Costa
Executive Producers by: The Osmond Brothers
Recorded at: Kolob Recording Studios Provo, Utah and Los Angeles, CA
Recording Engineers: Humberto Gatica, Ed Green, Wayne Osmond
Re-mix Engineer: Humberto Gatica
Arranged by: John D'Andrea and Don Costa
Vocal Arrangements by: Earl Brown and George Wyle
Strings and Horns arranged: by Sid Feller and Cesars Genfili
Art Direction: Beverly Parker
Design and Illustration: Fred Marcellino

Notes:
- Two LP Set
- This album was originally released on LP, cassette and 8-Track tape formats on December 18, 1976.
- Available on CD on Curb Records (10 tracks only) and Universal/Spectrum (18 track release)

The songbook marketed with this release.

Greatest Hits
PD-2-9005

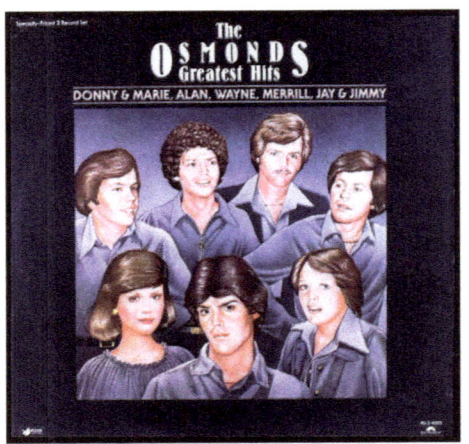

Track Listings:
One Bad Apple / Sweet and Innocent / Ain't Nothing Like The Real Thing / Love Me For A Reason / Are You Lonesome Tonight / C'mon Marianne / Puppy Love / Down By The Lazy River / This Is The Way That I Feel / Long Haired Lover From Liverpool / Let Me In / I'm Leaving It All Up to You / Go Away Little Girl / Crazy Horses / Back On The Road Again / Too Young / Goin' Home / Paper Roses / Hold Her Tight / Morning Side of the Mountain / Yo-Yo / The Twelfth of Never

Production Information:
Producers: Rick Hall, Sonny James, Mike Curb, Michael Lloyd, The Osmonds
Recording Studios: FAME Recording Studios / MGM Recording Studios / KOLOB Recording Studios / Columbia Recording Studios / Jack Clement Recording Studios / Independent Recorders
Engineers: Rick Hall / Michael Lloyd / Ed Greene / Umberto Gatica / Charlie Tallent / Don Daily / Ron Malo / Wayne Osmond / Donny Osmond

Cover Illustration: Vincent Topazio
Art Direction: Marilyn Romen / AGI
Design: David Larkham

Singles released from this album:
All!

Notes:
- Two LP Set
- This album was originally released on LP, cassette and 8-Track tape formats October 1977.

The Glory Of America
KM 11203

Track Listing:

Donny Osmond - America / Jimmy Osmond - Rock Medley / The Children Freedom Singers - It's A Small World/What's More American / Marie Osmond - City Medley / The Osmond Brothers - Mama Don't Allow / The Osmond Brothers - Mountain Music / Donny Osmond - Happy Birthday / You're A Grand Old Flag / The Osmond Family And Chorus Trilogy: Dixie, America The Beautiful, Battle Hymn Of The Republic

Production Information:

Record producers: Denny Crockett, Ike Egan
Executive Producers: Alan Osmond, Bill Critchfield, Merrill Osmond
Associate Producer: Vinny Trauth
Arranged By: Kurt Bestor, Merrill Jenson
Recording engineer: Tracy Jorgensen

Notes:

- Also released as "America-Fest"
- Original Cast Recording
- This album was originally released on LP and cassette tape formats.
- An Osmond Entertainment Production / 1983

Alternate album cover

Marie Osmond And The Osmond Brothers
Our Best to You
Case International

Track Listings:

Brothers:
Down By The Lazy River / Let Me In / Crazy Horses / Back Step Lovin' / You've Got Me Singin' Again

Marie:
Takin' Country To The City / Let's Make It Love Again (Duet with Merrill Osmond) / There's Gonna Be A Heartache Tonight / He's A Heartache / Memory

Production Information:
Produced by: Merrill Osmond
Executive Producers: Karl Engemann, Mike Williams and Allen Finlinson
Recorded at: The Record Lab, Orem, Utah
Engineer: Cliff Maag

Musical Director: Jerry Williams

Publicist: Ron Clark
Marie's cover photo: Greg Gorman
Brothers' cover photo: Stan Macbean
Case Tractor photo courtesy of Case, International

Special thanks to: Carole Blanchard, Gretchen Juergens, and Dick Smith

Notes:

- This 1985 album was pressed in limited numbers and used as a promotional give-away at Case International Conventions and is difficult to find.

50th Anniversary - Reunited Live In Las Vegas
OE-17727

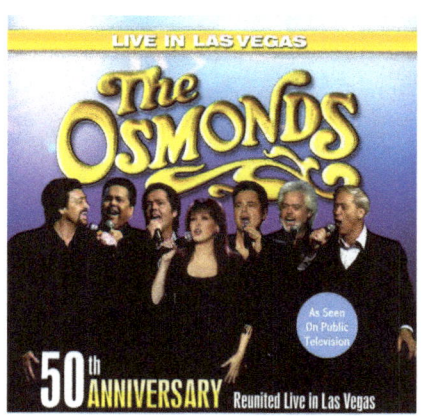

Track Listing:

Family:
Down By The Lazy River / Having A Party / One Bad Apple / Double Lovin' / Yo-Yo / The Proud One / Boogie Woogie Bugle Boy / Paper Roses / Soldier Of Love / Puppy Love

Donny And Marie Hits Medley:
Morning Side Of The Mountain / Make The World Go Away / I'm Leavin' It All Up To You Ain't Nothing Like The Real Thing / Deep Purple / It Takes Two / A Little Bit Country, A Little Bit Rock 'N' Roll / Through The Years

Brothers:
I Can't Live A Dream / Long Haired Lover From Liverpool / Let Me In / Love Me For A Reason / Crazy Horses / Hold Her Tight / Goin' Home / Are You Up There / I Believe / I'm Still Gonna Need You

Marie Hits Medley:
You're Still New To Me / Read My Lips / Meet Me In Montana / There's No Stoppin' Your Heart

Brothers:
One Way Rider / At The Rainbow's End / He Ain't Heavy, He's My Brother

Production Information:
Produced by Jimmy Osmond Productions in association with Osmond Entertainment. ©2007 / 2008 All Rights Reserved. Licensed and distributed by Pinnacle Vision. UK

50 Years - 50 Hits
B001 1007-2

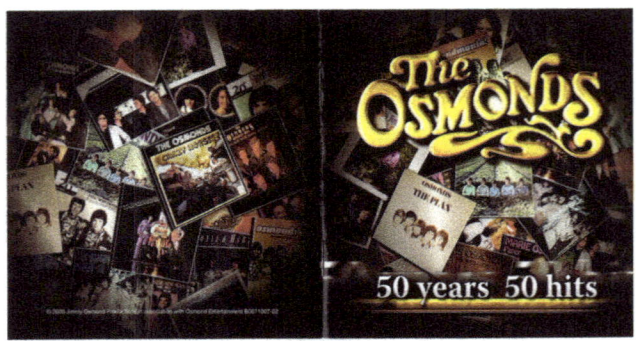

Track Listing:
Be My Little Baby Bumblebee / I Can't Stop / Flower Music / One Bad Apple / He Ain't Heavy, He's My Brother / Sweet And Innocent / Double Lovin' / Go Away Little Girl / Yo-Yo / Down By The Lazy River / Puppy Love / Hold Her Tight / Too Young / Why Crazy Horses / Utah / That's My Girl / Long Haired Lover From Liverpool / Mother Of Mine / Tweedle Dee / The Twelfth Of Never / Goin' Home / Young Love / Paper Roses / Let Me In / I'm Gonna Knock At Your Door / In My Little Corner Of The World / Love Me For A Reason / The Girl I Love / I'm Leaving It All Up To You / Morning Side Of The Mountain / Having A Party / Who's Sorry Now / The Proud One / I'm Still Gonna Need You / Make The World Go Away / Deep Purple / A Little Bit Country, A Little Bit Rock 'N Roll / I Can't Live A Dream / At The Rainbow's End / Back On The Road Again   / This Is The Way That I Feel / Steppin' Out / Baby's Back / (Put Your) Love On The Line / Hold On / Soldier Of Love / Sacred Emotion / Shine / Breeze On By

Production Information:
Producers: Jesse Kaye, Don Williams, Sonny James, Don Ovens, Mike Curb, Michael Lloyd, Don Costa, Rick Hall, Maurice Gibb, Donny Osmond, Evan Rogers, Carl Struken, Jeff Katz

Produced by Jimmy Osmond Productions in association with Osmond Entertainment.
©2008 Jimmy Osmond Productions.

Notes:

- 3 Compact Disc Collector's Edition with full color booklet.

Miscellaneous Osmond Recordings

Hugo The Hippo - UA-LA637-G - 1976
(Animated Motion Picture Soundtrack featuring Marie Osmond and Jimmy Osmond)

Track Listings:
It's Really True (Marie Osmond) / Harbor Chant (Rudy Clark, Ronald Bright, Ken Williams, J. R. Bailey) / Zing Zong (White Water) / H-I-P-P-O-P-O-T-A-M-U-S (Jimmy Osmond) / You Said A Mouthful (Burl Ives) / This Friendship Is Really True (Reprise) (Marie Osmond) / Mister M'-Bow-Wow (Jimmy Osmond) / The Day Ever Made (Burl Ives) / I Always Wanted To Have A Garden (Marie Osmond) / Somewhere You Call Home (Marie Osmond) / Wherever You Go Hugo (Jimmy Osmond) / H-I-P-P-O-P-O-T-A-M-U-S (End Title) (Jimmy Osmond)

Production Information:
George Barrie Presents a Brut Production "Hugo The Hippo"
Starring the singing voices of: Marie Osmond Jimmy Osmond and Burl Ives
Also sung by: Rudy Clark / Ronald Bright / Ken Williams / J.R. Bailey / White Water

Narration: Burl Ives

The of voices of:
Robert Morley as the Sultan
Paul Lynde as Aban Kahn

Words and Music by: Robert Larimer
Music Arranged, Scored, and Conducted by Bert Keyes

Animation Director: Jozsef Gemes
Design: Graham Percy
Marie Osmond and Jimmy Osmond Photo: Albert Mackenzie Watson

Screenplay: Thomas Baum
Executive Producer: George Barrie
Produced by: Robert Halmi
Directed by: William Feigenbaum

Notes:

- Film released through Twentieth Century-Fox.
- Soundtrack released through United Artists Records.

The Great Brain
(Original Motion Picture Soundtrack)
PRO-6778

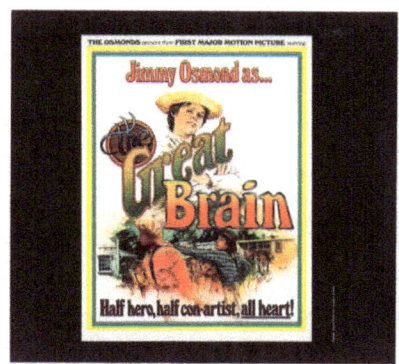 

Track Listings:
*You're There" Jimmy Osmond (Theme From the Great Brain) / Main Title (Utah) / Tom To The Rescue / A New Friendship / Swimming Lesson / J.D.'s Birthday / Andy's Accident / J. D. Gets the Mumps / The Brothers Visit J.D. / The Silent Treatment / That's What Brothers Are For / Come Come Ye Saints / Andy's Operation / Andy's Big Adjustment / The Downfall of Mr. Standish / Mr. Standish Accused / Andy's Drowning Attempt / Andy's Hanging Attempt / Learning to Live Again / Andy's Triumph / Andy's Attitude / You're There (Donny Osmond)

Production Information:
Osmond Distribution for Inter Planetary Pictures, Inc.
Promotional Album – Not For Sale

Music from Osmond Films "The Great Brain" Starring Jimmy Osmond

"You're There" (Theme from the Great Brain)
Produced by: Don Costa and Mike Curb
Arranged and Conducted by: Don Costa
©1978 Osmusic Publishing Company

All other selections conducted by Don Costa – ASCAP

©1978 Donarie Music Pub. Co. – ASCAP
(P)1978 Kolob Records
Manufactured by Kolob Records, Osmond Entertainment Center

Singles released from this album:
You're There / Life Is Just What You Make It - Mercury - 74005 (US)
You're There / You're There – Mercury – 74005 - promo single (US)

Notes:

- Most of this album is instrumental. The only tracks performed by an Osmond is the theme song, "You're There" by Jimmy and also later by Donny. This album was unfortunately rejected for release by Mercury Records. The Osmond's company KOLOB Records did press some copies as promotional items and this album has become a very rare and sought after collectible!

The promotional single for *You're There.*

Rose Petal Place
PB-7224

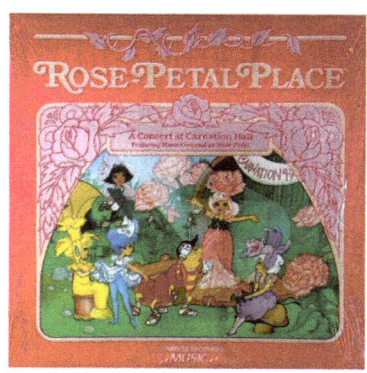

Track Listings:
Elmer's Song / A Special Place / Carnation Hall / Nastina, the Beauty Queen / Little Bit of Love / Rehearsal Song / Coral Bells / Amazing / Look Inside / If You Have Love In Your Heart

Production Information:
Produced by: Tom Chapin and Stephen Chapin
Executive Producers: William C. Coleburn and Fannie H. Cromwell
Production Coordinator: Jaime Chapin
Recorded at: Counterpoint Recording Studios
Engineer: Gary Chester
Assistant Engineer: Tommy "Monst" Civello

Starring the voices of:
Marie Osmond as Rose Petal
Marilyn Schreffler as Nastina
Susan Blu
Candy Ann Brown
Renae Jacobs
Frank Welker
Nicole Eggert as The girl in the garden

From the back jacket:
Welcome to Rose-Petal Place featuring Marie Osmond as Rose Petal. Rose-Petal Place is a beautiful fantasy world nestled in a corner of a Victorian garden. It is an enchanted haven full of music, laughter, and joy. Come join Rose-Petal and her glamorous friends as they sing about life in Rose-Petal Place. It is the place where dreams of little girls come true.

Rose-Petal Place is a trademark of David Kirschner Productions.
Rose-Petal Place Designs.

The Singles

→

OSMOND BROTHERS:
(PS) - Picture Sleeve

1963

Be My Little Baby Bumblebee / I Wouldn't Trade The Silver In My Mothers Hair - K13162 - US

Mr Sandman / My Mom - K13281 - US (PS)
Mr Sandman / My Mom - 13281X (Canada)

1964

Theme From "The Travels Of Jaimie Mcpheeters / Aura Lee* - K-13174 (US) (PS)
Theme From "The Travels Of Jaimie Mcpheeters / Aura Lee* - MGM-5394 - Australia
Theme From "The Travels Of Jaimie Mcpheeters / Aura Lee* - MGM-1245 - UK
(*from album SE-4146 Songs We Sang On The Andy Williams Show)

1965

Fem Smutsiga Sma Fingrar / A Jenta A Ja - MGM 6587 (Sweden) (PS)
Fem Smutsiga Sma Fingrar / A Jenta A Ja - 2006.352 (Sweden) (PS)

1966

Du Lasse, Lasse Liten / En Dag Fylld Av Kärlek (W/ Lasse Lonndahl) - X-8678 (RCA) (July 1966) (Sweden) Recorded at Europa Film Studio, Stockholm June 29, 1966

Ovan Regnbagen / Huldas Karin - X 8679 (Sweden)
(Likely also recorded at the June 29, 1966 session)

Chim Chim Cheree / That's What I Want (Japan) (PS)

1967

I Can't Stop / Flower Music - UNI55015 (Original issue)

1968

Mary Elizabeth / I Speak Like Child - ZS7 2002

I've Got Lovin' On My Mind / Mollie "A" - ZS7 2004 (US / Canada)
I've Got Lovin' On My Mind / Mary Elizabeth - CBS 3867 (Sweden)

Taking A Chance On Love / Groove With What You Got- SONG80099 Sept. 9, 1969 (Japan) (PS)
Taking A Chance On Love / Groove With What You Got- ZS7 2005 (US Promo)

1969

Andy Williams with the Osmond Brothers - Good Morning Starshine / Aquarius / Let The Sunshine In - SONG80150 - (Japan) (PS)

1970

Moving Along / Open Up Your Heart - K-14159 (US)
Moving Along / Open Up Your Heart - 2065 031 Polydor (Canada)

Make The Music Flow / Takin' On A Big Thing - CBSA82057- (Japan)

Young Love Swing / Sha La La - CD-77 (Both songs sung in Japanese) (July 1970)

Chance / Greensleeves - CD-92 (Japan) (PS)

One Bad Apple / He Ain't Heavy ...He's My Brother - K14193 (US) (PS)
One Bad Apple / Flirtin' - 20 06 026 (Spain)
One Bad Apple / He Ain't Heavy ...He's My Brother - 2006 021 (France) (PS)
One Bad Apple / Movin' Along - 2006 025 (Greece) (PS)
One Bad Apple / He Ain't Heavy ...He's My Brother - 2006 021 (Norway) (PS)
One Bad Apple / He Ain't Heavy ...He's My Brother - MG 70.040 (Italy) (PS)
One Bad Apple / He Ain't Heavy ...He's My Brother - 2006-021 (UK)

I Can't Stop / One Bad Apple - UNI-6073 026 (Turkey)

1971

One Bad Apple / Flirtin' - 2006 026 (Germany) (PS)
One Bad Apple / He Ain't Heavy ...He's My Brother - 3014 (Costa Rica)
One Bad Apple / He Ain't Heavy ...He's My Brother - CD-104 - Feb.1, 1971 (Japan) (PS)
One Bad Apple / He Ain't Heavy ...He's My Brother - 2065 044 - Polydor - Feb.1971 (Canada)
One Bad Apple / He Ain't Heavy ...He's My Brother - 2006021 (New Zealand)

I Can't Stop / Flower Music - UNI-55276 (Re-issue of 1967 single)

Double Lovin' / Chilly Winds - K-14259 (US)
Double Lovin' / Chilly Winds - 2006 058 (Australia)
Double Lovin' / Chilly Winds - 2006 058 (Germany) (PS)
Double Lovin' / Chilly Winds - 2006 058 (Norway) (PS)
Double Lovin' / Chilly Winds - CD-1003 (Japan) (PS)
Double Lovin' / Chilly Winds - 2065 066 Polydor (Canada)

Yo Yo / Keep On My Side - K-14295 (US)
Yo Yo / Keep On My Side - 2006 075 (Belgium) (PS)
Yo Yo / Keep On My Side - PS 170 (South Africa)
Yo Yo / Keep On My Side - 2006 075 (Australia)
Yo Yo / Keep On My Side - CD-1011-IN (Japan) (PS)
Yo Yo / Keep On My Side - 20 06 075 (Spain)
Yo Yo / Keep On My Side - 2006 075 (UK)
Yo Yo / Keep On My Side - 2006 075 (France)

Yo Yo / Keep On My Side - 2006 075 (New Zealand)
Yo Yo / Keep On My Side - 2006 075 (Germany)
Yo Yo / Keep On My Side - MG 70044 (Italy) (PS)
Yo Yo / Keep On My Side - S 53639 (Yugoslavia) (PS)
Yo Yo / Keep On My Side - 2065 082 Polydor (Canada)

Down By The Lazy River/ He's The Light Of The World - K 14324 (US)
Down By The Lazy River/ He's The Light Of The World - 2065-096 Polydor (Canada)
Down By The Lazy River/ He's The Light Of The World - 2006 096 (Norway) (PS)
Down By The Lazy River/ He's The Light Of The World - CD-1016-IN (Japan) (PS)
Down By The Lazy River/ He's The Light Of The World - 2006 096 (Portugal) (PS)
Down By The Lazy River/ He's The Light Of The World - 2006 096 (France) (PS)
Down By The Lazy River/ He's The Light Of The World - 2006 096 (Belgium) (PS)
Down By The Lazy River/ He's The Light Of The World - 2006-096 (UK)
Down By The Lazy River/ He's The Light Of The World - 2006 096 (Netherlands) (PS)
Down By The Lazy River/ He's The Light Of The World - 2006 096 (Germany) (PS)
Down By The Lazy River/ He's The Light Of The World - 2006 096 (Australia)
Down By The Lazy River / Hey Girl - 2006 097 (Greece)
Down By The Lazy River/ He's The Light Of The World - 2006 200 (Dutch) (PS)
Down By The Lazy River / Utah - 2006 200 (Netherlands) (PS)

Both Sides Now / Speak Like A Child - SONG 80164 (Japan)

1972

Down By The Lazy River / He's The Light Of The World - CD-1016-IN March. 9172 (Japan) (PS)

Hold Her Tight / Love Is - K 14405 (US)
Hold Her Tight / Love Is - DM-1231 (Japan) (PS)
Hold Her Tight / Love Is - 2006 115 (Australia)
Hold Her Tight / Love Is - 2065 137 Polydor (Canada)
Hold Her Tight / Love Is - 2006-115 (UK)
Hold Her Tight / Love Is - 2006-115 (Scandinavia)

Crazy Horses / That's My Girl - K 14450 (US)
Crazy Horses / That's My Girl - MGM-14-016 (Philippines)
Crazy Horses / That's My Girl - 2006 142 (Germany) (PS)
Crazy Horses / That's My Girl - 2006 142 (New Zealand)
Crazy Horses / That's My Girl - 2006 142 (Norway)
Crazy Horses / That's My Girl - 2065 156 Polydor (Canada)
Crazy Horses / That's My Girl - 2006-142 (UK)
Crazy Horses / That's My Girl - 2006 142 (Ireland)
Crazy Horses / That's My Girl - DM 1236 (Japan) (PS)
Crazy Horses / That's My Girl - 2006 142 (Belgium) (PS)
Crazy Horses / That's My Girl - 2006 142 (Australia)
Crazy Horses / That's My Girl - 2006 142 (Netherlands)
Crazy Horses / That's My Girl - PGP RTB – S 53 677 (Yugoslavia)

1973

Hold Her Tight / Down By The Lazy River - MGC 5021 (Asia)

Crazy Horses / That's My Girl - 2006 142 (Turkey)

Goin' Home / Are You Up There - K 14562 (US / Canada)
Goin' Home / Are You Up There - 2006 288 (Germany) (PS)
Goin' Home / Are You Up There - 2006 288 (Italy) (PS)
Goin' Home / Are You Up There - S 53 702 (Yugoslavia) (PS)
Goin' Home / Are You Up There - 2006 288 (New Zealand)
Goin' Home / Are You Up There - 2006 288 (France) (PS)
Goin' Home / Are You Up There - 2006 288 (Netherlands) (PS)
Goin' Home / Are You Up There - DM-1245 (Japan) (PS)
Goin' Home / Are You Up There - 2006 288 (Australia)
Goin' Home / Are You Up There - 2006 288 (Belgium)
Goin' Home / Are You Up There - 2006 288 (UK)

Let Me In/ One Way Ticket To Anywhere - K 14617 (PS)

Movie Man / Traffic in My Mind - 2006 357 (France / Belgium) (PS)

Hold Her Tight / Movie Man - 2006 438 (France / Belgium)

1974

Love Me For A Reason / Fever - M 14746 (US / Canada)
Love Me For A Reason / Fever - 2006 458 (UK)
Love Me For A Reason / Fever - S 53 794 (Yugoslavia) (PS)
Love Me For A Reason / Fever - 2006 458 (Austria)
Love Me For A Reason / Fever - 2006 458 (Netherlands) (PS)
Love Me For A Reason / Fever - 2006 458 (France) (PS)
Love Me For A Reason / Fever - 2006 458 (Ireland)
Love Me For A Reason / Fever - 2006 458 (Belgium) (PS)
Love Me For A Reason / Fever - 2006 458 (Australia)
Love Me For A Reason / Fever - 2006 458 (Germany) (PS)
Love Me For A Reason / Fever - 2006 458 (New Zealand)
Love Me For A Reason / Fever - MGM-14-076 (Philippines)
Love Me For A Reason / Fever - 2006 458 (Mexico)
Love Me For A Reason / Crazy Horses - 2006 469 (Brazil)

I Can't Stop / Flower Music - 4530 MCA (UK Re-issue) (PS)

Having A Party / Wanted - 2006 492 (UK)
Having A Party / Wanted - 2006 495 (Netherlands) (PS)
Having A Party / Wanted - 2006 495 (Italy)
Having A Party / Wanted - 2006 495 (Spain) (PS)
Having A Party / Wanted - 2006 495 (Germany) (PS)
Having A Party / Wanted - 2006 492 (New Zealand)
Having A Party / Wanted - 2006 492 (Australia)
Having A Party / Wanted - S - 53 862 (Yugoslavia) (PS)
Having A Party / Sun Sun Sun - 2006 495 (France) (PS)
Having A Party / Sun, Sun, Sun - (Belgium) (PS)

1975

Having A Party / Wanted - 2006 492 (Germany) (PS)
Having A Party / Wanted - 2006 492 (Spain) (PS)

The Proud One / The Last Day Is Coming Is Coming - M 14791 (US / Canada)
El Orgulloso (The Proud One) / El Final Se Acerca (The Last Day Is Coming Is Coming) - MGM-562 (Mexico)
The Proud One / The Last Day Is Coming Is Coming - 20 06 520 (Spain) (PS)
The Proud One / The Last Day Is Coming Is Coming - 2006 520 (France) (PS)
The Proud One / The Last Day Is Coming Is Coming - 2006 520 (Australia)
The Proud One / The Last Day Is Coming Is Coming - 2006 520 (New Zealand)
The Proud One / The Last Day Is Coming Is Coming - 2006 520 (Austria) (PS)
The Proud One / The Last Day Is Coming Is Coming - 2006 520 (Germany) (PS)
The Proud One / The Last Day Is Coming Is Coming - 2006 520 (Belgium) (PS)
The Proud One / The Last Day Is Coming Is Coming - 2006 520 (Netherlands) (PS)
The Proud One / The Last Day Is Coming Is Coming - 2006 520 (Ireland)
The Proud One / The Last Day Is Coming Is Coming - 2006 520 (UK)
The Proud One / The Last Day Is Coming Is Coming - DM-1267 (Japan))PS)

I'm Still Gonna Need You / Thank You - M 14831 (US) (PS)
I'm Still Gonna Need You / Thank You - M 14831(Canada)
I'm Still Gonna Need You / Thank You - 2006 551(Germany) (PS)

1976

I Can't Live A Dream / Check It Out - PD 14348 (US / Canada)
I Can't Live A Dream / Check It Out - 2066 726 (UK)
I Can't Live A Dream / Check It Out - 20 66 726 (New Zealand)
I Can't Live A Dream / Check It Out - 2066 726 (Netherlands) (PS)

1977

I'd Like To Be You For A Day - Disneyland Records – 566 A/B (Promo)
Theme Song for original screen release *Freaky Friday* but was never used in the film.
Credited as The Osmonds but Merrill Osmond vocals only,

1979

You're Mine / Put Your Love On The Line - Mercury74056 (US)
You're Mine / Put Your Love On The Line - Mercury74056 (US)
I, I, I / You're Mine - MK-91 (12" Single)
Emily - Mercury 74079 (US) (Promo)
Steppin' Out / Love On The Line - Mercury - 6167 761 (UK)
Rainin' / Hold On - Mercury - 6167 782 (France)
You're Mine / Hold On - Mercury - 6837 569 (France)

1982

I Think About Your Lovin' / Workin' Man Blues - E-47438 (US)

Pienso En Tu Amor (I Think About Your Lovin') / Blues Del Trabajador (Working Man's Blues)
Elektra F-ELK 0047438.9 (Peru)

Never Ending Song of Love For You / You'll Be Seeing Me - 7-69883 (US)

It's Like Fallin' Love (Over and Over Again) / Your Leavin' Was The Last Thing On My Mind 7-69969 (US)

1983

Where Does An Angel Go When She Cries / One More For Lovers - 7-29387 (US)

She's Ready For Someone To Love Her / You Make The Long Road Shorter (With Your Love) 7-29594 (US)

Heartache Tonight / Hello Darlin' Conway Twitty featuring the Osmond Brothers
Warner Bros. Records - 92-95057

1984

If Every Man Had A Woman Like You / Come Back To Me - 7-29312 (US)

1985

One Way Rider / I Think About Your Lovin' (UK) RANS-74 (Range)
(Taken from the UK Album "The Osmond Brothers - TODAY", RANGE 7005)

Baby When Your Heart Breaks Down / Love Burnin' Down - B-8298 (EMI) (US)

Anytime / Desperately - Warner Bros. Records - 7-28982

1986

Baby Wants / Lovin' Proof - B-8313 (EMI)
You Look Like The One I Love / It's Only Heartache - B-8325 (EMI) (US)
Looking For Suzanne / Back In Your Arms Again - B-8360 (EMI) (US)

1987

You're Here To My Remember, I'm Here To Forget* / The Price You Pay - B- 8388 (EMI) *Merrill Osmond & Jessica Boucher / The Osmonds
Slow Ride / Heartbreak Radio - B-43033 (EMI) (US)
(The seven EMI singles above are from an unreleased Osmond Brothers album to be titled *Baby Wants* on EMI/America.)

1988

One Bad Apple (Norman Cook 12" Remix) 12" 45 epm EP (Cat.#) (UK)
A1 - One Bad Apple (Norman Cook Remix) 5:53
B1 - One Bad Apple 2:46 / B2 - Crazy Horses 2:32

One Bad Apple PZ 18 UK 12" 45rpm EP (UK)
A1 - One Bad Apple / A2 - Let Me In
B1 - Crazy Horses / B2 - Love Me For A Reason

One Bad Apple / Let Me In - PO18 (UK) (PS)

1995

Crazy Horses (Utah Saints Remix) (PS)
This single was made available on 12" single / CD Single / CD Maxi-Single / Cass-Single of various re-mixes of the 1972 hit song Crazy Horses.
Mixed By – Bob Kearney, Michael Lloyd, Mark Haley, Paul Walton, Mark "Spike" Stent
Producer – Alan Osmond, Michael Lloyd
Remix, Producer [Additional] – Utah Saints

Label	Catalog #	Country	Year / Format
Polydor	579321-1	UK	1995 12" Single
Polydor	579321-2	UK	1995 CD Single
Polydor	577339-2	Europe	1995 CD Single
Polydor	579 321-4	UK	1995 Cassette Single
Polydor	Horse 1	UK	1995 12" Promo
Polydor	5 79325-1	UK	1995 12" Single
Polydor	5611370-2	UK	1999 CD Maxi Single
Polydor	561137-2	UK	1999 CD Single
Polydor	561137-4	UK	1999 Cassette Single

2012

I Can't Get There Without You - OSMDCD1 (US)

2019

The Last Chapter.
A last song by the original four Osmond Brothers.
Released on October 13, 2019 via digital download only.

MERRILL OSMOND

1987

*You're Here To Remember (I'm Here To Forget) - P-B-8388 (US) (Radio Station Promotional copy - Stereo / Mono) (*Duet with Jessica Boucher)

2001

America – MO-1001 (CD Single)
(In Support of Families Of Freedom Scholarship Fund for 9/11 Families)

2007

You Take My Breath Away / Coming Home (CD Single)

2016

It's Christmas Time (Duet with Heather Osmond Hallows) (CD Single)

DONNY OSMOND:
PS - Picture Sleeve

1971

Sweet and Innocent / Flirtin' - K 14227 (US) (PS)
Sweet and Innocent / Flirtin' - 2065 059 (Canada) (Polydor)
Sweet and Innocent / Flirtin' - 20 06 042 (Spain) (PS)
Sweet and Innocent / Flirtin' - 2006042 (Germany) (PS)
Sweet and Innocent / Flirtin' - 2006042 (Australia)
Sweet and Innocent / Flirtin' - 2006042 (New Zealand)

Go Away Little Girl / Time To Ride - K-14285 (US)
Go Away Little Girl / Time To Ride - 2162 008 (Brazil)
Go Away Little Girl / Time To Ride - CD - 1008 (Japan) (PS)
Go Away Little Girl / Time To Ride - 2006 071 (Germany) (PS)
Go Away Little Girl / Time To Ride - 2006 071 (New Zealand)
Go Away Little Girl / Time To Ride - 2006-071 (UK)
Go Away Little Girl / Time To Ride - S 53 636 (Yugoslavia) (PS)
Go Away Little Girl / Time To Ride - K-14285 (Jamaica)
Vete Lejos Chiquilla (Go Away Little Girl) / Un Poquito (Little Bit) - M-1701 (Mexico)
Both songs sung in English

*Bleib Bei Mir Little Girl / Little Bit Me - 2006 089 (Germany) (PS)
*Go Away Little Girl sung in German

Hey Girl / I Knew You When - K14322 (US)
Hey Girl / I Knew You When - 2006 087 (Germany) (PS)
Hey Girl / I Knew You When - 2065 095 (Canada) (Polydor)
Hey Girl / I Knew You When - 2006 087 (Netherlands) (PS)
Hey Girl / I Knew You When - 2006 087 (UK)
Hey Girl / I Knew You When - 2006087 (Peru)
Hey Girl / I Knew You When - 2006 087 (Australia)

1972

Puppy Love / Let My People Go - K 14367 (US)
Puppy Love / Let My People Go - 2006-104 (UK)
Puppy Love / Let My People Go - 2006 104 (Belgium) (PS)
Puppy Love / Let My People Go - 2006 111 (Lebanon)
Puppy Love / Let My People Go - 2006 104 (Brazil)
Puppy Love / Let My People Go - PS-199 (South Africa)
Puppy Love / Let My People Go - 2065 108 (Canada) (Polydor)
Puppy Love / Let My People Go - 20 06 104 (Spain) (PS)
Puppy Love / Let My People Go - 2006127 (Greece)
Puppy Love / Let My People Go - 2006 104 (Portugal) (PS)
Puppy Love / Let My People Go - 2006 104 (Austria)
Puppy Love / Let My People Go - 711 (Venezuela)
Puppy Love / Let My People Go - 2006 104 (Germany) (PS)
Puppy Love / Let My People Go - 2006 104 (Scandinavia)

Puppy Love / Let My People Go - 2006 104 (New Zealand) (Polydor)
Puppy Love / Let My People Go - 2006 104 (Turkey)
Puppy Love / Let My People Go - 2006 104 (Peru)
Puppy Love / Let My People Go - 2006 104 (Australia)
Puppy Love / Too Young - 2006 167 (France) (PS)
Puppy Love / Hey Girl - 2006 111 (Lebanon) (Multi-colored emerald vinyl)

Too Young / Love Me - 2006 113 (Germany) (PS)
Too Young / Love Me - 2006 113 (UK)
Too Young / Love Me - 2006 113 (Australia)
Too Young / Love Me - 2006 113 (Belgium) PS)
Too Young / Love Me - K 14407 (US)
Too Young / Love Me - 2065 133 (Canada) (Polydor)
Too Young / Love Me - 2065133 (Lebanon)

Why / Lonely Boy - 2006-119 (UK)
Why / Lonely Boy - 2006-119 (New Zealand)
Why / Lonely Boy - 2006-119 (Australia)
Why / Lonely Boy - K 14424 (US)
Why / Lonely Boy - 2065-143 (Canada) (Polydor)
Why / Lonely Boy - 2006-119 (France) (PS)
Why / Lonely Boy - K-14424 (Guatemala)
Lonely Boy / Why - 2006-119 (Belgium) (PS)
A Teenager In Love / Why - 2006 124 (Germany) (PS)

1973

The Twelfth of Never / Life Is Just What We Make It - K 14503 (US) (PS)
The Twelfth of Never / Life Is Just What We Make It - K 14503 (Canada)
The Twelfth of Never / Life Is Just What We Make It - 2006 199 (Germany) (PS)
The Twelfth of Never / Life Is Just What We Make It - 2006 199 (France) (PS)
The Twelfth of Never / Life Is Just What We Make It - 2006 199 (Scandinavia)
The Twelfth of Never / Life Is Just What We Make It - PS 246 (South Africa) (PS)
The Twelfth of Never / Life Is Just What We Make It - 2006 199 (Australia) (PS)
The Twelfth of Never / Life Is Just What We Make It - DM-1242 (Japan) (PS)
The Twelfth of Never / Life Is Just What We Make It - 20 06 199 (Spain) (PS)
The Twelfth of Never / Life Is Just What We Make It - 2006 199 (UK)
The Twelfth of Never / Life Is Just What We Make It - 20 06 199 (Ireland)
The Twelfth of Never / Life Is Just What We Make It - 2006 199 (Netherlands) (PS)
The Twelfth of Never / Life Is Just What We Make It - 2006 199 (Belgium) (PS)
The Twelfth of Never / Life Is Just What We Make It - S 53 687 (Yugoslavia) (PS)
The Twelfth of Never / Life Is Just What We Make It - 2006 199 (New Zealand)
The Twelfth of Never / Life Is Just What We Make It - K 14503 (Jamaica)

Young Love / A Million To One - K 14583 (US)
Young Love / A Million To One - K 14583 (Canada)
Young Love / A Million To One - K 14583 (Jamaica)
Young Love / A Million To One - 2006 300 (Belgium) (PS)
Young Love / A Million To One - 2006 300 (Germany) (PS)
Young Love / A Million To One - 2006 300 (France) (PS)
Young Love / A Million To One - 2006 300 (Scandinavia)

Young Love / A Million To One - 2006 300 (UK) (PS)
Young Love / A Million To One - 2006 300 (Portugal) (PS)
Young Love / A Million To One - DM-1246 (Japan) (PS)
Young Love / A Million To One - 2006 300 (Ireland)
Young Love / A Million To One - 2006 300 (Australia)

Amor Joven (Young Love) / lagrimas en mi almohada (Tears On My Pillow) MGM304 (New Zealand)
Amor Joven (Young Love) / lagrimas en mi almohada (Tears On My Pillow) MGM317 (Mexico)

Are You Lonesome Tonight / When I Fall In Love - K 14677 (US)
Are You Lonesome Tonight / When I Fall In Love - K 14677 (Canada)
Are You Lonesome Tonight / When I Fall In Love - 2006 365 (Australia)
Are You Lonesome Tonight / When I Fall In Love - 2006 365 (France) (PS)
Are You Lonesome Tonight / When I Fall In Love - 2006 365 (Guatemala)
Are You Lonesome Tonight / When I Fall In Love - 2006 365 (Netherlands) (PS)
Are You Lonesome Tonight / When I Fall In Love - 2006 365 (UK) (PS)
Are You Lonesome Tonight / When I Fall In Love - 2006 365 (Germany) (PS)
Are You Lonesome Tonight / When I Fall In Love - 2006 365 (New Zealand)
Are You Lonesome Tonight / When I Fall In Love - 2006 365 (Spain) (PS)
Are You Lonesome Tonight / When I Fall In Love - 2006 365 (Belgium) (PS)
Are You Lonesome Tonight / When I Fall In Love - DM-1250 (Japan) (PS)
Are You Lonesome Tonight / When I Fall In Love - AS 264 (Italy) (PS)
Are You Lonesome Tonight / When I Fall In Love - S - 53732 (Yugoslavia) (PS)
Are You Lonesome Tonight / When I Fall In Love - 2006 365 (Scandinavia)
A Time For Us / Guess Who - 2006 393 (France) (PS)
A Time For Us / Guess Who - 2006 393 (Belgium) (PS)
A Time For Us / Guess Who - 2006 393 (Australia)
A Time For Us / Guess Who - 2006 393 (Ireland)
A Time for Us / Hawaiian Wedding Song - DM1255 (Japan) (PS)

Hawaiian Wedding Song / A Boy Is Waiting - 2006 434 (Netherlands) (PS)

1974

¿Donde Fueron Los Buenos Tiempos? (Where Did All The Good Times Go) / Monalisa (Mona Lisa) - MGM 487 (Mexico)
Where Did All The Good Times Go / I'm Dyin' - 2006 468 (France) (PS)
Where Did All The Good Times Go / I'm Dyin' - 2006 468 (UK) PS)
Where Did All The Good Times Go / I'm Dyin' - 2006 468 (Netherlands) (PS)
Where Did All The Good Times Go / I'm Dyin' - 2006 468 (Germany) (PS)
Where Did All The Good Times Go / I'm Dyin' - 2006 468 (New Zealand)
Where Did All The Good Times Go / I'm Dyin' - 2006 468 (Belgium) (PS)
Where Did All The Good Times Go / I'm Dyin' - 2006 468 (Australia)
I Have A Dream / I'm Dyin' - 2006 491 (Belgium) (PS)
I Have A Dream / I'm Dyin' - 2006 491 (New Zealand)
I Have A Dream / I'm Dyin' - S 53 874 (Yugoslavia) (PS)
I Have A Dream / I'm Dyin' - 2006 491 (UK)
I Have A Dream / I'm Dyin' - 2006 491 (Australia)
I Have A Dream / I'm Dyin' - 2006 491 (Germany) (PS)
I Have A Dream / I'm Dyin' - 2006 491 (Netherlands) (PS)

I Have A Dream / I'm Dyin' - M 14781 (US)
I Have A Dream / I'm Dyin' - M14781 (Canada)

1976

C'mon Marianne / Old Man Auctioneer - 2066 688 (UK) (PS)
C'mon Marianne / Old Man Auctioneer - 2066 688 (Ireland) (June 1976)
C'mon Marianne / Old Man Auctioneer - 2066 688 (Germany) (PS)
C'mon Marianne / Old Man Auctioneer - 2066 688 (Belgium) (PS)
C'mon Marianne / Old Man Auctioneer - 2066 688 (New Zealand)
C'mon Marianne / Old Man Auctioneer - 2066 676 (Australia)
C'Mon Marianne / I Got Your Lovin' - 2066 676 (France)
Vamos Marianne (C'mon Marianne) / Viejo Rematador (Old Man Auctioneer) - 2066 688 (Uruguay)
C'mon Marianne / Old Man Auctioneer - PD 14320 (US)
C'Mon Marianne / I Got Your Lovin' - PD 14320 (US)
C'mon Marianne / Old Man Auctioneer - PD 14320 (Canada)
Hey Girl / Puppy Love - PDG-103 Polydor (Specialty Record) (Also: KGC-213 MGM)
Sweet and Innocent / C'mon Marianne - PDG-105 Polydor (Specialty Record)

1977

You've Got Me Dangling On A String / I'm Sorry PD 14417

1985

L.A. Street Scene (It's A Jubilee) (12") - LASS-1 (US) Featuring Donny Osmond, Phillip Ingram, Scherrie Payne & Freda Payne - The official song of the 1985 Los Angeles Street Scene Jubilee.

1987

I'm In It For Love / Keep Me Hummin' - Virgin - 109 387 (Europe) (PS)
I'm In It For Love / Keep Me Hummin' - Virgin - VSP994 (UK) (PS)
I'm In It For Love / Keep Me Hummin' - VIN - 45242 (Italy) (PS)
I'm In It For Love / Keep Me Hummin' - VIN - 009947 (France) (PS)
I'm In It For Love / Keep Me Hummin' / What Am I Here For (Instru) - Virgin 609 387 (Germany) (PS)
I'm In It For Love / Keep Me Hummin' / What Am I Here For (Instru) - Virgin 609 387 (UK) (PS)
I'm In It For Love / Keep Me Hummin' / What Am I Here For (Instru) - VG 2094Z (Greece) (PS)
I'm In It For Love / Keep Me Hummin' / What Am I Here For (Instru) - VG 2094Z (Australasia) (PS) VS99412

Groove (Club Mix) / Only Heaven Knows (Alternate Mix) VST1016 (UK) (PS)
Groove (Club Mix) / Only Heaven Knows (Extended Mix) F-609 584 (Spain) (PS)
Groove / Heaven Only Knows - VS 1016 (UK) (PS)

1988

Soldier of Love / Time Can't Erase - VSX 1094 (UK) (7" boxed set with postcards and badges)
Soldier of Love / Time Can't Erase - VS 1094 (UK)

Soldier of Love / Time Can't Erase - 111 784 (Germany) (PS)
Soldier of Love / Time Can't Erase - 90459 (France) (PS)
Soldier of Love / Time Can't Erase - 112 405 (Europe) (PS)
Soldier of Love / My Secret Touch - B-44369 (Canada) (PS)
Soldier of Love / My Secret Touch - B-44369 (US) (PS)
If It's Love That You Want / Come Down - VSP 1140 (UK) (PS / Poster)

12" singles
Soldier Of Love / Soldier Of Love (Dub Mix) / Time Can't Erase - 611 784-213 (Europe) (PS)
Soldier Of Love /Soldier Of Love (Dub Mix) / Time Can't Erase - VST 1094 (UK) (PS)
Soldier Of Love /Soldier Of Love (Dub Mix) / Time Can't Erase - 612 405 (Germany) (PS)
Soldier Of Love /Soldier Of Love (Dub Mix) / Time Can't Erase - VSTY 1094 (UK) (Picture Disc)
Soldier Of Love /Soldier Of Love (Dub Mix) / Time Can't Erase - VST 1094 (Australia)
If It's Love That You Want (Extended Remix) / If It's Love That You Want (7" Remix) / Come Down - VST 1140 (UK) (PS)
If It's Love That You Want (Extended Remix) / If It's Love That You Want - VST 1140 (Australia) (PS)
If It's Love That You Want / If It's Love That You Want - VS 1140 (Australia)

1989

Sacred Emotion / Groove - B-44379 (US) (PS)
Sacred Emotion / Sacred Emotion (Spanish Version) - 7PRO-79858 (US)
Sacred Emotion / Groove - VS 1211 (UK) (PS)

Hold On (7" Radio Version) / Only Heaven Knows - B-44423 (Canada)
Hold On (12" Club Mix) / Hold On (Perc-a-pella) / Hold On (Extended Mix) / Hold On (Instrumental) / Hold On (7" Version) - V-15505

I'll Be Good To You (1/2 Guitar Solo) / I'll Be Good To You (Extended Guitar Mix) - DPRO-79885 (Released on promo 7" single and CD)

1990

My Love Is A Fire (Edit) / Before It's Too Late - CL 600 (UK) (PS)
My Love Is A Fire (Edit) / Before It's Too Late - Cap. 016 20 4169 7 (Germany) (PS)

12" singles
My Love Is A Fire (D.J. Pierre's In-Da-House Mix) / My Love Is A Fire (D.J. Pierre's House Instrumental Mix) / My Love Is A Fire (Da-House Radio Mix) - V-15642 (US) (PS)

My Love Is A Fire (D.J. Pierre's In-Da-House Mix) / My Love Is A Fire (D.J. Pierre's House Instrumental UK Edit) / My Love Is A Fire (Da-House Radio Version) - 12CL 600 (UK) (PS)

Sure Lookin' (Radio Remix) / Sure Lookin' (LP Version) / Sure Lookin' (Soul To Jack R&B Mix) / Sure Lookin' (Sho'Housin Club Mix) / Sure Lookin' (Soul To Jack Instrumental) / Sure Lookin' (Sho'Housin Instrumental) - Cap.5666 (US) (PS)

Sure Lookin' (Sho' Housin' Club Mix) / Sure Lookin' (Sho' Housin' Instrumental) / Sure Lookin' (Radio Remix) Sure Lookin' (Soul To Jack R&B Mix) / Sure Lookin' (Soul To Jack Instrumental) - V-15666 (US) (PS)

Love Will Survive / Just Between You And Me - 4JM-44707

1992

Any Dream Will Do / Joseph Remix - PRCDP 00232 (Polydor)

1997

I've Been looking For Christmas / The Echo Of Your Whisper - (Promo CD only / Not for sale)

1998

I'll Make A Man Out of You (Promotional single only) Walt Disney Records

2000

This Is The Moment

Without You

2001

Seasons Of Love (Radio Remix) / Luck Be A Lady / Seasons Of Love (Original Version) - PCD 20011 (Promotional only single)

Seasons Of Love / It's Possible - DONNY1

2004

Breeze on By / Right Here Waiting - 9863140 (UK and Europe)
Breeze on By - UCGR-00094-2 (US)

Christmas Time / What I Meant To Say - Radio issued promo CD single.

2005

Keep Her In Mind (Radio Edit) / Whenever You're In Trouble / Just The Way You Are
Bonus CD Video: Whenever You're In Trouble (Director – Phil Griffin) - LC 00171 (UK)

2007

Sometimes When We Touch

2015

Could She Be Mine - promo CD single.

Whenever You're In Trouble / If Every Day Could Be Christmas - Limited Edition CD single - (US)

MARIE OSMOND
PS - Picture Sleeve

1973

*Paper Roses / Least of All You - K 14609 (US) (PS)
*Peaked at #1 on 11/9/1973 (US) - Weeks on Chart: 16
Paper Roses / Least of All You - 2006 315 (Netherlands) (PS)
Paper Roses / Least of All You - S-53.725 (Yugoslavia) (PS)
Paper Roses / Least of All You - 2006 315 (France) (PS)
Paper Roses / Least of All You - 2006 315 (Scandinavia) (PS)
Paper Roses / Least of All You - DM1248 (Japan) (PS)
Paper Roses / Least of All You - 2006 315 (Germany) (PS)
Paper Roses / Least Of All You - R-0496 (Poland) (6" 45 rpm, Single Side, Picture Card)
Paper Roses / Least of All You - 2006 315 (Ireland)
Paper Roses / Least of All You - 2006 315 (UK)
Paper Roses / Least of All You - 2006 315 (Australia)
Paper Roses / Least of All You - K 14609 (Canada)
Paper Roses / Least of All You - 2006 315 (New Zealand)
Paper Roses / Least of All You - 2006 315 (Turkey)

1974

In My Little Corner Of The World / It's Just The Other Way Around - K 14694 (US)
In My Little Corner Of The World / It's Just The Other Way Around - K 14694 (Canada)
In My Little Corner Of The World / It's Just The Other Way Around - 2006 429 (UK)
In My Little Corner Of The World / It's Just The Other Way Around - 2006 429 (Australia)
In My Little Corner Of The World / It's Just The Other Way Around - DM-1254 (Japan) (PS)
In My Little Corner Of The World / It's Just The Other Way Around - 2006 429 (Germany) (PS)
In My Little Corner Of The World / It's Just The Other Way Around - 2006 429 (Belgium) (PS)

1975

Who's Sorry Now / This I Promise You - M 14786 (US)
Who's Sorry Now / This I Promise You - M 14786 (Canada)
Who's Sorry Now / This I Promise You - 2006496 (Peru)
Who's Sorry Now / This I Promise You - 2006496 (Spain)
Who's Sorry Now / This I Promise You - 2006 496 (New Zealand)
Who's Sorry Now / This I Promise You - 2006 496 (Belgium) (PS)
Who's Sorry Now / This I Promise You - 2006 496 (Netherlands) (PS)
Who's Sorry Now / This I Promise You - 2006 496 (Germany) (PS)
Who's Sorry Now / This I Promise You - 2006 496 (UK) (PS)
Who's Sorry Now / This I Promise You - DM-1265 (Japan) (PS)

1976

'A' My Name Is Alice / Weeping Willow - PD 14333 (US)
'A' My Name Is Alice / Weeping Willow - 2066 697 (New Zealand)
Paper Roses / Who's Sorry Now - PDG-105 Polydor (Specialty Record)

1977

This Is The Way That I Feel / Play The Music Loud - (PD-14385) (US) (PS)
This Is The Way That I Feel / Play The Music Loud - 2066 793 (Belgium) (PS)
This Is The Way That I Feel / Play The Music Loud - 2066 793 (Germany) (PS)
This Is The Way That I Feel / Play The Music Loud - DPQ-6053 (Japan) (PS)
This Is The Way That I Feel / Play The Music Loud - 2066 793 (Spain) (PS)
This Is The Way That I Feel / Play The Music Loud - 2066 793 (Belgium) (PS)
This Is The Way That I Feel / Play The Music Loud - 2066 793 (France) (PS)
This Is The Way That I Feel / Play The Music Loud - 2066 793 (Scandinavia) (PS)
This Is The Way That I Feel / Play The Music Loud - PD 14385 (Canada)
This Is The Way That I Feel / Play The Music Loud - 2066 793 (Peru)
This Is The Way That I Feel / Play The Music Loud - 2066 793 (UK)
This Is The Way That I Feel / Play The Music Loud - 2066 793 (Scandinavia)
This Is The Way That I Feel / Play The Music Loud - PD 14385 (Promo, Seafare Fun Days / 95 KJR / Coca Cola / Pay 'N Save)
Asi Es Como Yo Siento (This Is The Way That I Feel) / Toca La Musica Fuerte (Play The Music Loud) - 2066 793-827 (Mexico) Both songs sung in English.

Please Tell Him That I Said Hello / Cry, Baby, Cry - PD-14405 (US / Canada)

1980

Your Gonna Get Me To Heaven / L.A. Song - POSP 147 (UK Only)

1982

I've Got A Bad Case Of You / You Still Get The Best Of Me - E-47430 (US)
I've Got A Bad Case Of You / You Still Get The Best Of Me - F-ELK0047430-3 (Spain)
I'm Learnin' / I'm Learnin' - Unreleased -7-69882 (US) (Promo)
Back To Believin' Again / Look Who's Getting Over Who - 7-69995 (US)

1984

Who's Counting / Our Song - PB-13680 (US)

1985

Until I Fall in Love Again / I Don't Want To Go Too Far - B-5445 (US)
Until I Fall in Love Again / I Don't Want To Go Too Far - B-5445 (Canada)
Until I Fall in Love Again / I Don't Want To Go Too Far - B-5445 (UK) (PS)

Meet Me In Montana (with Dan Seals)* / What Do Lonely People Do - B-5478 (US / Canada)
*Peaked at #1 on 10/1985 (US) (PS)

Meet Me In Montana (with Dan Seals) / Meet Me In Montana (with Dan Seals) P-B-5478 (US) (Promotional single - Stereo / Mono)

There's No Stopping Your Heart / Blue Sky Shinin' - B-5521 (US) (PS)
There's No Stopping Your Heart / Love Will Find Its Way To You - CL 390 (UK) (PS)

Puedes Detener Tu Corazon (There's No Stopping Your Heart) / Lee Mis Labios (Read My Lips) - 121-0053 (Ecuador) (Both songs sung in English)

Read My Lips / That Old Devil Moon - B-5563 (US / Canada) (PS)

1986

Cry Just A Little / More Than Dancing - B-44044 (US) (PS)
Cry Just A Little / Cry Just A Little - P-B-44044 (US) (Radio Station Promotional copy - Stereo / Mono)

You're Still New To Me* (with Paul Davis) / New Love B-5613 (US) (PS)
*Peaked at #1 on 11/21/1986 (US) (PS)

I Only Wanted You / We're Gonna Need A Love Song - B-5663 (US) (PS)
I Only Wanted You / I Only Wanted You - P-B-5663 (US) (Radio Station Promotional copy - Stereo / Mono)

Everybody's Crazy 'Bout My Baby / Making Magic - B-5703 (US)
Everybody's Crazy 'Bout My Baby / Everybody's Crazy 'Bout My Baby (US) (Radio Station Promotional copy - Stereo / Mono)

1988

Without A Trace / Baby's Blue Eyes - B-44176 (US / Canada)
Without A Trace / Without A Trace - P-B-44176 (US) (Radio Station Promotional copy - Stereo / Mono)
Sweet Life (with Paul Davis) / Somebody Else's Moon - B-44215
Sweet Life (with Paul Davis) / Sweet Life (with Paul Davis) - P- B-44215 (US) (Radio Station Promotional copy - Stereo / Mono)
I'm In Love and He's In Dallas / My Hometown Boy - B-44269 (US)
I'm In Love and He's In Dallas / I'm In Love and He's In Dallas - P-B-44269 (US) (Radio Station Promotional copy - Stereo / Mono)

1989

Steppin' Stone / What Would You Do About You (If You Were Me) - B-44412 (US)
Steppin' Stone / Steppin' Stone P-B-44412 (US) (Radio Station Promotional copy - Stereo / Mono)
Slowly But Surely / What Would You Do About You (If You Were Me) - B-44468 (US)
Slowly But Surely /Slowly But Surely - 7PRO-79808 (US) (Radio Station Promotional copy - Stereo / Mono)
Let Me Be the First / What's A Little Love between Friends - B-44505 (US)
Let Me Be the First / Let Me Be the First - P-B-44505 (US) (Radio Station Promotional copy - Stereo / Mono)

1990

Like A Hurricane / I'll Be Faithful To You - NR-76840 (US)
Think With Your Heart / Paper Roses* - NR-76851 (US)
(*1990 Re-recorded version)

1991

Boogie Woogie Bugle Boy / Think With Your Heart – NR-76868 (US)

1992

True Love Never Goes Away - CURBD-092 (US) (Promotional CD - Not For Sale)

1995

What Kind of Man (Walks On A Woman) - WEA-76943 (Cass-single only) (Cass-single also included: The Loft (Preview) 1:06 / Baby, It's Tonight (Preview) 1:06 on side B from Curb CD "True Love (Never Goes Away)" (D-77542) which remains unreleased.
What Kind of Man (Walks On A Woman) - D-1096 (Promotional CD - Not For Sale)

1997

From God's Arms (Cassette tape © 1997 Shining Star Music)
Promo release with Knickerbocker / Marie Osmond Doll Purchase only.

2010

Pie Jesu (Digital download only)

2011

Naughty List / Angels We Have Heard On High / Away In A Manger
CD single released for sale through concert venues / tour outlets.
(Now a highly sought after collectible. Autographed copies also sold.)

2016

Music Is Medicine (Digital download only)
Baby You're Crazy (Digital download only)

DONNY & MARIE
PS - Picture Sleeve

1974

I'm Leaving It All Up To You / The Umbrella Song - M 14735 (*US / Canada / Guatemala)
(*Certified Gold on September 20, 1974 for selling 1,000,000+ copies)
I'm Leaving It All Up To You / The Umbrella Song - 2006 446 (Ireland)
I'm Leaving It All Up To You / The Umbrella Song - 2006 446 (UK)
I'm Leaving It All Up To You / The Umbrella Song - 2006 446 (Australia)
I'm Leaving It All Up To You / The Umbrella Song - 2006 446 (Spain) (PS)
I'm Leaving It All Up To You / The Umbrella Song - 2006 446 (France) (PS)
I'm Leaving It All Up To You / The Umbrella Song - 2006 446 (Turkey) (PS)
I'm Leaving It All Up To You / The Umbrella Song - 2006 446 (Germany) (PS)
I'm Leaving It All Up To You / The Umbrella Song - 2006 446 (Belgium) (PS)
I'm Leaving It All Up To You / The Umbrella Song - 2006 446 (Austria) (PS)
I'm Leaving It All Up To You / The Umbrella Song - 2006 446 (Switzerland) (PS)
I'm Leaving It All Up To You / The Umbrella Song - 2006 446 (Yugoslavia) (PS)
I'm Leaving It All Up To You / The Umbrella Song - 2006 446 (Netherlands) (PS)
I'm Leaving It All Up To You / The Umbrella Song - DM-1256 (Japan) (PS)

Morning Side Of The Mountain / One of These Days - M 14765 (US)
Morning Side Of The Mountain / One of These Days - 2006 474 (Ireland)
Morning Side Of The Mountain / One of These Days - 2006 474 (UK)
Morning Side Of The Mountain / One of These Days - 2006 474 (Uruguay)
Amanecer En la Montaña (Morning Side Of The Mountain) / Amor Verdadero (True Love) - 2006 486 (Mexico) (Both songs are sung in English)
Morning Side Of The Mountain / One of These Days - 2006 474 (Germany) (PS)
Morning Side Of The Mountain / One of These Days - 2006 474 (Austria) (PS)
Morning Side Of The Mountain / One of These Days - 2006 474 (Belgium) (PS)
Morning Side Of The Mountain / One of These Days - DM-1262 (Japan) (PS)
Morning Side Of The Mountain / One of These Days - 2006 474 (Yugoslavia) (PS)

1975

Morning Side Of The Mountain / True Love - 2006 486 (Australia)

Make The World Go Away / Living On My Suspicion - M 14807 (US / Canada)
Make The World Go Away / Living On My Suspicion - 2006 523 (New Zealand)
Make The World Go Away / Living On My Suspicion - 2006 523 (Australia)
Make The World Go Away / Living On My Suspicion - 2006 523 (Ireland)
Make The World Go Away / Living On My Suspicion - 2006 523 (UK)
Make The World Go Away / Living On My Suspicion - 2006 523 (Austria)
Make The World Go Away / Living On My Suspicion - 2006 523 (Belgium) (PS)
Make The World Go Away / Living On My Suspicion - 2006 523 (France) (PS)
Make The World Go Away / Living On My Suspicion - 2006 523 (Germany) (PS)
Make The World Go Away / Living On My Suspicion - 2006 523 (Netherlands) (PS)

Deep Purple / Take Me Back Again - 2006 561 (Belgium) (PS)
Deep Purple / Take Me Back Again - 2006 561 (France) (PS)

Deep Purple / Take Me Back Again - DM-1272 (Japan) (PS)
Deep Purple / Take Me Back Again - 2006 561 (Germany) (PS)
Deep Purple / Take Me Back Again - M 14840 (US / Canada)
Deep Purple / Take Me Back Again - 2006 561 (UK)
Deep Purple / Take Me Back Again - 2006 561 (Ireland)
Deep Purple / Take Me Back Again - 2006 561 (New Zealand)
Deep Purple / Take Me Back Again - S 53946 (Yugoslavia)
Deep Purple / Take Me Back Again - 2006 561 (Australia)
Purpura Escondido (Deep Purple) / Aceptame Otra Vez (Take Me Back Again) - 2006 561-624 (Mexico) (Both songs are sung in English)

1976

Deep Purple / I'm Leaving It All Up To You - PDG-102 Polydor (Specialty Record)

Ain't Nothing Like The Real Thing / Sing - DPQ 6037 (Japan) (PS)
Ain't Nothing Like The Real Thing / Sing - 2066 756 (Germany) (PS)
Ain't Nothing Like The Real Thing / Sing - S 53990 (Yugoslavia) (PS)
Ain't Nothing Like The Real Thing / Sing - PD 14363 (US / Canada)
Ain't Nothing Like The Real Thing / Sing - 2006 756 (UK)

1977

You're My Soul and Inspiration / Now We're Together - DPQ-6076 (Japan) (PS)
You're My Soul and Inspiration / Now We're Together - 2066 879 (Germany) (PS)
You're My Soul and Inspiration / Now We're Together - 2066 879 (Germany) (PS)
You're My Soul and Inspiration / Now We're Together - PD 14439 (US / Canada)
You're My Soul and Inspiration / Now We're Together - 2066 879 (UK)
You're My Soul and Inspiration / Now We're Together - 2066 879 (New Zealand)
(Tu Eres) Mi Alma E Inspiración ((You're My) Soul And Inspiration) / Ahora Estamos Juntos (Now We're Together) - 2066 879 (Guatemala) (Both songs sung in English)

Baby, I'm Sold On You / Sure Would Be Nice - PD-14456 (US)
Baby, I'm Sold On You / Sure Would Be Nice - 2066 905 (France) (PS)

I Want To Give You My Everything / May Tomorrow Be A Perfect Day - PD-14474 (US)

1978

On The Shelf / Certified Honey - PD-14510 (US / Canada)
En La Repisa (On The Shelf) / Dame Tiempo (Gimme Some Time) - 75225 (Ecuador)

On The Shelf / Certified Honey - DPQ-6117 (Japan) (PS)

12" Singles:
On The Shelf (12") - Polydor - PRO 054 (US)
A1 - On The Shelf 4:28 / B1 - On The Shelf 4:28

2009

Vegas Love (Digital download only)

2011

The Good Life (Digital download only)

A Beautiful Life (Digital download only)

Donny and Marie during the run of their ABC-TV variety series in 1977.

JIMMY OSMOND
PS - Picture Sleeve

1969

Santa No Chimney / I Hope You Have A Very Merry Christmas - CBS/Sony - CBSA 82031 (Japan) (PS)

1970

My Little Darling / Peg O' My Heart - CD 62 (Japan) (PS)

Chuk Chuk / Jimmy's Lullaby - CD-90 (Japan) (PS)

Jingle Bells / I Saw Mommy Kissing Santa Claus - CD-94 (PS) (Japan)

1971

If Santa Were My Daddy / Silent Night - K14328 (US) (PS)
If Santa Were My Daddy / Silent Night - 2006 090 (Australia)
If Santa Were My Daddy / Silent Night - 2065 097 (Canada) (Polydor)

Jimmy's The Happy Robbers / I Found A Little Happiness - CD-103 (Japan) (PS)

Put Your Hand In the Hand* / Flirtin'+ - CD-1001 (Japan) (PS)
*Jimmy Osmond with Osmond Brothers / +Osmond Brothers

Goodbye Mr. Tears / Utopia - CD-1014-IN (Japan) (PS)

1972

Long Haired Lover From Liverpool / Mother of Mine - K 14376 (US)
Long Haired Lover From Liverpool / Mother of Mine - 2006-109 (UK)
Long Haired Lover From Liverpool / Mother of Mine - 2006 109 (Australia)
Long Haired Lover From Liverpool / Mother of Mine - 2006 109 (Belgium) (PS)
Long Haired Lover From Liverpool / Mother of Mine - 2006 109 (Ireland)
Long Haired Lover From Liverpool / Mother of Mine - 2006 109 (France) (PS)
Long Haired Lover From Liverpool / Mother of Mine - 2006 109 (Netherlands) (PS)
Long Haired Lover From Liverpool / Mother of Mine - 2065 111 (Canada) (Polydor)
Long Haired Lover From Liverpool / Mother of Mine - PS240 (South Africa)
Long Haired Lover From Liverpool / Mother of Mine - 2006 109 (Portugal) (PS)
Long Haired Lover From Liverpool / Mother of Mine - S 53 676 (Yugoslavia) (PS)
Long Haired Lover From Liverpool / Mother of Mine - 2006 109 (Spain) (PS)
Long Haired Lover From Liverpool / Mother of Mine - 2006 109 (India)

Tweedlee Dee/ Mama'd Know What To Do - K 14468 (US / Canada)
Tweedlee Dee/ Mama'd Know What To Do - 2006-175 (UK) (PS)
Tweedlee Dee/ Mama'd Know What To Do - PS-253 (South Africa) (PS)
Tweedlee Dee/ Mama'd Know What To Do - 2006 175 (New Zealand)
Tweedlee Dee/ Mama'd Know What To Do - 2006 175 (Netherlands) (PS)

Tweedlee Dee/ Mama'd Know What To Do - 2006 175 (Belgium) (PS)
Tweedlee Dee/ Mama'd Know What To Do - 2006 175 (Portugal) (PS)
Tweedlee Dee/ Mama'd Know What To Do - 2006 175 (Australia)
Tweedlee Dee/ Mama'd Know What To Do - 2006 175 (France) (PS)

Killer Joe / Let Me Be Your Teddy bear - 2006 279 (France) (PS)

She Is Good Lookin' / Bye Bye Suzanne (CD-1019-IN) (Japan) (PS)

1973

I'm Gonna Knock On Your Door / Good Ole Mammy Song - K 14687 (US / Canada)
I'm Gonna Knock On Your Door / Good Ole Mammy Song - S 53 762 (Yugoslavia) (PS)
I'm Gonna Knock On Your Door / Good Ole Mammy Song - 2006 389 (Belgium) (PS)
I'm Gonna Knock On Your Door / Good Ole Mammy Song - 2006 389 (Germany) (PS)
I'm Gonna Knock On Your Door / Good Ole Mammy Song - 2006 389 (New Zealand)
I'm Gonna Knock On Your Door / Good Ole Mammy Song - 2006 389 (Netherlands) (PS)
I'm Gonna Knock On Your Door / Good Ole Mammy Song - 2006 389 (France) (PS)
I'm Gonna Knock On Your Door / Good Ole Mammy Song - 2006 389 (UK) (PS)
I'm Gonna Knock On Your Door / Good Ole Mammy Song - 2006 389 (Australia)

Give Me A Good Old Mammy Song / I'm Gonna Knock On Your Door - DM-1252 (Japan) (PS)

Teddy Bear / Rubber Ball (Australia)

1974

*Yes Virginia, There Is A Santa Claus / If Santa Were My Daddy - M14770 (US)
(*Yes Virginia, There Is A Santa Claus is from the 1974 TV Special of the same name.)

Little Arrows / Don't You Remember - M 14771 (US / Canada)
Little Arrows / Don't You Remember - 2006 478 (Germany) (PS)
Little Arrows / Don't You Remember - 2006 478 (UK)
Little Arrows / Don't You Remember - 2006 478 (Netherlands) (PS)
Little Arrows / Don't You Remember - 2006 478 (New Zealand)
Little Arrows / Don't You Remember - 2006 478 (France) (PS)

1975

Little Arrows / Don't You Remember - 2006 478 (Australia)
Some Little Girl / Breakaway (From That Boy) - 2006 556 (UK)

1976

Swing Bike - SB-44145-2 (Promo - no label)
(This has the same rhythm as the 1976 Donny & Marie song "Sing.")

1978

*You're There / Life Is Just What You Make It Mercury - 74005 (US)
(*Theme from the motion picture "The Great Brain")

1980

*She Put The Light On / +Uncertain (Japan) - A.I.R. Broadcasting Corp - OSM-8681
*1974 / +1980 - +Produced by Donny Osmond.

1981

Ring Ring / After All - (Japan) - A.I.R. Broadcasting Corp - 07-5H-77 (PS)

Kimi Wa Pretty / Tokyo Savannah - (Japan) - A.I.R. Broadcasting Corp - (07-5H-93) (PS)

1982

Livin' In Love / One More Chance - 07-5H-113 - Epic Records (Japan) (PS)

1985

Ontonyo Y Primavera / Tu Me Haces Falta (Mexico)

2001

Shine / This Much I Know Is True / Long Haired Lover From Liverpool - ADCDS01 (UK)
(This was a special promotional CD that was made in England in 2001)

Jimmy enjoyed his time on The Donny & Marie Show as a frequent guest.

Extended Play (EP's)
Vinyl and CD

The Osmond Bothers / Be My Little Baby Bumble Bee
MGM-EP - EPD 126 (Sweden) 1964 (Picture Sleeve)
A1 - Be My Little Baby Bumble Bee / A2 - Down Our Way
B1 - By The Light Of The Silvery Moon / B2 - Bye Bye Blues

The Osmond Brothers / med Lasse Lönndahl
MGM-EP 7EGS 346 (Sweden) 1967 (Picture Sleeve)
A1 - Ovan Regnbagen / A2 - Huldas Karin
B1 - Du, Lasse Liten (W/ Lasse Lönndahl) / B2 - En Dag Fylld Av Kärlek (May Each Day) (W/ Lasse Lönndahl)

The Osmond Brothers / Merry X'mas
MGM-EP - KM-1082 (Japan) 1968 (Picture Sleeve)
A1 - Silent Night / A2 - Deck The Halls With Boughs Of Holly / A3 - Joy To The World
B1 - Jingle Bells / B2 - Christmas Means More Ev'ry Year / B3 - The First Noel & O Come All Ye Faithful

Calpis's Song / Moomin's Song
Calpis EP 1970 (Japan) (Picture Sleeve)
A1 - The Osmond Brothers Calpis Song
B1 - Yoshiko Fujita Moomin Song / B2 - Hiroyuki Nishimoto Snufkin Song

Christmas Holiday With The Osmonds
Denon-EP - CD-3001 (Japan) 1970 (Picture Sleeve)
A1 - Jingle Bells / A2 - White Christmas
B1 - Santa Claus Is Coming To Town / B2 - Silent Night

Jimmy Osmond / My Little Darling
Denon-EP - CD-3005 (Japan) 1970 (Picture Sleeve)
A1 - My Little Darling / A2 - Sha La La
B1 - Chuk Chuk / B2 - Jimmy's Lullaby

The Osmonds / One Bad Apple
MGM-EP - 2202008 (Portugal) 1970 (Picture Sleeve)
A1 - One Bad Apple / A2 - Think
B1 - Flirtin' / B2 - Most Of All

Donny Osmond / Hey Girl
MGM-EP - 2202 021 - (Singapore) 1971 (Picture Sleeve)
A1 - Hey Girl / A2 - I Knew You When
B1 - I'm Your Puppet / B2 - Burning Bridges

Donny Osmond /Sweet And Innocent
MGM-EP - 2202 024 - (Australia) 1971 (Picture Sleeve)
A1 - Sweet And Innocent / A2 - Go Away Little Girl
B1 - Hey Girl / B2 - Burning Bridges

The Osmonds / Down By The Lazy River
MGM-EP - 2202 028 - (Mexico) 1971 (Picture Sleeve)
A1 - Rio Abajo (Down By The Lazy River) / A2 - El Es La Luz Del Mondo (He's The Light Of The World)
B1 - Es Amor (Love Is) / B2 - En Lo Que Queda De Mi Vida (In The Rest Of My Life)

The Osmonds / Down By The Lazy River
MGM-EP - 2202 034 - (Australia) 1971 (Picture Sleeve)
A1 - Down By The Lazy River / A2 - He Ain't Heavy He's My Brother
B1 - One Bad Apple / B2 - Yo-Yo

Donny Osmond / Puppy Love
MGM-EP - 2202 035 - (France) 1972 (Picture Sleeve)
A1 - Puppy Love / A2 - Let My People Go
B1 - Too Young / B2 - Love Me

Donny Osmond / Too Young
MGM-EP - 2202 040 - (Brazil) 1971 (Picture Sleeve)
A1 - Too Young / A2 - Puppy Love
B1 - Love Me / B2 - Go Away Little Girl

Donny Osmond / The Osmonds
MGM-EP - 2202 046 - (Portugal) 1972 (Picture Sleeve)
A1 - Why / A2 - Lonely Boy - Donny Osmond
B1 - Crazy Horses / B2 - That's My Girl - The Osmonds

Jimmy Osmond / Mother of Mine
MGM-EP - 2218 - (Mexico) 1972 (Picture Sleeve)
A1 - Madre Mia / A2 - Soy Tu Titere
B1 - Soy Tu Titere / B2 - Puentes Quemados

Donny Osmond / Puppy Love
MGM-EP - 2202 047 - (Australia) 1972 (Picture Sleeve)
A1 - Puppy Love / A2 - Lonely Boy
B1 - Too Young / B2 - Why

Donny Osmond / Puppy Love
MGM-EP - POE-9 - (Bolivia) 1972 (Picture Sleeve)
A1 - Puppy Love / A2 - Going, Going Gone
B1 - Love Me / B2 - Let My People Go

The Osmonds / Crazy Horses
MGM-EP - 2202 058 - (Brazil) 1973 (Picture Sleeve)
A1 - Hold Her Tight / A2 - Hey, Mr. Taxi
B1 - Crazy Horses / B2 - That's My Girl

The Osmonds / Best 6
MGM-EP - 2005 - (Japan) 1973 (Picture Sleeve)
A1 - Crazy Horses / A2 - Hold Her Tight / A3 - Utah
B1 - One Bad Apple / Side B2 - Yo-Yo / B3 - Down By The Lazy River

Marie Osmond / Paper Roses
MGM-EP - 2202 061 - (Mexico) 1973 (Picture Sleeve)
A1 - Rosas De Papel (Paper Roses) / A2 - Cualquier Detalle Tuyo (Least Of All You)
B1 - Tonta No. 1 (Fool No. 1) / B2 - Todo Es Bello (Everything Is Beautiful)

The Osmonds / Goin' Home
MGM-EP - 2297 - (Mexico) 1973 (Picture Sleeve)
A1 - Yendo A Casa (Goin' Home) / A2 - Boleto De Ida A Cualquier Lugar (One Way Ticket Anywhere)
B1 - Estas Ahi Arriba (Are You Up There?) / B2 - Guerra En El Cielo (War In Heaven)

Donny Osmond / Young Love
MGM-EP - MGM-2359 - (Mexico) 1973 (Picture Sleeve)
A1 - Young Love (Amor Joven / A2 - Are You Lonesome Tonight (¿Estas Sola Esta Noche?)
B1 - A Time For Us ("Romeo Y Julieta) / B2 - The Twelfth Of Never (Hasta El Final Del Tiempo)

The Osmonds / Love Me For A Reason
MGM-EP - 2202 076 - (Mexico) 1975 (Picture Sleeve)
A1 - Una Razón Para Amar (Love Me For A Reason) / A2 - Caballos Locos (Crazy Horses)
B1 - Rio Bajo (Down By The Lazy River) / B2 - Abrazala Fuertemente (Hold Her Tight)

Donny Osmond / Disco Train
Polydor-EP - POE-11078 - (Bolivia) 1976 (Picture Sleeve)
A1 - C'Mon Marianne / A2 - Disco Train
B1 - I'M Dyin' / B2 - Disco Dancin'

Donny & Marie / Winning Combination
Polydor-EP - POE-11083 - (Bolivia) 1977 (Picture Sleeve)
A1 - (You're My) Soul And Inspiration / A2 - I Want To Be In Your World
B1 - Winning Combination / B2 - I Want To Give You My Everything

Donny Osmond / Four
Nightstar Records -70002-2 / CD - (US) 1997
1.) The Echo Of Your Whisper
2.) And Still Run Out Of Time
3.) What Shall I Do?
4.) What You Won't Do For Love

Marie Osmond / Stocking Stuffer
HiFi Recordings, LLC / CD - (US) 2007
1.) White Christmas
2.) Sleigh Ride
3.) Have Yourself A Merry Little Christmas
4.) It's Beginning To Look A Lot Like Christmas / Pine Cones And Holly Berries
5.) My Favorite Things
    (Five Track Promo EP for purchase of Marie's *Magic Of Christmas* album through QVC)

Unknown Singles
Beauty And The Sweet Talk / Good News - The Osmond Brothers (Japan)
*Go Away Little Girl / +Yo Yo - *Donny Osmond +Osmond Brothers (Picture Disc from Japan)
Someone To Go Home To / Where Are You Going To My Love - The Osmonds (UK)
Double Lovin' / Crazy Horses - The Osmonds
Secret Love / Message - Jimmy Osmond (Japan)
Stayin' Alive - Donny Osmond with Dweezil Zappa 1991
Now I Know - Suzy K and Donny Osmond 2000

Osmond Related Singles:

We Can Make It Together* / E Fini - Steve Lawrence and Eydie Gorme (*Featuring The Osmond Brothers) K-14383 (US / Canada) 1972 (PS) *Written by: A. Osmond, M. Osmond, W. Osmond

We Can Make It Together* / E Fini - Steve Lawrence and Eydie Gorme (*Featuring The Osmond Brothers) 2006 137 (UK / Netherlands) 1972 (PS) *Written by: A. Osmond, M. Osmond, W. Osmond

And You Love Me* Petula Clark (Featuring The Osmond Brothers) 73-L-58?? MGM 1975 *Written and produced by Wayne Osmond. (Going by the master # this was likely recorded in 1973. The "L" in the number signifies this master was stored in Los Angeles and may have been lost in the Universal Studios fire on June 1, 2008.)

*Heartache Tonight / Hello Darlin' - Conway Twitty (*Featuring the Osmond Brothers) Recorded February 1–2, 1983 at Sound Stage Studio, Nashville, Tennessee. Released on Warner Bros. Records in August 1983. (WB7-29505)

Other Known Recordings:

THE OSMONDS "GUEST STAR" GXTV-108244 (1006) 7-4-1966. Host: Merv Griffin.
This is on a record from The Treasury Department / US Savings Bonds.

An album from The Osmond Brothers for Warner Brothers Records was recorded in Nashville and St. Louis and tentatively titled "Yes Ma'am" but was rejected by the label. All the material has been issued on singles.

There is at least one unreleased Osmond album from Mercury Records, but I could not find song titles or recording dates in time for publication. This could be The Great Brain album.

Marie recorded a demo prior to signing with MGM Records of "Coat of Many Colors" written by Dolly Parton that has never been heard by anyone outside the business… unfortunately. Also Donny & Marie recorded a demo of "Where Is The Love" that has never been released.

The Osmonds — What's It All About? - TRAV – 22775 - 1972 (US) This release is a 45RPM of the Osmonds being interviewed by Bill Huie for Presbyterian Church for public AM broadcast. Also has snippets of their song Crazy Horses.

Osmonds World Magazine Welcome Message - LYN 2705 - November 1973. The Osmonds talk about their new magazine. Made in England. Single sided 7" flexi-disc.

Personal Christmas Message To Members Of The Official Fan Club Europe - LYN 2753 December 1973. Made in England. Single sided 7" flexi-disc.

The Osmonds — All About Love
Cardboard 7" with band picture and corresponding member names, and the words "Each Osmond tells you personally, in his own words, what LOVE means to him!" This is thought to have come from TigerBeat Magazine in 1971.

The Osmonds — Everything You Always Wanted To Know About The Osmond Brothers.
This is an interview LP from SuperStar Records (SSR-201) that contains such ditties as Their Music, Their Magic, Their Secret Passions and what happened to Jimmy in Japan! I wonder if it was when he broke his arm in a revolving door? 1972

Other recordings made by various family members and possibly shelved:

Gotcha Goin' My Way / Music Through The Ages / I'm So Glad / Feelin' Alright / Old Cape Cod / Say Wonderful Things.

For the 1976 Osmond Christmas Album these songs were recorded and initially shelved:
*These recordings were finally issued on the heavily edited Curb Records release of the Osmond Family Christmas Album that contained only 10 songs and was released in 1991.
A Very Merry Christmas - Master #: 76-L-2181 - (Merrill vocal)
*The Christmas Waltz - Master #: 76-L-2184 - (Family)
*Winter Wonderland - Master #: 76-L-2169 Re-1 - US Promo (radio single edit version)

Also of note concerning 1970's Osmond Christmas material. Jimmy has recorded "If Santa Were My Daddy" three times- 1971, 1974 and 1976!

We're Gettin' Together - 21677AS (Mattel, Inc. 9830-9029) Sold with the 1976 Donny & Marie TV Show Playset by Mattel. Has an original song and skits for use with the dolls.

Mother and Father Osmond were rumored to have done some recording and though I have seen pictures of father Osmond in the recording studio standing before the microphone I have not been able to locate any releases. It could have been only issued on cassette tape through the fan club.

In 1984 Donny recorded an album with Grammy winning producer **Jay Graydon** with a working title of "411" that remains unreleased. Jay also played guitar on many of the Osmonds recordings such as: Old Man Auctioneer, Don't Need No Money, I Got Your Lovin', Let It Be Me, It Takes Two, Jigsaw, Ain't Nothing Like The Real Thing, It's All Been Said Before, Which Way You Goin' Billy, Show Me, Hold Me, Thrill Me, Kiss Me, We Got Love, Oh, Sweet Lovin', (You're My) Soul And Inspiration, On The Shelf, Don't Play With The One Who Loves You, You Don't Have To Say You Love Me, Gimme Some Time, Let's Fall In Love, Let Me In, I Can't Live A Dream, Boogie Down, It'll Be Me, Check It Out.

As well as many unreleased Osmond titles such as: Believin' In Love (Osmond Brothers), Dancin' Man (Donny Osmond), You Betcha (Donny Osmond), Sugar Candy (Donny & Marie), Can't Help Falling In Love (Donny & Marie), Can't Stop Loving You (Donny & Marie), Rhythm of the Rain (Donny & Marie. Recorded two different times July 14 and 24, 1978!), Don't You Love It (Donny & Marie). See the listing at back of the book for the recording session information on these and many other unreleased gems! Jay Graydon was also in the "house band" for the Donny & Marie Show for one season!

Sometime back in the very late 1990's and by way of my old Osmond web page I was contacted by Jay Graydon's assistant, Kerstin, who wrote to me for a while for help when Jay was researching some of his past session work. They were curious if I knew about some song titles...had they been released? Reading the titles I replied that the songs were likely shelved, since I had not heard of them. She replied:

"Thanks for your kind responses, Daniel! Yea, I suspected that these songs Jay and I are trying to track down (mentioned above) **were likely just shelved after the sessions for some reason. Maybe we'll hear them some day... One thing that is puzzling though is "Rhythm of the Rain" since it was recorded at two sessions (July 14 and 24, 1978) and then just never released! Seems like such a waste of time** (and money) **recording material and then just never using it!**

You have a fantastic website for Donny & Marie and the Osmond Family. If you have direct contact with them please give them Jay's best! I know for a fact Jay thinks Donny is one of the *best* singers of all time and he only has three on his list of great voices!"

I know many of you readers will agree with Jay Graydon. I do as well, but I would also have to include **Marie** in that category of great American voices in music! Their talent is in-born! Phenomenal!

There is no further information available on the album and I am unaware of what label it may have been recorded for or released on. Sheet music scans I have from the sessions do not give this information.

The Bootlegs:

Every popular group has been bootlegged. The Osmond's more so than most. Bootlegs are unauthorized copies of records made in just about every country, including the US. Here are pictures of a few bootleg Osmond records in my collection. I don't have many. The only reason I bought these, decades after they were made, were for the graphics.

Recording Information: Master #'s, Dates and <u>Release #'s</u>

About Master #'s: L= Los Angeles / N= Nashville / NY= New York / NP= New York Polydor.

So for example— "73-L-5321" is for the song "Paper Roses." It shows it was recorded in 1973 and the original master is stored in Los Angeles. 5321 is the master catalog # used to store the tape for easy retrieval in the mast tape vault. I'm unsure what "XY" stands for as shown in Master #'s 5 — 58. Here you will find a wealth of unreleased titles! Sadly a lot of these masters could have perished in the June 1, 2008 Universal fire that destroyed hundreds of thousands of master recordings, many unreleased.

If the "Album/45" column is blank that means the song likely went unreleased or I did not have the information at the time of publication. Why time and money is spend recording a song and then never releasing it (even later as bonus material) is beyond me. Most sessions last three hours or more and at least three songs are recorded during a live session.

As you will see below Marie herself has at least twelve (*12!*) unreleased songs from her first solo recording sessions in Nashville. **That kills me!** A whole album could have been edited together and released in 1976 to make a US solo 1976 Marie album to bridge the gap between 1975's "Who's Sorry Now" and 1977's "This Is The Way That I Feel." I can't believe having heard the songs released from those early sessions that those still unreleased could sound anything other than *spectacular!* But unfortunately I've come to find through the years in the music business it is all about money. The record labels in truth do not care about the consumers… only their wallets. I can no longer recall where this information came from since so many people sent me information via email and snail mail so many years ago!

	A	B	C	D	E	F
1	Master #	Title	Artist	Recording Date	Album/45	Time
2	UNIVERSAL MUSIC ENTERPRISES					
3	Masters From MGM, MGM Sweden, UNI, Osbro/Kolob, Polydor, Mercury, Mercury Japan, Decca & Island/Def Jam!					
4	Note: All Japanese Language Denon and Live In Tokyo still are owned by Denon Japan.					
5	63-XY-29	Kentucky Babe	Osmond Bros	18-Apr-63	4146	
6	63-XY-30	Be My Little Baby Bumble Bee	Osmond Bros	18-Apr-63	4146	02:22
7	63-XY-30	Be My Little Baby Bumble Bee (mono single edit)	Osmond Bros	18-Apr-63	4146	01:53
8	63-XY-31	Keep Your Eye On The Girlie You Love	Osmond Bros	18-Apr-63	4146	
9	63-XY-32	Just A Song At Twilight	Osmond Bros	18-Apr-63	4146	
10	63-XY-33	Mighty Lak A Rose	Osmond Bros	18-Apr-63	4146	
11	63-XY-34	Bye Bye Blues	Osmond Bros	25-Apr-63	4146	
12	63-XY-35	By The Light Of The Silvery Moon	Osmond Bros	25-Apr-63	4146	
13	63-XY-36	Down Our Way	Osmond Bros	25-Apr-63	4146	
14	63-XY-37	In The Good Old Summertime	Osmond Bros	25-Apr-63	4146	
15	63-XY-38	Aura Lee	Osmond Bros	25-Apr-63	4146	
16	63-XY-39	I Wouldn't Trade The Silver In My Mother's Hair	Osmond Bros	29-Apr-63	4146	
17	63-XY-40	Take Me Back To Babyland	Osmond Bros	29-Apr-63	4146	
18	63-?? OM7	Preview	Osmond Bros		PM-9	
19	63-XY-84	Theme From "The Travels Of Jamie Mc Pheeters"	Osmond Bros	19-Aug-63	13174	
20	63-XY-85	The Little Drummer Boy	Osmond Bros	19-Aug-63	4187	
21	63-XY-86	Christmas Means More Ev'ry Year	Osmond Bros	19-Aug-63	4187	
22	63-XY-87	Winter Wonderland	Osmond Bros	19-Aug-63	4187	
23	63-XY-88	Silent Night, Holy Night	Osmond Bros	19-Aug-63	4187	
24	63-XY-89	Deck The Hall With Boughs Of Holly	Osmond Bros	19-Aug-63	4187	
25	63-XY-90	White Christmas	Osmond Bros	19-Aug-63	4187	
26	63-XY-91	The First Noel / O Come All Ye Faithful	Osmond Bros	19-Aug-63	4187	
27	63-XY-92	Jingle Bells	Osmond Bros	12-Sep-63	4187	
28	63-XY-93	Santa, No Chimney	Osmond Bros	12-Sep-63	4187	
29	63-XY-94	O Little Town Of Bethlehem	Osmond Bros	12-Sep-63	4187	
30	63-XY-95	Joy To The World	Osmond Bros	12-Sep-63	4187	
31	64-XY-67	My Task	Osmond Bros	8-May-64	4235	
32	64-XY-68	Whispering Hope	Osmond Bros	8-May-64	4235	
33	64-XY-69	Come, Come Ye Saints	Osmond Bros	8-May-84	4235	
34	64-XY-70	In The Garden	Osmond Bros	8-May-64	4235	
35	64-XY-71	Now The Day Is Over	Osmond Bros	8-May-64	4235	
36	64-XY-72	Oh, My Father	Osmond Bros	8-May-64	4235	
37	64-XY-73	Softly And Tenderly	Osmond Bros	8-May-64	4235	
38	64-XY-74	Abide With Me	Osmond Bros	8-May-64	4235	
39	64-XY-75	At The End Of The Road	Osmond Bros	8-May-64	4235	
40	64-XY-76	Softly Now, The Light Of Day	Osmond Bros	8-May-64	4235	
41	64-XY-77	Lead Me Gently Home Father	Osmond Bros	8-May-64	4235	
42	64-XY-78	I Need Thee Ev'ry Hour	Osmond Bros	8-May-64	4235	
43	64-XY-119	Mister Sandman	Osmond Bros	20-Jul-64	4291	
44	64-XY-120	My Mom	Osmond Bros	20-Jul-64	4291	
45	65-XY-10	Ragtime Cowboy Joe	Osmond Bros	17-Mar-65	4291	
46	65-XY-11	Life Is Just A Bowl Of Cherries	Osmond Bros	30-Mar-65	4291	
47	65-XY-12	Sing A Rainbow	Osmond Bros	17-Mar-65	4291	
48	65-XY-13	When The Red, Red Robin Comes Bob, Bob Bobbin' Along	Osmond Bros	17-Mar-65	4291	
49	65-XY-14	May Each Day	Osmond Bros	17-Mar-65	4291	
50	65-XY-15	Chim Chim Cher-ee	Osmond Bros	30-Mar-65	4291	

	A	B	C	D	E	F
1	Master #	Title	Artist	Recording Date	Album/45	Time
51	65-XY-16	Downtown	Osmond Bros	30-Mar-65	4291	
52	65-XY-17	That's What I Want	Osmond Bros	30-Mar-65	4291	
53	65-XY-18	Hello! Dolly	Osmond Bros	30-Mar-65	4291	
54	65-XY-19	Sweet And Low	Osmond Bros	30-Mar-65	4291	
55	65-XY-20	unknown title	Osmond Bros			
56	65-XY-21	unknown title	Osmond Bros			
57	65-XY-22	unknown title	Osmond Bros			
58	65-XY-23	unknown title	Osmond Bros			
59	65-LSW-1	Fem Smutsiga Sma Fingreg (Five Sticky Fingers)	Osmond Bros		6587	
60	65-LSW-2	A Janta, A Ja	Osmond Bros		6587	
61	. 034	Flower Music	Osmond Bros	May-67	55015	
62	. 035	I Can't Stop	Osmond Bros	May-67	55015	03:03
63	*Note: most of the above songs were recorded in both mono and stereo!!!!*					
64	70-L-1365	Movin' Along	Osmond Bros	5-Apr-70	14159/J	
65	70-L-1366	Taking On A Big Thing	Osmond Bros	5-Apr-70		
66	70-L-1385	Open Up Your Heart	Osmond Bros	6-Apr-70	14159/J	
67		Golden Rainbows			J	
68		Keep The Customer Satisfied			J	
69		Raindrops Keep Fallin' On My Head			J	
70		Bridge Over Troubled Water			J	
71		Scarborough Fair			J	
72		Aquarius/Let The Sunshine In			J	
73		Greensleeves			J	
74		Santa Claus Is Coming To Town	Osmonds		4744/J	
75		Rudolph The Red-Nosed Reindeer	Osmonds		4744/J	
76		This Christmas Eve	Osmonds		4744/J	
77		Silent Night	Osmonds		4744/J	
78		Jingle Bells	Osmonds		4744/J	
79		O Come All Ye Faithful	Osmonds		4744/J	
80		I Saw Mommy Kissing Santa Claus	Osmonds		4744/J	
81		Blue Christmas	Osmonds		4744/J	
82		God Rest Ye Merry Gentlemen	Osmonds		4744/J	
83		The Night Before Christmas	Osmonds		4744/J	
84	70-L-1742	One Bad Apple (Merrill & Donny Lead)	Osmond Bros	26-Oct-70	4724	02:48
85	70-L-1742	One Bad Apple (Merrill Lead)	Osmond Bros	26-Oct-70		
86	70-L-1742	One Bad Apple (Donny Lead)	Osmond Bros	26-Oct-70		
87	70-L-1743	Flirtin'	Osmond Bros	26-Oct-70	4724/82	
88	70-L-1838	Lonesome They Call Me, Lonesome I Am	Osmonds	10-Nov-70	4724	
89	70-L-1839	Catch Me Baby	Osmonds	10-Nov-70	4724	
90	70-L-1840	Sweet And Innocent	Osmonds	10-Nov-70	4724/82	03:05
91	70-L-1840 Rev 1	Sweet And Innocent (mono enhanced single edit)	Osmonds/Donny	10-Nov-70	4724/82	02:49
92	70-L-1841	(Would It Make You) Think	Osmonds	10-Nov-70	4724	
93	70-L-1842	He Ain't Heavy... He's My Brother	Osmonds	10-Nov-70	4724	03:58
94	70-L-1843	Holly For The Holidays	Osmonds	10-Nov-70		
95	70-L-1844	Sign Of The Dove	Osmonds	10-Nov-70		
96	70-L-1845	Most Of All	Osmonds	10-Nov-70	4724	
97	70-L-1846	Find 'Em, Fool 'Em and Forget 'Em	Osmonds	10-Nov-70	4724	
98	70-L-1893	Santa, No Chimney	Jimmy	9-Nov-70	4744/J	
99	70-L-1894	I Hope You Have A Very Merry Christmas	Jimmy	9-Nov-70	4744/J	

	A	B	C	D	E	F
1	Master #	Title	Artist	Recording Date	Album/45	Time
100	70-L-1896	Motown Special	Osmonds	13-Nov-70	4770	
101	71-L-2160	Double Lovin'	Osmonds	16-Feb-71	4770	02:37
102	71-L-2161	Shuckin' And Jivin'	Osmonds	16-Feb-71	4770	
103	71-L-2164	Carrie	Osmonds	16-Feb-71	4770	
104	71-L-2165	The Promised Land	Osmonds	16-Feb-71	4770	
105	71-L-2166	If You're Gonna Leave Me	Osmonds	17-Feb-71	4770	
106	71-L-2167	Sho' Would Be Nice	Osmonds	17-Feb-71	4770	
107	71-L-2168	She Makes Me Warm	Osmonds	18-Feb-71	4770	
108	71-L-2169	We Never Said Forever	Osmonds	18-Feb-71	4770	
109	71-L-2170	Chilly Winds	Osmonds	20-Feb-71	4770	03:00
110	71-L-2170	Chilly Winds (alternate mix)	Osmonds	20-Feb-71		
111	71-L-2170	Chilly Winds (movie version)	Osmonds	20-Feb-71		
112	71-L-2381	The Honey Bee Song (A Taste Of Honey)	Osmonds	21-Feb-71	4770	
113		Put Your Hand In The Hand	Jimmy		J	
114	71-L-2414	Hey Little Johnny	Donny	May-71	4797	
115	71-L-2415	I'm Your Puppet	Donny	May-71	4782	
116	71-L-2416	Hey Little Girl	Donny	May-71	4782	
117	71-L-2417	Don't Say No	Donny	May-71	4782	
118	71-L-2418	So Shy	Donny	May-71	4782	
119	71-L-2419	Lollipops, Lace and Lipstick	Donny	May-71	4782	
120	71-L-2420	Go Away Little Girl	Donny	May-71	4797	02:42
121	71-L-2420	Go Away Little Girl (single edit)	Donny	May-71	14285	02:23
122	71-L-2421	Burning Bridges	Donny	May-71	4782	
123	71-L-2422	Wild Rover, The (Time To Ride)	Donny	May-71	4782	
124	71-L-2423	Wake Up Little Susie	Donny	May-71	4782	
125	71-L-2579	Yo-Yo (album version)	Osmonds	21-Jun-71	4796	03:16
126	71-L-2579	Yo-You (mono single edit)	Osmonds	21-Jun-71	14295	02:50
127	71-L-2580	A Taste Of Ryhytm And Blues	Osmonds	21-Jun-71	4796	
128	71-L-2581	Don't Shut Me Out	Osmonds	21-Jun-71		
129	71-L-2582	Lay It Down	Osmonds	21-Jun-71		
130	71-L-2583	Keep On My Side (stereo mix)	Osmonds	22-Jun-71		
131	71-L-2583 M	Keep On My Side (mono single mix)	Osmonds	22-Jun-71	14295	
132	71-L-2708	Standing In The Need Of Love	Donny	7-Sep-71	4797	
133	71-L-2709	Sit Down, I Think I Love You	Donny	7-Sep-71	4797	
134	71-L-2710	All I Have To Do Is Dream	Donny	7-Sep-71	4820	
135	71-L-2711	I'm Into Something Good	Donny	7-Sep-71	4797	
136	71-L-2712	Bye Bye Love	Donny	8-Sep-71	4797	
137	71-L-2713	Sit Down, I Think I Love You (alternate version)	Donny	8-Sep-71	4797	
138	71-L-2714	A Little Bit Me, A Little Bit You	Donny	8-Sep-71	4797	
139	71-L-2715	I Knew You When	Donny	10-Sep-71	4797	02:50
140	71-L-2716	Big Man	Donny	10-Sep-71	4820	
141	71-L-2717	Hey Girl	Donny	10-Sep-71	4820	03:14
142	71-L-2717	Hey Girl (single edit)	Donny	10-Sep-71	14322	03:06
143	71-L-2718	Finders Aren't Always Keepers	Donny	10-Sep-71		
144	71-L-2719	Little Bit	Donny	10-Sep-71	4797	
145	71-L-2724	Don't Panic	Osmonds	29-Jul-71	4796	
146	71-L-2725	Down By The Lazy River	Osmonds	29-Jul-71	4796	02:53
147	71-L-2725 M	Down By The Lazy River (mono single edit)	Osmonds	29-Jul-71	14324	02:37
148	71-L-2726	Everybody	Osmonds	29-Jul-71		

	A	B	C	D	E	F
1	Master #	Title	Artist	Recording Date	Album/45	Time
149	71-L-2727	We Can Make It Together	Osmonds	29-Jul-71		
150	71-L-2734	We Can Make It Together (Do You Want Me?)	Donny	24-Sep-71	4797	
151	71-L-2746	Business	Osmonds	20-Sep-71	4796	
152	71-L-2747	Sho' Would Be Nice	Osmonds	20-Sep-71		
153	71-L-2748	It's A Blue World	Osmonds	20-Sep-71		
154	71-L-2749	Hear Ye Hymn	Osmonds	20-Sep-71		
155	71-L-2780	If Santa Were My Daddy	Jimmy	Sep-71	14328	
156	71-L-2785	Silent Night	Jimmy	Sep-71	14328	
157	71-L-2832	Bleib Bei Mir Little Girl (Go Away Little Girl)	Donny	24-Sep-71	2006 089	02:32
158	71-L-2833	Sweet And Innocent (Deutsch)	Donny	24-Sep-71		
159	71-L-2868	Hey There Lonely Girl	Donny	20-Sep-71	4820	
160	71-L-2869	Puppy Love	Donny	20-Sep-71	4820	03:09
161	71-L-2869	Puppy Love (single edit)	Donny	20-Sep-71	14367	02:58
162	71-L-2871	Love Is	Osmonds	25-Sep-71	4796	
163	71-L-2872	My Drum	Osmonds	25-Sep-71	4796	
164	71-L-2902	We Can Make It Together	Steve & Eydie	9-Nov-71	4803/81	
165	71-L-2902 M	We Can Make It Together (mono single edit)	Steve & Eydie	9-Nov-71	14438	
166	71-L-2955	He's The Light Of The World	Osmonds	1-Nov-71	4796	
167	71-L-2955 M	He's The Light Of The World (mono mix)	Osmonds	1-Nov-71	14324	
168	71-L-2956	It's You Babe	Osmonds	1-Nov-71	4796	
169	71-L-2966	In The Rest Of My Life	Osmonds	8-Dec-71	4796	
170	71-L-3014	Why	Donny	8-Dec-71	4854	02:47
171	71-L-3015	Last Of The Red Hot Lovers	Donny	8-Dec-71	4854	02:27
172	72-L-3109	Let My People Go	Donny	Jan-72	4820	
173	72-L-3159	This Guy's In Love With You	Donny	2-Feb-72	4820	
174	72-L-3160	Going Going Gone (To Somebody Else)	Donny	2-Feb-72	4820	
175	72-L-3161	Don't You Remember	Osmonds	2-Feb-72		
176	72-L-3162	Osmond Special (Live)	Osmonds	27-Dec-71	4826	
177	72-L-3163	Motown Special Medley (Live)	Osmonds	27-Dec-71	4826	
178	72-L-3164	Double Lovin' (Live)	Osmonds	27-Dec-71	4826	
179	72-L-3165	Your Song (Live)	Donny	27-Dec-71	4826	
180	72-L-3166	Sweet And Innocent (Live)	Donny	27-Dec-71	4826	
181	72-L-3167	You've Lost That Lovin' Feelin' (Live)	Wayne	27-Dec-71	4826	
182	72-L-3168	Proud Mary/Free (Live)	Jay	27-Dec-71	4826	
183	72-L-3169	Free	Jay	27-Dec-71	4826	
184	72-L-3170	Go Away Little Girl (live)	Donny	27-Dec-71	4826	
185	72-L-3171	Sometimes I Feel Like A Motherless Child/Where Could I Go But To The Lord/Everytime I Feel The Spirit (Live)	Osmonds	27-Dec-71	4826	
186	72-L-3172	We Gotta Live Together (Live)	Osmonds	27-Dec-71	4826	
187	72-L-3173	Trouble/I Got A Woman (Live)	Little Jimmy	27-Dec-71	4826	
188	72-L-3174	I Got A Woman	Little Jimmy	27-Dec-71	4826	
189	72-L-3175	Hey Girl (Live)	Donny	27-Dec-71	4826	
190	72-L-3176	Down By The Lazy River (Live)	Osmonds	27-Dec-71	4826	
191	72-L-3177	Yo-Yo (Live)	Osmonds	27-Dec-71	4826	
192	72-L-3178	One Bad Apple (Live)	Osmonds	27-Dec-71	4826	
193	72-L-3197	Mother Of Mine	Little Jimmy	Jan-72	4855	
194	72-L-3198	My Father Told So	Little Jimmy	Jan-72 J		
195	72-L-3226	Long Haired Lover From Liverpool	Little Jimmy		4855	
196	72-L-3273	Donna	Donny	9-Feb-72	4854	

	A	B	C	D	E	F
1	Master #	Title	Artist	Recording Date	Album/45	Time
197	72-L-3274	I've Got Plans For You	Donny	9-Feb-72	4820	02:18
198	72-L-3275	Pretty Blue Eyes	Donny	20-Sep-71	4854	
199	72-L-3276	Promise Me	Donny	2-Mar-72	4820	
200	72-L-3277	Love Me	Donny	2-Mar-72	4820	
201	72-L-3320	Your World	Osmonds	17-Mar-72		
202	72-L-3321	Somewhere	Osmonds	17-Mar-72		
203	72-L-3322	And You Love Me	Osmonds	17-Mar-72	4851	
204	72-L-3367	Morning Light	Osmonds	27-Mar-72		
205	72-L-3368	What Could It Be	Osmonds	27-Mar-72	4851	03:12
206	72-L-3438	Anybody Out There?	Osmonds	17-Mar-72		
207	72-L-3439	Julie	Osmonds	21-Mar-72	4851	
208	72-L-3440	Hold Her Tight	Osmonds	21-Mar-72	4851	03:18
209	72-L-3440	Hold Her Tight (single edit)	Osmonds	21-Mar-72	14405	03:07
210	72-L-3441	Girl	Osmonds	21-Mar-72	4851	03:38
211	72-L-3441	Girl (edit)	Osmonds	21-Mar-72		02:45
212	72-L-3481	Movie Man	Osmonds	15-Apr-72	4902	03:36
213	72-L-3484	A Teenager In Love	Donny	17-Apr-72	4854	
214	72-L-3485	Unchained Melody	Donny	17-Apr-72	4930	
215	72-L-3486	Too Young	Donny	17-Apr-72	4854	03:10
216	72-L-3517	Mama'd Know What To Do	Little Jimmy	10-May-72	4855	
217	72-L-3518	If My Dad Were President	Little Jimmy	10-May-72	4855	
218	72-L-3522	Little Girls Are Fun	Little Jimmy	10-May-72	4855	
219	72-L-3523	That's My Girl	Osmonds	3-May-72	4851	03:15
220	72-L-3524	Rubber Ball	Little Jimmy	3-May-72	4855	
221	72-L-3536	Let Me Be Your Teddy Bear	Little Jimmy	1-May-72	4855	
222	72-L-3537	Tweedlee Dee	Little Jimmy	1-May-72	4855	03:33
223	72-L-3537 M	Tweedlee Dee (mono radio mix)	Little Jimmy	1-May-72	14468	02:00
224	72-L-3538	Killer Joe	Little Jimmy	1-May-72	4855	
225	72-L-3666	To Run Away	Donny	Jun-72	4854	
226	72-L-3667	Lonely Boy	Donny	Jun-72	4854	02:57
227	72-L-3668	Run To Him	Donny	8-Nov-71	4854	
228	72-L-3669	Take Good Care Of My Baby	Donny	9-Nov-71	4854	
229	72-L-3719	Crazy Horses	Osmonds	23-Jun-72	4851	02:40
230	72-L-3720	Utah	Osmonds	23-Jun-72	4851	
231	72-L-3721	Hey, Mr. Taxi	Osmonds	23-Jun-72	4851	
232	72-L-3722	We All Fall Down	Osmonds	23-Jun-72	4851	
233	72-L-3736	Life Is Hard Enough Without Goodbyes	Osmonds	23-Jun-72	4851	
234	72-L-3737	Big Finish	Osmonds	23-Jun-72	4851	
235	72-L-3865	Sunshine Rose	Donny	31-Aug-72	4886	
236	72-L-3866	The Other Side Of Me	Donny	31-Aug-72	4886	
237	72-L-3867	Who Can I Turn To?	Donny	31-Aug-72	4886	
238	72-L-3868	The Tears On My Pillow	Donny	31-Aug-72	4886	
239	72-L-4078	My Girl	Little Jimmy	3-May-72	4855	
240	72-L-4511	Young Love	Donny	27-Nov-72	4886	02:35
241	72-L-4511	Young Love (single edit)	Donny	27-Nov-72	14583	02:18
242	72-L-4512	The Twelfth Of Never	Donny	27-Nov-72	4886	02:44
243	72-L-4513	A Million To One	Donny	27-Nov-72	4930	03:02
244	72-L-4514	Lovin' You Could Be So Easy	Donny	27-Nov-72		
245	72-L-4538	Life Is Just What You Make It	Donny	1-Dec-72	4886	

	Master #	Title	Artist	Recording Date	Album/45	Time
246	72-L-4539	Do You Want Me?	Donny	1-Dec-72	4886	
247	72-L-4540	It Takes A Lot Of Love	Donny	1-Dec-72	4886	
248	72-L-4541	It's Hard To Say Goodbye	Donny	1-Dec-72	4886	
249	73-L-4802	Traffic In My Mind	Osmonds	7-Feb-73	4902	03:55
250	73-L-4895	Are You Up There ? (version 2)	Osmonds	5-Mar-73	4902	04:43
251	73-L-4896	Darlin'	Osmonds	5-Mar-73	4902	03:11
252	73-L-4897	Mirror, Mirror	Osmonds	5-Mar-73	4902	02:25
253	73-L-4902	Before The Beginning	Osmonds	7-Mar-73	4902	04:06
254	73-L-4903	Let Me In	Osmonds	7-Mar-73	4902	03:39
255	73-L-5161	Goin' Home	Osmonds	Apr-73	4902	02:29
256	73-L-5161 M	Goin' Home (mono single edit)	Osmonds	Apr-73	14562	02:10
257	73-L-5162	War In Heaven	Osmonds	Apr-73	4902	01:40
258	73-L-5163	One Way Ticket To Anywhere	Osmonds	Apr-73	4902	03:08
259	73-L-5164	It's Allright	Osmonds	Apr-73	4902	02:37
260	73-L-5165	The Last Days	Osmonds	Apr-73	4902	03:01
261	73-L-5321	Paper Roses	Marie	7-Jun-73	4910	02:42
262	73-L-5321 M	Paper Roses (mono radio mix)	Marie	7-Jun-73	14609	02:39
263	73-L-5322	In My Little Corner Of The World	Marie	7-Jun-73	4944	02:52
264	73-L-5322 M	In My Little Corner Of The World (mono radio mix)	Marie	7-Jun-73	14694	02:48
265	73-L-5323	Louisiana Bayou	Marie	8-Jun-73	4910	02:20
266	73-L-5326	Too Many Rivers	Marie	8-Jun-73	4910	
267	73-L-5327	You're The Only World I Know	Marie	8-Jun-73	4910	02:19
268	73-L-5328	Sweet Dreams	Marie	8-Jun-73	4910	
269	73-L-5329	It's Such A Pretty World Today	Marie	8-Jun-73	4910	
270	73-L-5330	True Love Last Forever	Marie	8-Jun-73	4910	03:18
271	73-L-5331	Everything Is Beautiful	Marie	8-Jun-73	4910	
272	73-L-5332	Fool Number One	Marie	6-Jun-73	4910	02:10
273	73-L-5333	Least Of All You	Marie	6-Jun-73	4910	02:41
274		*The Plan album radio spot*				
275	73-L-5437	A Time For Us	Donny	18-Jul-73	4930	
276	73-L-5438	Are You Lonesome Tonight?	Donny	18-Jul-73	4930	03:12
277	73-L-5439	I Believe	Donny	18-Jul-73	4930	
278	73-L-5440	Hawaiian Wedding Song	Donny	18-Jul-73	4930	
279	73-L-5441	A Boy Is Waiting	Donny	19-Jul-73	4930	
280	73-L-5442	When I Fall In Love	Donny	19-Jul-73	4930	03:00
281	73-L-5443	Young And In Love	Donny	19-Jul-73	4930	
282	73-L-5444	Guess Who	Donny	19-Jul-73	4930	
283	73-L-5479	Purple People Eater	Jimmy	20-Jul-73	4916	
284	73-L-5480	I'm Gonna Knock On Your Door	Jimmy	20-Jul-73	4916	
285	73-L-5481	Give Me A Good Ole Mammy Song	Jimmy	20-Jul-73	4916	
286	73-L-5751	Day O	Jimmy	13-Oct-73	4916	
287	73-L-5752	*Hang On Sloopy*	Jimmy	13-Oct-73		
288	73-L-5754	Angry	Jimmy	15-Oct-73	4916	
289	73-L-5755	Keep Your Eye On The Girlie You Love	Jimmy	15-Oct-73	4916	
290	73-L-58??	And You Love Me	Petula Clark/Osm			
291	73-N-5987	True Love's A Blessing	Marie	10-Dec-73	4944	02:22
292	73-N-5988	It's The Little Things	Marie	10-Dec-73	4979	02:48
293	73-N-5989	*I'm Satisfied*	Marie	10-Dec-73		
294	73-N-5990	Crazy Arms	Marie	10-Dec-73	4944	

	A	B	C	D	E	F
1	Master #	Title	Artist	Recording Date	Album/45	Time
295	73-N-5991	Invisible Tears	Marie	10-Dec-73	4944	
296	73-N-5992	The Only One We Truly Heart	Marie	10-Dec-73		
297	73-N-5993	Why Don't You Haul Off And Love Me	Marie	10-Dec-73		
298	73-N-5994	Making Believe	Marie	10-Dec-73		
299	73-N-5995	Singing The Blues	Marie	10-Dec-73	4944	
300	73-N-5996	Big Hurts Can Come (From Little White Lies)	Marie	11-Dec-73	4944	02:28
301	73-N-5997	Please Help Me I'm Falling	Marie	11-Dec-73		
302	73-N-5998	He's Got The Whole World In His Hands	Marie	11-Dec-73		
303	73-N-5999	Everybody's Somebody's Fool	Marie	11-Dec-73	4979	
304	73-N-6000	Dawn	Marie	11-Dec-73		
305	73-N-6001	I Love You Because	Marie	11-Dec-73	4944	
306	73-N-6002	The Things I Tell My Pillow	Marie	11-Dec-73	4979	02:47
307	73-N-6003	Don't Worry	Marie	11-Dec-73		
308	73-N-6004	I Love You So Much It Hurts	Marie	11-Dec-73	4944	
309	73-N-6005	Don't Keep Me Hangin' On	Marie	12-Dec-73		
310	73-N-6006	Jealous Heart	Marie	12-Dec-73	4979	
311	73-N-6007	Love's Gonna Make A Fool Of You	Marie	12-Dec-73		
312	73-N-6008	I Guess It Doesn't Matter Anymore	Marie	12-Dec-73		
313	73-N-6009	Somehow Your Name Comes Again	Marie	12-Dec-73		
314	73-N-6010	Room In My Heart	Marie	13-Dec-73		
315	73-N-6011	It's Just The Other Way Around	Marie	13-Dec-73	4944	
316	73-N-6011-M	It's Just The Other Way Around (mono mix)	Marie	13-Dec-73	14694	
317	74-L-6185	The Good Old Bad Old Days	Jimmy	5-Feb-74	4916	
318	74-L-6186	Candy	Jimmy	5-Feb-74		
319	74-L-6215	Sing	Osmonds	Feb-74		
320	74-L-6216	Medicine Man	Osmonds	Feb-74	6077	
321	74-L-6217	High Tide	Osmonds	Feb-74		
322	74-L-6218	You're Wanted	Osmonds	Feb-74	2006 492	
323	74-L-6219	Suzanne	Osmonds	Feb-74		
324	74-L-6220	The Last Day Is Coming	Osmonds	Feb-74	4993	
325	74-L-6221	Living On My Suspicion	Donny & Marie	Feb-74	4996	
326	74-L-6297	Morning Side Of The Mountain	Donny & Marie	26-Mar-74	4968	03:06
327	74-L-6297	Morning Side Of The Mountain (single edit)	Donny & Marie	26-Mar-74	14765	02:55
328	74-L-6297 M	Morning Side Of The Mountain (mono radio mix)	Donny & Marie	26-Mar-74	14765	02:55
329	74-L-6298	True Love	Donny & Marie	26-Mar-74	4968	
330	74-L-6299	It Takes Two	Donny & Marie	26-Mar-74	4968	02:53
331	74-L-6305	Don't You Remember	Jimmy	7-Jun-74	4916	
332	74-L-6307	That's You	Osmonds	7-Feb-74		
333	74-L-6308	Stop! Look And Listen To Love	Jimmy	7-Jun-74		
334	74-L-6316	Everything Good Reminds Me Of You	Donny & Marie	11-Apr-74	4968	02:15
335	74-L-6317	A Day Late And A Dollar Short (original lyrics)	Donny & Marie	11-Apr-74	R113422	02:23
336	74-L-6317	A Day Late And A Dollar Short (re-written lyrics)	Donny & Marie	11-Apr-74	4968	02:23
337	74-L-6318	I'm Leaving It (All) Up To You	Donny & Marie	11-Apr-74	4968	02:55
338	74-L-6318	I'm Leaving It (All) Up To You (single edit)	Donny & Marie	11-Apr-74	14734	02:46
339	74-L-6318 M	I'm Leaving It (All) Up To You (Mono radio mix)	Donny & Marie	11-Apr-74	14734	02:46
340	74-L-6331	The Umbrella Song	Donny & Marie	11-Apr-74	4968	03:27
341	74-L-6366	I Can't Get Next To You	Osmonds	3-May-74	4939	
342	74-L-6367	Sixteen Candles	Donny	3-May-74	4978	
343	74-L-6368	A Mother's Love	Osmonds	3-May-74		

	A	B	C	D	E	F
1	Master #	Title	Artist	Recording Date	Album/45	Time
344	74-L-6402	Ballin' The Jack	Osmonds	21-May-74	4939	
345	74-L-6403	Love Me For A Reason	Osmonds	21-May-74	4939	
346	74-L-6403	Love Me For A Reason (single edit)	Osmonds	21-May-74	14746	04:05
347	74-L-6403 M	Love Me For A Reason (mono radio mix)	Osmonds	21-May-74	14746	03:45
348	74-L-6404	Fever	Osmonds	21-May-74	4939	
349	74-L-6405	Gabrielle	Osmonds	21-May-74	4939	
350	74-L-6406	The Girl I Love	Osmonds	21-May-74	4939	
351	74-L-6407	Having A Party	Osmonds	21-May-74	4939	
352	74-L-6408	Sun, Sun, Sun	Osmonds	21-May-74	4939	
353	74-L-6424	Peace	Osmonds	5-Jun-74	4939	
354	74-L-6425	One More Bridge To Cross	Osmonds	5-Jun-74		
355	74-L-6426	Send A Little Love	Osmonds	5-Jun-74	4939	
356	74-L-6441	Let It Be Me	Donny & Marie	6-Jun-74	4968	03:14
357	74-L-6442	Gone	Donny & Marie	6-Jun-74	4968	
358	74-L-6443	Take Me Back Again	Donny & Marie	6-Jun-74	4968	02:53
359	74-L-6444	I Can See Love In You And Me	Osmonds	6-Jun-74	4939	
360	74-L-6503	Ours	Donny	22-Jul-74	4978	02:49
361	74-L-6504	Maybe	Donny	22-Jul-74		
362	74-L-6505	This Time	Donny	22-Jul-74	4978	
363	74-L-6512	What's He Doin' In My World	Donny	8-Feb-74	4978	
364	74-L-6513	Mona Lisa	Donny	8-Feb-74	4978	
365	74-L-6514	Where Did All The Good Times Go	Donny	8-Feb-74	4978	03:24
366	74-L-6514	Where Did All The Good Times Go (single edit)	Donny	8-Feb-74	2006 468	03:09
367	74-L-6515	I Have A Dream	Donny	8-Feb-74	4978	
368	74-L-6515 M	I Have A Dream (mono radio mix)	Donny	8-Feb-74	14781	
369	74-L-6516	If Someone Ever Breaks Your Heart	Donny	8-Feb-74	4978	03:03
370	74-L-6577	I'm So Lonesome I Could Cry	Donny	24-Aug-74	4978	
371	74-L-6581	Tic Tac Toe	Jimmy	7-Jun-74		
372	74-L-6582	A Mother's Love	Jimmy	7-Jun-74		
373	74-L-6585	Little Arrows	Jimmy	7-Jun-74	4916	
374	74-L-6585 M	Little Arrows (mono radio mix)	Jimmy	7-Jun-74	14771	
375		I'm Leaving It All Up To You album radio spot				
376		Love Me For A Reason album radio spot				
377	74-L-6611	I'm Dyin' (Broken Heart)	Donny	6-Oct-74	4978	
378	74-L-6612	One Of These Days	Donny & Marie	6-Oct-74	4996	04:24
379	74-L-6619	Yes Virginia, There Is A Santa Claus	Jimmy	25-Oct-74	14770	
380	74-L-6619 M	Yes Virginia, There Is A Santa Claus (mono radio mix)	Jimmy	25-Oct-74	14770	
381	74-L-6620	If Santa Were My Daddy	Jimmy	25-Oct-74	14770	
382	74-L-6621	????	Jimmy	25-Oct-74		
383	74-L-6639	Where Would I Be Without You	Osmonds	11-Nov-74	4993	
384	74-L-6640	The Proud One	Osmonds	11-Nov-74	4993	03:07
385	74-L-6640 M	The Proud One (mono radio mix)	Osmonds	11-Nov-74	14791	
386	74-L-6641	Where Are You Going To My love	Osmonds	11-Nov-74	4993	
387	74-L-6642	Believing In Love	Osmonds	12-Nov-74		
388	74-L-6643	Jigsaw	Donny & Marie	12-Nov-74	4996	
389	74-L-6665	I Will	Donny & Marie	25-Nov-74	4996	02:27
390	74-L-6666	Make The World Go Away	Donny & Marie	25-Nov-74	4996	02:52
391	74-L-6666 M	Make The World Go Away (mono radio mix)	Donny & Marie	25-Nov-74	14807	
392	74-L-6667	When Somebody Cares For You	Donny & Marie	25-Nov-74	4996	03:20

	A	B	C	D	E	F
1	Master #	Title	Artist	Recording Date	Album/45	Time
393	74-L-6668	All You Had To Do	Donny & Marie	25-Nov-74		
394	74-L-6669	Take Love If Ever You Find Love	Osmonds	25-Nov-74	4993	02:32
395	74-L-6670	Someone To Go Home To	Osmonds	25-Nov-74	4993	
396	74-L-6671	I'm Still Gonna Need You	Osmonds	25-Nov-74		04:11
397	74-L-6671	I'm Still Gonna Need You (single edit)	Osmonds	25-Nov-74	4993	03:21
398	74-L-6671 M	I'm Still Gonna Need You (mono single edit radio mix)	Osmonds	25-Nov-74	14831	03:14
399	74-L-6672	More Love	Donny & Marie	26-Nov-74		
400	74-L-6673	Together	Donny & Marie	26-Nov-74	4996	03:12
401	74-L-6674	Mama Didn't Lie	Donny & Marie	13-Dec-74	4996	
402	74-L-6675	It's All In The Game	Donny & Marie	26-Nov-74	4996	03:26
403	74-N-6703	Clinging Vine	Marie	3-Dec-74	4979	
404	74-N-6704	Anytime	Marie	3-Dec-74	4979	
405	74-N-6705	Who's Sorry Now?	Marie	3-Dec-74	4979	02:11
406	74-N-6705 M	Who's Sorry Now? (mono radio mix)	Marie	3-Dec-74	14786	02:08
407	74-N-6706	I Fall To Pieces	Marie	3-Dec-74		
408	74-N-6707	This I Promise You	Marie	4-Dec-74	4979	
409	74-N-6708	Amoung My Souvenirs	Marie	4-Dec-74	4979	
410	74-N-6709	Love Letters In The Sand	Marie	6-Dec-74	4979	
411	74-L-6710	When You're Young And In Love	Donny & Marie	13-Dec-74	4996	02:29
412	74-L-6711	Denver	Donny & Marie	13-Dec-74		
413	74-L-6752	Thank You	Osmonds	28-Dec-74	4993	
414	74-L-6753	Kind Of A Woman That A Man Wants	Osmonds	28-Dec-74	4993	
415	74-L-6754	Frightened Eyes	Osmonds	28-Dec-74	4993	
416	74-L-6760	Dandelion	Marie	6-Jan-75	6068	
417	74-L-6761	I'd Rather Be Your Friend	Marie	6-Jan-75		
418	75-L-6856	One Of These Days	Osmonds	8-Jan-75		
419	75-L-6877	A Little Bit Country (Marie solo version)	Marie	3-Apr-75		
420	75-L-6877	A Little Bit Country	Donny & Marie	3-Apr-75	6068	02:31
421	75-L-6878	Butterfly	Marie	3-Apr-75	6068	
422	75-L-6879	Weeping Willow	Marie	3-Apr-75	6068	
423	75-L-6903	Some Little Girl	Jimmy	30-Apr-75	2006 556	
424	75-L-6904	Break Away (From That Boy)	Jimmy	30-Apr-75	2006 556	
425	75-L-6926	Pick Up The Pieces		28-May-75	5012	
426	75-L-6931	Introduction (Live)		28-May-75	5012	
427	75-L-6927	Feelin' Alright (Live)	Osmonds	28-May-75	5012	
428	75-L-6928	Crazy Horses (Live)	Osmonds	28-May-75	5012	
429	75-L-6929	Your Mama Don't Dance (Live)	Donny	28-May-75	5012	
430	75-L-6930	Hold Her Tight / Dialogue...Hey Look Me Over (live)	Osmonds	28-May-75	5012	
431	75-L-6932	Hey Look Me Over (Live)		28-May-75	5012	
432	75-L-6933	Love Me For A Reason (Live)	Osmonds	28-May-75	5012	
433	75-L-6934	Music Makin'/Girl I Love, The/I Can't Get Next To You (Live)	Osmonds	28-May-75	5012	
434	75-L-6939	Proud One, The (Live)	Osmonds	28-May-75	5012	
435	75-L-6940	Long Haired Lover From Liverpool (Live)	Jimmy	28-May-75		
436	75-L-6941	Jimmy Medley: Long Haired Lover From Liverpool/You Are So Beautiful/Never Can Say Goodbye (Live)	Jimmy	28-May-75	5012	
437	75-L-6942	Stevie Wonder Medley (Live)	Osmonds	28-May-75	5012	
438	75-L-6943	Are You Lonesome Tonight (live)	Donny	28-May-75	5012	
439	75-L-6935	Mona Lisa (Live)	Donny	28-May-75	5012	

	A	B	C	D	E	F
1	Master #	Title	Artist	Recording Date	Album/45	Time
440	75-L-6936	Donny & Marie Medley (Live)	Donny & Marie	28-May-75	5012	
441	75-L-6937	Make The World Go Away (Live)	Donny & Marie	28-May-75	5012	
442	75-L-6938	Some Kind Of Wonderful (Live)	Jay	28-May-75	5012	
443	75-L-6944	Merrill's Banjo Medley (Live)	Merrill	28-May-75	5012	
444	75-L-6945	50's Medley (Live)	Osmonds	28-May-75	5012	
445	75-L-6946	*Elvis Presley Medley (Live)*	Osmonds	28-May-75		
446	75-L-6947	Down By The Lazy River (Live)	Osmonds	28-May-75	5012	
447	75-L-6948	*I Have A Dream (Live)*	Donny	28-May-75		
448	75-L-7101	C'mon Marianne	Donny	1-Aug-75	6067	02:23
449	75-L-7101 M	C'mon Marianne (mono radio mix)	Donny	1-Aug-75	14320	02:21
450	75-L-7102	Deep Purple	Donny & Marie	1-Aug-75	6068	02:50
451	75-L-7102 M	Deep Purple (mono radio mix)	Donny & Marie	1-Aug-75	14840	02:42
452	75-L-7102	Deep Purple (alternate mix)	Donny & Marie	1-Aug-75		
453	75-L-7103	Sunshine Lady	Donny	1-Aug-75	6068	
454	75-L-7104	Disco Train	Donny	1-Aug-75	6067	
455	75-L-7140	Old Man Auctioneer	Donny		6067	
456	75-L-7141	I Got Your Lovin'	Donny		6067	
457	75-L-7143	"A" My Name Is Alice	Marie		6068	02:29
458	75-L-7143 M	"A" My Name Is Alice (mono radio mix)	Marie		14333	02:25
459		Swinging City Gal	Donny		6067	
460		I Follow The Music (Disco Donny)	Donny	21-Aug-75	6067	
461		Don't Need No Money	Donny		6067	
462		I Can't Put My Finger On It	Donny	25-Aug-75	6067	
463		Reachin' For The Feeling	Donny	25-Aug-75	6067	
464		Disco Dancin'	Donny	21-Aug-75	6067	
465		Never Gonna Let You Go	Donny	25-Aug-75	6067	
466		Never Gonna Let You Go (12" Mix)	Donny	25-Aug-75		
467		*You Betcha*	Donny	21-Aug-75		
468		*Dancin' Man*	Donny	25-Aug-75		
469	76-NP-2008	I Can't Live A Dream	Osmonds	17-May-76	6077	02:59
470	76-NP-2008 M	I Can't Live A Dream (mono radio mix)	Osmonds	17-May-76	14348	02:52
471	76-NP-2009	Gotta Get Love	Osmonds		6077	
472	76-NP-2010	Back On The Road Again	Osmonds		6077	
473	76-NP-2011	*Put The Light ?*	Osmonds			
474	76-NP-2012	Boogie Down	Osmonds	22-Jul-76	6077	
475	76-NP-2013	Walkin' In The Jungle	Osmonds		6077	
476	76-NP-2014	At The Rainbow's End	Osmonds		6077	
477	76-NP-2015	Learnin' How To Love Again	Osmonds		6077	
478	76-NP-2016	It'll Be Me	Osmonds	17-May-76	6077	
479	76-NP-2017	Check It Out	Osmonds	22-Jul-76	6077	
480	76-L-2098	Ain't Nothing Like The Real Thing	Donny & Marie		6083	02:25
481	76-L-2098 M	Ain't Nothing Like The Real Thing (mono radio mix)	Donny & Marie		14363	02:25
482	76-L-2099	Anytime Sunshine	Donny & Marie		6083	
483	76-L-2100	It's All Been Said Before	Donny & Marie		6083	
484	76-L-2101	Which Way You Goin' Billy	Marie	1-Jun-76	6083	
485	76-L-2102	Show Me	Donny & Marie		6083	
486	76-L-2103	You Broke My Heart	Donny & Marie		6083	
487	76-L-2104	Now We're Together	Donny & Marie		6083	
488	76-L-2105	Hold Me, Thrill Me, Kiss Me	Donny & Marie	27-May-76	6083	

	A	B	C	D	E	F
1	Master #	Title	Artist	Recording Date	Album/45	Time
489	76-L-2106	Sing	Donny & Marie		6083	
490	76-L-2107	We Got Love	Donny & Marie		6083	
491		Sugar Candy	Donny & Marie	27-May-76		
492		Can't Help Falling In Love	Donny & Marie	1-Jun-76		
493		Can't Stop Loving You	Donny & Marie	2-Jun-76		
494		She's Got You	Donny & Marie	2-Jun-76		
495		Don't You Love It	Donny & Marie	22-Jul-76		
496	76-L-2168	I'll Be Home For Christmas	Osmonds		8001	03:08
497	76-L-2169	Winter Wonderland	Donny & Marie		8001	02:41
498	76-L-2169	Winter Wonderland (promo single edit)	Donny & Marie		X-1	02:27
499	76-L-2170	Kay Thompson's Jingle Bells	Osmonds		8001	02:23
500	76-L-2171	If Santa Were My Daddy (1976)	Jimmy		8001	02:22
501	76-L-2172	Blue Christmas	Marie		8001	02:31
502	76-L-2173	Silver Bells	Donny & Marie		8001	03:00
503	76-L-2174	Sleigh Ride	Osmonds		8001	03:40
504	76-L-2175	This Christmas Eve	Donny		8001	02:47
505	76-L-2176	Pine Cones And Holly Berries with It's Beginning To Look A Lot Like Christmas	Osmonds		8001	02:12
506	76-L-2177	White Christmas	Osmonds		8001	02:25
507	76-L-2178	What Are You Doing New Year's Eve	Donny		8001	03:30
508	76-L-2179	It Never Snows In L.A.	Jimmy		8001	03:00
509	76-L-2180	Christmas Song, The	Osmonds		8001	02:58
510	76-L-2181	A Verry Merry Christmas	Merrill		8001	
511	76-L-2182	Caroling Medley	Osmonds		8001	04:13
512	76-L-2183	Let It Snow! Let It Snow! Let It Snow!	Marie		8001	02:17
513	76-L-2184	Christmas Waltz, The	Osmonds		8001	03:18
514	76-L-2185	Old Fashioned Christmas, An	Donny		8001	03:16
515	76-L-2186	When He Comes Again	Jimmy		8001	03:13
516	76-L-2187	Silent Night	Osmonds		8001	02:52
517	76-NP-2544	This Is The Way That I Feel	Marie	Oct-76	6099	03:25
518	76-NP-2544 M	This Is The Way That I Feel (mono radio mix)	Marie	Oct-76	14385	03:20
519	76-NP-2545	Play The Music Loud	Marie	Oct-76	6099	
520	76-NP-2546	Didn't I Love You, Boy?	Marie	Oct-76	6099	
521	76-NP-2547	Please Tell Him That I Said Hello	Marie	Oct-76	6099	
522	76-NP-2547 M	Please Tell Him That I Said Hello (mono radio mix)	Marie	Oct-76	14405	
523	76-NP-2548	Miss You Nights	Marie	Oct-76	6099	
524	76-NP-2549	Where Did Our Love Go	Marie	Oct-76	6099	
525	76-NP-2550	Cry, Baby, Cry	Marie	Oct-76	6099	
526	76-NP-2551	You're My Superman (You're My Everything)	Marie	Oct-76	6099	
527	76-NP-2552	All He Did Was Tell Me Lies (And Try To Woo Me)	Marie	Oct-76	6099	
528	76-NP-2553	Run To Me	Marie	Oct-76	6099	
529	77-NP-2827	You've Got Me Dangling On A String	Donny		6109	
530	77-NP-2827 M	You've Got Me Dangling On A String (mono radio mix)	Donny		14417	
531	77-NP-2835	I'm Sorry	Donny		6109	
532		I Can't Stand It	Donny		6109	
533		The More I Live (The More I Love)	Donny		6109	
534		Fly Into The Wind	Donny		6109	
535		You Are The Music In My Life	Donny		6109	
536		I Haven't Had A Heartache All Day	Donny		6109	
537		Oh, It Must Be Love	Donny		6109	

	A	B	C	D	E	F
1	Master #	Title	Artist	Recording Date	Album/ 45	Time
538		I Discovered You, You Discovered Me	Donny		6109	
539		You'll Be Glad	Donny		6109	
540	77-NP-3233	(You're My) Soul And Inspiration	Donny & Marie		6127	03:16
541	77-NP-3233 M	(You're My) Soul And Inspiration (mono radio mix)	Donny & Marie		14439	
542		I Want To Give You My Everything	Donny & Marie		6127	
543	77-NP-3279	Baby I'm Sold On You (album version)	Donny & Marie		6127	
544	77-NP-3279	Baby I'm Sold On You (single remix)	Donny & Marie		14456	
545	77-NP-3279 M	Baby I'm Sold On You (mono single remix)	Donny & Marie		14456	
546	77-NP-3280	Sure Would Be Nice	Donny & Marie		6127	
547		Winning Combination	Donny & Marie		6127	
548		Winning Combination (alternate mix)	Donny & Marie			
549		The Best Of Me	Donny & Marie		6127	
550		Angel Love (Heaven Is Where You Are)	Marie		6127	
551		Oh Sweet Lovin'	Donny & Marie		6127	
552		I Can't Do Without You	Donny & Marie		6127	
553		You Remind Me	Donny		6127	
554		I Want To Be In Your World	Donny & Marie		6127	
555	2-54641	You're There	Jimmy	May-78	74005	
556	2-54642	Life Is Just What You Make It	Jimmy	May-78	74005	
557	PWM-3372	Secret Love	Jimmy		SFL-2306	
558	PWM-3373	Message	Jimmy		SFL-2306	
559	78-NP-3752	On The Shelf	Donny & Marie		6169	03:58
560	78-NP-3752	On The Shelf (single edit)	Donny & Marie		14510	03:38
561	78-NP-3752	On The Shelf (12" Mix)	Donny & Marie		PD-054	
562	78-NP-3752 M	On The Shelf (mono radio mix)	Donny & Marie		14510	03:28
563	78-NP-3753	Don't Play With The One Who Loves You	Donny & Marie	14-Jul-78	6169	
564	78-NP-3754	You Don't Have To Say You Love Me	Marie	14-Jul-78	6169	
565	78-NP-3755	Baby Now That I've Found You	Donny & Marie		6169	
566	78-NP-3756	Gimme Some Time	Donny & Marie	14-Jul-78	6169	
567	78-NP-3757	Let's Fall In Love	Donny & Marie	14-Jul-78	6169	
568	78-NP-3758	You Bring Me Sunshine	Donny & Marie		6169	
569	78-NP-3759	Fallin' In Love Again	Donny & Marie		6169	
570	78-NP-3760	Doctor Dancin'	Donny & Marie		6169	
571	78-NP-3761	You Never Can Tell	Donny & Marie		6169	
572	78-NP-3762	May Tomorrow Be A Perfect Day (instrumental Theme From Donny & Marie)			6169	
573	78-NP-3763	Certfied Honey	Donny & Marie		6169	
574		Rhythm Of The Rain	Donny & Marie	14-Jul-78		
575	2-55062	Steppin' Out	Osmonds	Dec-78	3766	
576	2-55063	Emily	Osmonds	Dec-78	3766	
577	2-55064	You're Mine	Osmonds	Dec-78	3766	
578	2-55064	You're Mine (single edit)	Osmonds	Dec-78	74056	
579	2-55064	You're Mine (12" Mix)	Osmonds	Dec-78	MK-91	
580	2-55065	Baby's Back	Osmonds	Dec-78	3766	
581	2-55066	Love On The Line	Osmonds	Dec-78	3766	
582	2-55067	Rainin'	Osmonds	Dec-78	3766	
583	2-55068	I,I,I	Osmonds	Dec-78	3766	
584	2-55068	I,I,I (12" Mix)	Osmonds	Dec-78	MK-91	
585	2-55069	Love Ain't An Easy Thing	Osmonds	Dec-78	3766	
586	2-55070	Hold On	Osmonds	Dec-78	3766	

	A	B	C	D	E	F
1	Master #	Title	Artist	Recording Date	Album/45	Time
587	2-55071	Rest Your Love	Osmonds	Dec-78	3766	
588		I'm So Glad	Jimmy			
589		It's The Fallin' In Love	Marie			
590		You're Gonna Get Me To Heaven	Marie		POSP-147	
591		LA Song	Marie		POSP-147	
592		Tenderly	Marie			
593		Cryin'	Marie			
594		I'm A Woman	Marie			
595			Marie			
596			Marie			
597			Marie			
598			Marie			
599		Crazy Horses (Utah Saints Remix)	Osmonds	1994	579 321 2	
600		Seasons Of Love	Donny	2000	013 052 2	
601		Seasons Of Love (radio edit)	Donny	2000	DONNY 1	
602		This Is The Moment	Donny	2000	013 052 2	
603		Luck Be A Lady	Donny	2000	013 052 2	
604		Our Kind Of Love	Donny	2000	013 052 2	
605		At The Edge Of The World	Donny	2000	013 052 2	
606		Not While I'm Around	Donny	2000	013 052 2	
607		Solla Sollew	Donny	2000	013 052 2	
608		No Matter What	Donny	2000	013 052 2	
609		Immortality	Donny	2000	013 052 2	
610		I Know The Truth	Donny	2000	013 052 2	
611		You've Got A Friend In Me	Donny	2000	013 052 2	
612		Give My Regards To Broadway	Donny	2000	013 052 2	
613		Puppy Love (2001 Accoustic)	Donny	2000	158 777 2	
614		Too Young (2001 Accoustic)	Donny	2000	158 777 2	
615		Young Love (2001 Accoustic)	Donny	2000	158 777 2	
616		The Twelfth Of Never (2001 Accoustic)	Donny	2000	158 777 2	
617		Why (2001 Accoustic)	Donny	2000	158 777 2	
618		When I Fall In Love (2001 Accoustic)	Donny	2000	158 777 2	
619		Goin' Down	Stephen Craig	2002		
620		Bend Me, Shape Me	Stephen Craig	2002		
621		100 Days, 100 Nights	Stephen Craig	2002		
622		Just Say So	Stephen Craig	2002		
623		Right Here Waiting	Stephen Craig	2002		
624		That's What You Get	Stephen Craig	2002		
625		In My Life	Stephen Craig	2002		
626		Be That Way	Stephen Craig	2002		
627		Back In Love Again	Stephen Craig	2002		
628		What's Wrong With My Heart	Stephen Craig	2002		
629		4 Ever 1	Stephen Craig	2002		
630		Without You	Donny	2002	018 912 2	
631		Without You (Radio edit)	Donny	2002		
632		I Can't Go For That	Donny	2002	018 912 2	
633		All Out Of Love	Donny	2002	018 912 2	
634		Could It Be I'm Falling In Love	Donny	2002	018 912 2	
635		Don't Dream It's Over	Donny	2002	018 912 2	

	A	B	C	D	E	F
1	Master #	Title	Artist	Recording Date	Album/45	Time
636		After The Love Is Gone	Donny	2002	018 912 2	
637		Would I Lie To You	Donny	2002	018 912 2	
638		Happy Together	Donny	2002	018 912 2	
639		Don't Give Up On Us Baby	Donny	2002	018 912 2	
640		No One Has To Be Alone (from The Land Before Time)	Donny	2002	018 912 2	
641		I Wish	Donny	2002	066 530 2	
642		Crazy Horses (2002)	Donny	2002	018 912 2	
643		An Audience With Promo Interviews	Donny			
644		Could It Be I'm Falling In Love [Live 2003]	Donny	2003	920 873 9	
645		All Out Of Love [Live 2003]	Donny	2003	920 873 9	
646		Puppy Love [Live 2003]	Donny	2003	920 873 9	
647		Seasons Of Love [Live 2003]	Donny	2003	920 873 9	
648		Luck Be A Lady Tonight [Live 2003]	Donny	2003	920 873 9	
649		Not While I'm Around [Live 2003]	Donny	2003	920 873 9	
650		Any Dream Will Do [Live 2003]	Donny	2003	920 873 9	
651		I Can't Go For That [Live 2003]	Donny	2003	920 873 9	
652		Don't Dream It's Over [Live 2003]	Donny	2003	920 873 9	
653		This Is The Moment [Live 2003]	Donny	2003	920 873 9	
654		Soldier Of Love [Live 2003]	Donny	2003	920 873 9	
655		Go Away Little Girl [Live 2003]	Donny	2003	920 873 9	
656		Too Young [Live 2003]	Donny	2003	920 873 9	
657		The Twelfth Of Never [Live 2003]	Donny	2003	920 873 9	
658		Love Me For A Reason [Live 2003]	Donny	2003	920 873 9	
659		I'm Not In Love [Live 2003]	Donny	2003	920 873 9	
660		Would I Lie To You [Live 2003]	Donny	2003	920 873 9	
661		I Wish [Live 2003]	Donny	2003	920 873 9	
662		Immortality [Live 2003]	Donny	2003	920 873 9	
663		Crazy Horses [Live 2003]	Donny	2003	920 873 9	
664		Never Gonna Say Goodbye [Live 2003]	Donny	2003	920 873 9	
665		Breeze On By	Donny	2004	986 313 9	
666		Breeze On By (radio edit)	Donny	2004	BREEZE 1	
667		Breeze On By (single edit)	Donny	2004	863 140 9	
668		Keep Her In Mind	Donny	2004	986 313 9	
669		In It For Love	Donny	2004	986 313 9	
670		I Wanna Know What Love Is	Donny	2004	986 313 9	
671		My Perfect Rhyme	Donny	2004	986 313 9	
672		Faith	Donny	2004	986 313 9	
673		What I Meant To Say	Donny	2004	986 313 9	
674		What I Meant To Say (single edit)	Donny	2005		
675		Whenever You're In Trouble	Donny	2004	986 313 9	
676		Shoulda Known Better	Donny	2004	986 313 9	
677		Broken Man	Donny	2004	986 313 9	
678		This Guy's In Love With You	Donny	2004	986 313 9	
679		Insecurity	Donny	2004	986 313 9	
680		One Dream	Donny	2004	986 313 9	
681		Christmas Time	Donny	2004	986 313 9	
682		Christmas Time (Radio Edit)	Donny	2004	210 335 5	
683		Right Here Waiting	Donny	2004	B 0003737-2	
684		Climbing	Donny	2004	Download	

	A	B	C	D	E	F
1	Master #	Title	Artist	Recording Date	Album/ 45	Time
685		Just The Way You Are	Donny	2004	988 028 2	
686		Could It Be I'm Falling In Love [Live 2004]	Donny	2004	986 874 9	
687		Seasons Of Love [Live 2004]	Donny	2004	986 874 9	
688		Puppy Love [Live 2004]	Donny	2004	986 874 9	
689		In It For Love [Live 2004]	Donny	2004	986 874 9	
690		Keep Her In Mind [Love 2004]	Donny	2004	986 874 9	
691		Any Dream Will Do [Live 2004]	Donny	2004	986 874 9	
692		Don't Dream It's Over [Live 2004]	Donny	2004	986 874 9	
693		This Is The Moment [Live 2004]	Donny	2004	986 874 9	
694		Soldier Of Love [Live 2004]	Donny	2004	986 874 9	
695		Whenever You're In Trouble [Live 2004]	Donny	2004	986 874 9	
696		Go Away Little Girl [Live 2004]	Donny	2004	986 874 9	
697		Too Young [Live 2004]	Donny	2004	986 874 9	
698		Young Love [Live 2004]	Donny	2004	986 874 9	
699		The TWelfth Of Never [Live 2004]	Donny	2004	986 874 9	
700		Love Me For A Reason [Live 2004]	Donny	2004	986 874 9	
701		What I Meant To Say [Live 2004]	Donny	2004	986 874 9	
702		Would I Lie To You [Live 2004]	Donny	2004	986 874 9	
703		Shoulda' Known Better [Live 2004]	Donny	2004	986 874 9	
704		Breeze On By [Live 2004]	Donny	2004	986 874 9	
705		Immortality [Live 2004]	Donny	2004	986 874 9	
706		Crazy Horses [Live 2004]	Donny	2004	986 874 9	
707		Flower Of Scotland [Live 2004]	Donny	2004	986 874 9	
708		Red Red Rose [Live 2004]	Donny	2004	986 874 9	
709		Never Gonna Say Goodye [Live 2004]	Donny	2004	986 874 9	
710		I Can See Clearly Now	Donny	2006	172 556 0	
711		Sometimes When We Touch	Donny	2006	172 556 0	
712		Sometimes When We Touch (radio edit)	Donny	2007		
713		Let's Stay Together	Donny	2006	172 556 0	
714		Laughter In The Rain	Donny	2006	172 556 0	
715		Oh Girl	Donny	2006	172 556 0	
716		When I Need You	Donny	2006	172 556 0	
717		How Long	Donny	2006	172 556 0	
718		Mandy	Donny	2006	172 556 0	
719		How Deep Is Your Love	Donny	2006	172 556 0	
720		Will It Go Round In Circles	Donny	2006	172 556 0	
721		Alone Again (Naturally)	Donny	2006	172 556 0	
722		You Are So Beautiful	Donny	2006	172 556 0	
723		If	Donny	2006	B-0008291-02	
724		You Are The Sunshine Of My Life	Donny	2006		
725		**Songs Recorded that I cannot find master numbers**				
726		Gotcha Goin' My Way	Osmonds			
727		I Am Certain				
728		Before You Know It, It Will Be Christmas				
729		Christmas People				
730		The Christmas Song (Chestnuts Roasting On A Open Fire)				
731		Dream My Little One				
732		Happy New Year, Mom				
733		It's That Time Of Year Again				

	A	B	C	D	E	F
1	Master #	Title	Artist	Recording Date	Album/45	Time
734		Silver Bells				
735		Star Of The East				
736		We Need A Little Christmas				
737		I Hope You Have A Merry Christmas				
738		This Christmas Eve [1971]				
739		Winter Wonderland [1971]				
740		*Feelin' Alright*				
741		The Coat Of Many Colors	Marie		Demo	
742		Where Is The Love?	Donny & Marie		Demo	
743		Fire	Donny			
744		The Great Brain Soundtrack				
745		Goin' Coconuts				
746						
747						

Master #	Title	Artist	Recording Date	Album/45	Time
\multicolumn{6}{l}{MASTERS OWNED BY DENON RECORDS/NIPPON COLUMBIA LTD. JAPAN}					
SN-153	Chitchana Koibito (My Little Darling)	Little Jimmy	Mar-70	CD-7004	03:25
SN-154	Peg O' My Heart	Little Jimmy	Mar-70	CD-7028	02:43
SN-191	Young Love Swing	Osmond Bros	Mar-70	CD-7004	
SN-192	Sha La La	Osmond Bros + J	Mar-70	CD-7004	02:50
SN-211	Chuk Chuk	Little Jimmy	Mar-70	CD-7028	02:58
SN-212	Jimmy's Lullaby	Little Jimmy	Mar-70	CD-7028	03:02
SN-219	Chance	Osmond Bros D	Mar-70	CD-7004	
SN-243	Jimmy's The Happy Robbers	Little Jimmy	Mar-70	CD-7028	02:33
	Golden Rainbow	Osmond Bros	Mar-70	CD-7004	
	Keep The Customer Satisfied	Osmond Bros	Mar-70	CD-7004	
	Raindrops Keep Falling On My Head	Donny & Marie	Mar-70	CD-7004	02:39
	Bridge Over Troubled Water	Osmond Bros	Mar-70	CD-7004	
	Scarborough Fair	Osmond Bros	Mar-70	CD-7004	
	Aquarius Let The Sushine In	Osmond Bros	Mar-70	CD-7004	
SN-220	Greensleeves	Osmond Bros	Mar-70	**CD-92**	
	Hello From The Osmond Brothers	Osmond Bros	Mar-70	Soundsheet	
	Santa Claus Is Coming To Town	Osmonds, The	Nov-70	CD-7006	
	Rudolph The Red-Nosed Reindeer	Osmonds, The	Nov-70	CD-7006	
	Silent Night	Osmonds, The	Nov-70	CD-7006	
	This Christmas Eve	Osmonds, The	Nov-70	CD-7006	
SN-221	Jingle Bells	Osmonds, The	Nov-70	CD-7006	
	O Come All Ye Faithful	Osmonds, The	Nov-70	CD-7006	
SN-222	I Saw Mommy Kissing Santa Claus	Osmonds, The	Nov-70	CD-7006	
	Blue Christmas	Osmonds, The	Nov-70	CD-7006	
	God Rest Ye Merry Gentlemen	Osmonds, The	Nov-70	CD-7006	
	Night Before Christmas, The	Osmonds, The	Nov-70	CD-7006	
	White Christmas	Osmonds, The	Nov-70	CD-7006	
	Winter Wonderland	Osmonds, The	Nov-70	CD-7006	
SN-244	I Found A Little Happiness	Little Jimmy	Apr-71	CD-7028	03:36
SN-289	Put Your Hand In The Hand	Little Jimmy	Apr-71	CD-7028	03:04
	Moon Was Watching	Little Jimmy	Apr-71	CD-7028	02:26
SN-341	We Wish You A Merry Christmas/Whispering Hope	Osmonds, The	Apr-71	**CD-1010**	
SN-342	Christmas Medley	Osmonds, The	Apr-71	**CD-1010**	
SN-367	Good-bye Mr. Tears	Little Jimmy	Apr-71	CD-7028	02:42
SN-368	Utopia	Little Jimmy	Apr-71	CD-7028	02:15
SN-391	She Is Good Looking	Little Jimmy	Apr-71	CD-7028	02:48
SN-392	Bye Bye Suzanne	Little Jimmy	Apr-71	**CD-1019**	
	Movin' Along (Live)	Osmonds, The	Apr-71	CD-7015	
	Motown Special (Live)	Osmonds, The	Apr-71	CD-7015	
	Introductions (Live)	Osmonds, The	Apr-71	CD-7015	
	Close To You (Live)	Osmonds, The	Apr-71	CD-7015	
	Sweet And Innocent (Live)	Donny	Apr-71	CD-7015	
	He Ain't Heavy...He's My Brother (Live)	Osmonds, The	Apr-71	CD-7015	
	Trouble/I Got A Woman (Live)	Jimmy	Apr-71	CD-7015	
	Put Your Hand In The Hand (Live)	Jimmy	Apr-71	CD-7015	
	My Little Darling (Live)	Jimmy	Apr-71	CD-7015	
	Jimmy's The Happy Robbers (Live)	Jimmy	Apr-71	CD-7015	
	Your Song (Live)	Donny	Apr-71	CD-7015	

	A	B	C	D	E	F
1	Master #	Title	Artist	Recording Date	Album/45	Time
797		We Gotta Live Together (Live)	Osmonds, The	Apr-71	CD-7015	
798		Proud Mary/Free (Live)	Jay	Apr-71	CD-7015	
799		Sometimes I Feel Like A Motherless Child/Where Could I Go But To The Lord/Everytime I Feel The Spirit (live)	Osmonds, The	Apr-71	CD-7015	
800		One Bad Apple (Live)	Osmonds, The	Apr-71	CD-7015	
801		He Ain't Heavy...He's My Brother (Reprise -Live)	Osmonds, The	Apr-71	CD-7015	
802		Calpis Commercials CF Song				
803		Calpis Commercials CF Song				
804	Items Denon released in Japan as leased from MGM/Universal and not released on album in US.					
805	63-XY-87	Winter Wonderland	Osmond Bros.	19-Aug-63	CD-7006	
806	63-XY-90	White Christmas	Osmond Bros.	19-Aug-63	CD-7006	
807	70-L-1365	Movin' Along	Osmond Bros.	5-Apr-70	CD-7004	
808	70-L-1385	Open Up Your Heart	Osmond Bros.	6-Apr-70	CD-7004	
809	70-L-1893	Santa No Chimney	Jimmy	9-Nov-70	CD-7006	
810	70-L-1894	I Hope You Have A Very Merry Christmas	Jimmy	9-Nov-70	CD-7006	
811	72-L-3198	My Father Told Me So	Little Jimmy	Jan-72	CD-4038/39	
812	Items Denon may have recorded but never released					
813		Down On The Corner	Osmond Bros.	1970		
814		Lookin' Out My Back Door	Osmond Bros.	1970		
815		Didn't We	Osmond Bros.	1970		
816		Everybody Wants To Be A Cat	Osmond Bros.	1970		
817		This Is My Country	Osmond Bros.	1970		
818		Something	Osmond Bros.	1970		
819		Moon River	Osmond Bros.	1970		
820		Woodstock	Osmond Bros.	1970		
821		Sunshine	Osmond Bros.	1970		
822		Black Cat Tango	Little Jimmy	Apr-71		
823	**ALBUM MASTERS:**					
824	JX-101	Hello! The Osmond Brothers Side 1			CD-7004	
825	JX-102	Hello! The Osmond Brothers Side 2			CD-7004	
826	JX-109	Christmas Holiday With The Osmonds Side 1			CD-7006	
827	JX-110	Christmas Holiday With The Osmonds Side 2			CD-7006	
828	JX-151	The Osmonds In Tokyo Side 1			CD-7015	
829	JX-152	The Osmonds In Tokyo Side 2			CD-7015	
830	JX-173	The Best Of The Osmonds Side 1			CD-4038	
831	JX-174	The Best Of The Osmonds Side 2			CD-4038	
832	JX-175	The Best Of The Osmonds Side 3			CD-4039	
833	JX-176	The Best Of The Osmonds Side 4			CD-4039	
834	JX-247	Little Jimmy Side 1			CD-7028	
835	JX-248	Little Jimmy Side 2			CD-7028	
836	**EP MASTERS:**					
837	DN-1	Christmas Holiday Side 1			CD-3001	
838	DN-2	Christmas Holiday Side 2			CD-3001	
839	DN-9	Little Jimmy Volume 1 Side 1			CD-3005	
840	DN-10	Little Jimmy Volume 1 Side 2			CD-3005	
841	DN-21	Scarborough Fair Side 1			CD-3011	
842	DN-22	Scarborough Fair Side 2			CD-3011	

Although I admire all the Osmonds and have held them in very high regard for decades now, Marie has always been my favorite. From the time I first saw her up to this very day I still see absolute beauty in the lady. And not just an outside beauty. Her heart glows with beauty in my opinion. Those who do not know her as a friend, and while that is not possible for everyone, are certainly missing out! Marie has been a light in my life for many years. Her music has brought me so much joy. More than mere words could ever express. So for that reason I am putting Marie's solo Nashville recording log here on it's own to show more detail than above. It shows year recorded, title, date recorded, producer and studio. It also shows that MGM really cranked out the material on the Osmonds! It also shows those 12 sadly unreleased songs!

MARIE OSMOND - NASHVILLE SESSIONS 1973-1974

73 L 5321 Paper Roses 06/07/1973 Sonny James - Columbia, Nashville
73 L 5322 In My Little Corner of the World 06/07/1973 Sonny James - Columbia, Nashville
73 L 5323 Louisiana Bayou 06/07/1973 Sonny James - Columbia, Nashville
73 L 5326 Too Many Rivers 06/08/1973 Sonny James - Columbia, Nashville
73 L 5327 You're the Only World I know 06/08/1973 Sonny James - Columbia, Nashville
73 L 5328 Sweet Dreams 06/08/1973 Sonny James - Columbia, Nashville
73 L 5329 It's Such a Pretty World Today 06/08/1973 Sonny James - Columbia, Nashville
73 L 5330 True Love Lasts Forever 06/08/1973 Sonny James - Columbia, Nashville
73 L 5331 Everything is Beautiful 06/08/1973 Sonny James - Columbia, Nashville
73 L 5332 Fool No. 1 06/06/1973 Sonny James - Columbia, Nashville
73 L 5333 Least of all You 06/06/1973 Sonny James - Columbia, Nashville
73 N 5987 True Love's a Blessing 12/10/1973 James, Curb, Ovens - Jack Clement Studio, Nashville
73 N 5988 It's the Little Things 12/10/1973 James, Curb, Ovens - Jack Clement Studio, Nashville
73 N 5989 I'm Satisfied **(UNRELEASED)** 12/10/1973 James, Mullins - Jack Clement Studio, Nashville
73 N 5990 Crazy Arms 12/10/1973 James, Curb, Ovens - Jack Clement Studio, Nashville
73 N 5991 Invisible Tears 12/10/1973 James, Curb, Ovens - Jack Clement Studio, Nashville
73 N 5992 The Only One We Truly Hurt **(UNRELEASED)** 12/10/1973 James, Mullins - Jack Clement Studio, Nashville
73 N 5993 Why Don't You Haul off and Love Me **(UNRELEASED)** 12/10/1973 James, Mullins - Jack Clement Studio, Nashville
73 N 5994 Making Believe 12/10/1973 James, Curb, Ovens - Jack Clement Studio, Nashville
73 N 5995 Singing The Blues 12/10/1973 James, Curb, Ovens - Jack Clement Studio, Nashville
73 N 5996 Big Hurts Can Come 12/11/1973 James, Curb, Ovens - Jack Clement Studio, Nashville
73 N 5998 He's Got the Whole World in His Hands **(UNRELEASED)** 12/11/1973 James, Mullins - Jack Clement Studio, Nashville
73 N 5999 Everybody's Somebody's Fool 12/11/1973 James, Curb, Ovens - Jack Clement Studio, Nashville
73 N 6000 Dawn **(UNRELEASED)** 12/11/1973 James, Mullins - Jack Clement Studio, Nashville
73 N 6001 I Love You Because 12/11/1973 James, Curb, Ovens - Jack Clement Studio, Nashville
73 N 6002 The Things I Tell My Pillow 12/11/1973 James, Curb, Ovens - Jack Clement Studio, Nashville
73 N 6003 Don't Worry **(UNRELEASED)** 12/11/1973 James, Mullins - Jack Clement Studio, Nashville
73 N 6004 I Love You so Much it Hurts 12/11/1973 James, Curb, Ovens - Jack Clement Studio, Nashville
73 N 6005 Jealous Heart 12/11/1973 James, Curb, Ovens - Jack Clement Studio, Nashville
73 N 6006 Don't Keep Me Hanging On **(UNRELEASED)** 12/12/1973 Jack Clement Studio, Nashville
73 N 6007 Love's Gonna Make a Fool of You **(UNRELEASED)** 12/12/1973 Jack Clement Studio, Nashville
73 N 6008 I Guess it Doesn't Matter Anymore **(UNRELEASED)** 12/12/1973 Jack Clement Studio, Nashville
73 N 6009 Somehow Your Name Comes Again **(UNRELEASED)** 12/12/1973 Jack Clement Studio, Nashville
73 N 6010 Room in Your Heart **(UNRELEASED)** 12/13/1973 James, Mullins - Jack Clement Studio, Nashville
73 N 6011 It's Just the Other Way Round 12/13/1973 James, Mullins - Jack Clement Studio, Nashville

74 L 6703 Clinging Vine 12/03/1974 James, Curb Arr. Mullins, Nashville
74 L 6704 Anytime 12/03/1974 James, Curb Arr. Mullins, Nashville
74 L 6705 Who's Sorry Now 12/03/1974 James, Curb Arr. Mullins, Nashville
74 L 6706 I Fall to Pieces **(UNRELEASED)** 2/03/1974 James, Curb Arr. Mullins, Nashville
74 L 6707 This I Promise You 12/04/1974 James, Curb Arr. Mullins, Nashville
74 L 6708 Among My Souvenirs 12/04/1974 James, Curb Arr. Mullins, Nashville
74 L 6709 Love Letters in the Sand 12/06/1974 James, Curb Arr. Mullins, Nashville

Recording "Paper Roses" was a highlight for Marie.

Marie is surrounded by paper roses as she sings her famous hit tune.

Visit Marie Osmond's Little Corner of the World

'In My Little Corner of the World'

2315 287 SUPER
Also available on
Musicassette and 8 Track

MARKETED BY POLYDOR LIMITED

THE *DONNY & MARIE* SHOW

Donny and Marie were offered a prime time special by then ABC-TV President Fred Silverman after he saw the duo co-host a week on The Mike Douglas Show in 1975. The ratings were so good ABC-TV in turn offered them a series of their own in 1976. Donny & Marie (18 and 16 years old, respectively, when the program premiered) were the youngest entertainers in TV history to host their own variety show at the time.

0-0   Donny & Marie Special — November 16, 1975
       Kate Smith / Paul Lynde / Lee Majors / Osmond Brothers

Season 1

1-1   Jan. 23, 1976 - Farrah Fawcett Majors / Lee Majors / Vincent Price
1-2   Jan. 30, 1976 - Bob Hope / Ted Knight / The Harlem Globetrotters
1-3   Feb. 06, 1976 - Paul Lynde / Jimmy Walker / Andy Williams
1-4   Feb. 20, 1976 - Edgar Bergen / Ruth Buzzi / Kate Smith
1-5   Feb. 27, 1976 - Charo / Roy Clark / George Gobel
1-6   Mar. 06, 1976 - Raymond Burr / Esther Rolle
1-7   Mar. 12, 1976 - Pearl Bailey / Ruth Buzzi / Sherman Hemsley
1-8   Mar. 19, 1976 - Milton Berle / Paul Lynde / Anne Meara / Nipsey Russell
1-9   Mar. 26, 1976 - Ruth Buzzi / Jerry Lewis / Jim Nabors
1-10   Apr. 02, 1976 - Karen Valentine / Hal Linden / Cast Of Welcome Back Kotter
1-11   Apr. 09, 1976 - Rick Hurst / Minnie Pearl / McLean Stevenson#
1-12   Apr. 16, 1976 - Ruth Buzzi / Gabe Kaplan
1-13   Apr. 23, 1976 - Jack Albertson / Barbara Eden
1-14   Apr. 30, 1976 - Don Knotts / Michael Landon

Season 2

2-1   Sept. 24, 1976 - Desi Arnaz / Arthur Godfrey / Art Linkletter
2-2   Oct. 01, 1976 - George Burns / Chubby Checker / Evel Knievel
2-3   Oct. 08, 1976 - Ruth Buzzi / Chad Everett / Florence Henderson
2-4   Oct. 15, 1976 - Edgar Bergen / Sonny & Cher / Loretta Swit
2-5   Oct. 22, 1976 - Roz Kelly / Charly Pride / Cindy Williams
2-6   Oct. 29, 1976 - Rich Little / Roy Rogers & Dale Evans
2-7   Nov. 05, 1976 - Bo Didley / Andy Griffith
2-8   Nov. 12, 1976 - George Gobel / Little Richard / Isabelle Sandford
2-9   Dec. 03, 1976 - Charo / Paul Lynde / Carl Reiner#
2-10   Dec. 17, 1976 - (Christmas Show) Paul Lynde / The Osmonds / Andy Williams
2-11   Dec. 31, 1976 - (New Years Eve) Show Tina Turner / Rip Taylor / Billy Preston
2-12   Jan. 07, 1977 - Chuck Berry / Gary Burghoff / Buddy Hackett
2-13   Jan. 14, 1977 - Merle Haggard / Kaptain Kool & the Kongs
2-14   Jan. 21, 1977 - The Brady Bunch / Cyde Charise / Robert Hegyes / Tony Martin
2-15   Jan. 28, 1977 - Milton Berle / Connie Stevens
2-16   Feb. 04, 1977 - Paul Anka / Paul Lynde
2-17   Feb. 11, 1977 - Ruth Buzzi / Roy Clark
2-18   Feb. 18, 1977 - Bert Convy / Anne Meara / Fred Travalena
2-19   Feb. 25, 1977 - George Gobel / Paul Williams
2-20   Mar. 04, 1977 - Don Knotts / Paul Lynde / Keely Smith
2-21   Mar. 11, 1977 - Lorne Greene / Bob Hegyes
2-22   Mar. 18, 1977 - Sonny James / McLean Stevenson

Season 3

3-1	Sep. 23, 1977 - Redd Fox / Kris Kristofferson / Paul Lynde (Star Wars Episode)
3-2	Sep. 30, 1977 - Lucille Ball / Ray Bolger / Paul Lynde
3-3	Oct. 07, 1977 - Robert Young / Neil Sedaka / Paul Lynde
3-4	Oct. 21, 1977 - Glen Campbell / Bernadette Peters / Big Bird
3-5	Oct. 28, 1977 - Billy Crystal / Kristy McNichol / Ben Vereen
3-6	Nov. 04, 1977 - Ken Berry / What's Happening Cast
3-7	Nov. 11, 1977 - Cheryl Ladd / Bob Hope / Ruth Buzzi / Jay Osmond#
3-8	Nov. 18, 1977 - Paul Lynde / Cindy Williams / Bruce Kimmel
3-9	Dec. 02, 1977 - The Sylvers / Milton Berle / Charo
3-10	Dec. 09, 1977 - Mac Davis / Mackenzie Phillips / Paul Lynde
3-11	Dec. 23, 1977 - (Christmas Show) The Osmond Family / Paul Lynde
3-12	Jan. 06, 1978 - Andy Grffith / Charo
3-13	Jan. 13, 1978 - Danny Thomas / Desi Arnaz Jr / Ruth Buzzi
3-14	Jan. 20, 1978 - Suzanne Somers / Buddy Hackett / Ruth Buzzi
3-15	Jan. 27, 1978 - Andy Gibb / Betty White / Paul Lynde
3-16	Feb. 03, 1978 - Cheryl Ladd / Paul Lynde
3-17	Feb. 10, 1978 - Ron Howard / Ruth Buzzi
3-18	Feb. 10, 1978 - Englebert Humperdink / Parker Stevenson
3-19	Mar. 03, 1978 - Tom Jones / Loretta Swit
3-20	Mar. 24, 1978 - Roy Clark/ Ruth Buzzi / Johnny Dark
3-21	May. 12, 1978 - Connie Stevens / McLean Stevenson
3-22	May. 19, 1978 - Rita Coolidge / Mel Tillis / Paul Lynde

Season 4

4-1	Sep. 22, 1978 - Olivia Newton-John / Bob Hope
4-2	Sep. 29, 1978 - Jaclyn Smith / Dirk Benedict / Rita Coolidge / Paul Lynde
4-3	Oct. 13, 1978 - Kris Kristofferson / Paul Lynde / Robert Young
4-4	Oct. 20, 1978 - Robert Conrad / Johnny Dark / Andy Gibb / Ted Knight
4-5	Oct. 27, 1978 - Ruth Buzzi / Johnny Dark / Sherman Hemsley
4-6	Nov. 24, 1978 - Lorne Greene / Bruce Kimmel / Cindy Williams
4-7	Dec. 01, 1978 - Paul Lynde / Suzanne Somers / Betty White
4-8	Dec. 07, 1978 - Ruth Buzzi / Gavin MacLeod / Racquel Welch
4-9	Dec. 15, 1978 - (Christmas Show) The Osmond Family+
4-10	Dec. 29, 1978 - Betty White / What's Happening Cast
4-11	Jan. 05, 1979 - Cheryl Tiegs / Harvey Korman / Buddy Hackett
4-12	Jan. 12, 1979 - Dick Van Patten / Joey Travolta / Ruth Buzzi#
4-13	Jan. 19, 1979 - Debbie Boone / Dirk Benedict / Paul Lynde

Notes:

- # Available on The Best of Donny & Marie Volume 1 – Two Disc DVD Set
- + Available on The Donny & Marie 1978 Christmas Show DVD

The Osmond Family Show

From here the *Donny & Marie* series became *The Osmond Family Show* and aired from January 21, 1979 - May 27, 1979.

1-1   Jan. 21, 1979 - Roy Clark / David Copperfield / Lassie
1-2   Feb. 11, 1979 - Andy Gibb / Ruth Buzzi / Paul Lynde
1-3   Feb. 18, 1979 - Leif Garrett / Royal Command Performance
1-4   Mar. 04, 1979 - Joyce DeWitt / LeVar Burton / Johnny Dark
1-5   Mar. 11, 1979 - Ron Palillo / Debbie Reynolds / Susan Richardson
1-6   Mar. 18, 1979 - K.C. and the Sunshine Band / Tanya Tucker / Larry Mahan
1-7   May 06, 1979 - Johnny Dark / Cathy Rigby / Andrea McArdle / Adam Rich
1-8   May 13, 1979 - Loretta Lynn / Chuck Berry / Chubby Checker / Wolfman Jack
1-9   May 20, 1979 - Andy Williams / Connie Stevens / Adam Rich / Grant Goodeve
1-10   May 27, 1979 - Johnny Dark - On this final episode the program's staff and production crew join the Osmonds and Johnny Dark for an inside look at what goes into the making of a variety show. Included is a tour of the Osmond TV studio conducted by Jay, scenes of rehearsals and rewrite sessions, and outtakes of bloopers and pratfalls from earlier programs. None of these programs have been released.

TV Guide ad for the January 21, 1979 Premiere

The

Marie

Show

In this solo show Marie set out to show she can hold her own. And she does. The music alone shows growth as an artist. From well known songs like: "Hit Me With Your Best Shot," "I'm Coming Out," "Another One Bit's the Dust," "In My Life" to her own composition "Tenderly" (from her unreleased 1979 album) Marie only hints at what she will show us musically in the coming years.

This show, from what I understand, was unfortunately only meant to last for these seven episodes. None of these programs have been released.

1-1   Dec. 12, 1980 - Gavin MacLeod / Jeff Conaway
1-2   Dec. 19, 1980 - Andy Williams / Fred Willard / Scott Baio
1-3   Dec. 26, 1980 - Tony Orlando / The Pointer Sisters / Jay Johnson
2-1   Jan. 02, 1981 - Sally Struthers / David Copperfield
2-2   Sept. 12, 1981 - Andy Gibb / Stephen Stucker
2-3   Sept. 19, 1981 - Grant Goodeve / The Commodores
2-4   Sept. 26, 1981 - Nell Carter / Jimmy Osmond / Bob Hope

An NBC-TV promo from the *MARIE* press kit.

WE'RE PROUD

MARIE

ANOTHER GREAT NEW SERIES! She's beautiful! She just turned 21! And she finally has her own apartment in L.A.! She's Marie Osmond, starring in her own comedy-variety series about a young woman out to establish her own life...and live it on her own terms.

Comedy sketches will evolve from the various new situations Marie must face, with top guest stars and a talented troupe of regulars appearing in both the sketches and the show's lavish musical numbers.

"Marie" is produced by Terry Hughes, noted for his comedy touch on "Monty Python's Flying Circus" and "The Two Ronnies."

CAST AND PRODUCTION CREDITS TBA

NBC STATION ADVERTISING AS OF NOV. 11

A full page promotional from the *MARIE* press kit.

The Osmond Brothers Cartoons

The Osmond Brothers cartoons ran on the ABC-TV Network from September 9, 1972 to December 30, 1972. A total of 17 thirty minute episodes were produced by Rankin/Bass Productions in association with British company Halas and Batchelor.

1.) **"And Away We Go" (September 9, 1972)**+
The pilot episode introduces the six brothers, their pet dog Fuji, and Donny's biggest fan Hortense Bird. The brothers have a chance to audition to go around the world, but Jimmy and Fuji almost ruin their chances. Songs: "One Bad Apple" (Osmonds), "Go Away Little Girl" (Donny solo, To You With Love, Donny)

2.) **"China" (September 16, 1972)**+
The brothers arrive in China and there are bad vibes between Jimmy and Fuji. The brothers play a ping pong game for America vs. China. Songs: "Don't Panic" (Phase III), "Sweet and Innocent" (Osmonds album and The Donny Osmond)

3.) **"Jimmy and James in London" (September 23, 1972)**+
The brothers visit London and Jimmy is mistaken for a prince who looks exactly like him.
Songs: "In the Rest of My Life" (Phase III), "Why" (Donny solo, Too Young)

4.) **"Sir Donald of Bavaria" (September 30, 1972)**
The brothers arrive in Bavaria and Donny is sent back in time and meets a princess.
Songs: "Do You Want Me (We Can Make it Together)" (Donny solo, To You With Love, Donny), "Business" (Phase III)

5.) **"Paris" (October 7, 1972)**
The brothers are in Paris and they must save a restaurant from going out of business.
Songs: "Promise Me" (Donny solo, Portrait Of Donny), "Shuckin' and Jivin'" (Homemade)

6.) **"Monte Carlo" (October 14, 1972)**
The brothers are in Monte Carlo and Jimmy makes a very popular movie. Donny falls for the wrong girl. Songs: "Wake Up Little Susie" (Donny solo, The Donny Osmond), "Getcha Goin' My Way" (non-album song) **Note:** The Osmonds' single, "Crazy Horses", and their album of the same name, were released on this date.

7.) **"Denmark" (October 21, 1972)**
The brothers arrive in Denmark and Jimmy travels with a mermaid underwater.
Songs: "Love Me" (Donny solo, Portrait Of Donny), "Hold Her Tight" (Crazy Horses)

8.) **"India" (October 28, 1972)**
The brothers arrive in India and Jimmy makes friends with a genie. Songs: "And You Love Me" (Crazy Horses), "Hey Girl" (Donny solo, Portrait Of Donny)

9.) **"The Yukon" (November 4, 1972)**
Jimmy accidentally books the brothers to go to the Yukon. Songs: "All I Have to Do Is Dream" (Donny solo, Portrait Of Donny), "My Drum" (Phase III)

10.) **"The Black Forest" (November 11, 1972)**
The brothers have to fix a clock or a whole town will be put to sleep forever. Songs: "Going Going Gone (To Somebody Else)" (Donny solo, Portrait Of Donny), "Girl" (Crazy Horses)

11.) **"Italy"** (November 18, 1972)
Jimmy finds a coin worth a lot of money and a girl tries to get it from him by going on a date with Donny. Songs: "What Could It Be" (Crazy Horses), "This Guy's in Love with You" (Donny solo, Portrait Of Donny)

12.) **"Australia"** (November 25, 1972)
The Osmonds hope over to Australia where a kangaroo falls in love with Jimmy. Songs: "It's You Babe" (Phase III), "Lonely Boy" (Donny solo, Too Young)

13.) **"Transylvania"** (December 2, 1972)
The Osmonds are invited to a vampire's party. Songs: "Killer Joe" (Jimmy solo, Killer Joe), "We All Fall Down" (Crazy Horses)

14.) **"Rio"** (December 9, 1972)
The brothers visit Rio and Jimmy gets lost at a costume contest. Songs: "Pretty Blue Eyes" (Donny solo, Too Young), "Hey Mr. Taxi" (Crazy Horses) **Note:** This episode was aired on Donny's 15th birthday.

15.) **"Don Osmondo in Spain"** (December 16, 1972)+
The brothers arrive in Spain and Donny becomes a bullfighter to impress a girl. Songs: "Puppy Love" (Donny solo, Portrait Of Donny), "Yo-Yo" (Phase III)

16.) **"Luck of The Osmonds"** (December 23, 1972)+
The brothers arrive in Ireland and Jimmy is mistaken for a leprechaun. Songs: "Down by the Lazy River" (Phase III), "Long Haired Lover from Liverpool" (Jimmy solo, Killer Joe)
Note: This episode's air date coincided with Jimmy's "Long Haired Lover from Liverpool" reaching "Christmas number one" in the United Kingdom.

17.) **"Coming Home to Utah"** (December 30, 1972)
After 15 weeks of touring around the world, the Osmonds return home to Utah and this episode wraps up the series. Songs: "Utah" (Crazy Horses), "Too Young" (Donny solo, Too Young)

Notes:

- The complete Jackson 5ive's Animated series has been issued on Blu-ray, but sadly only five of the seventeen episodes of the Osmond animated series have been issued and only on VHS / DVD! But unlike the Jackson 5ive's series the actual Osmond brothers voices are used in their series. Also the complete The Brady Kids series (see next page) has been issued on DVD along with scores of the other ABC-TV Saturday morning line-up programs.

- +Available on The Osmonds Cartoons DVD.

TV Guide Ad for Saturday Morning Cartoons in 1972

www.ingramcontent.com/pod-product-compliance
Lightning Source LLC
Chambersburg PA
CBHW061127010526
44116CB00023B/2993